917.8967 Boye, Alan.
BOY
          Tales from the
          journey of the
          dead.

$26.95

DATE			

Indian River County Main Library
1600 21st Street
Vero Beach, Florida 32960

B4T 2/07

BAKER & TAYLOR

Tales from the Journey of the Dead

Tales from the Journey of the Dead

Ten Thousand Years on an American Desert

Alan Boye

UNIVERSITY OF NEBRASKA PRESS LINCOLN AND LONDON

♾

Library of Congress Cataloging-in-Publication Data
Boye, Alan, 1950–
Tales from the journey of the dead: ten thousand years on an American desert / Alan Boye.
p. cm.
Includes bibliographical references.
ISBN-13: 978-0-8032-1358-6 (cloth: alk. paper)
ISBN-10: 0-8032-1358-1 (cloth: alk. paper)
1. Jornada del Muerto Wilderness (N.M.)—Description and travel. 2. Jornada del Muerto (N.M.)—Description and travel. 3. Boye, Alan, 1950-—Travel—New Mexico—Jornada del Muerto Wilderness. 4. Jornada del Muerto Wilderness (N.M.)—History. 5. Natural history—New Mexico—Jornada del Muerto Wilderness. 6. Jornada del Muerto Wilderness (N.M.)—Biography—Anecdotes. 7. Oral history.
I. Title.
F802.J67B695   2006
917.89′670454—dc22   2005033455
Text set in Robert Slimbach's Adobe Minion by Keystone Typesetting, Inc. Designed by Richard Eckersley.

For Bill Price;
and for Cathy Russell and Mel Mann:
companions

The men whom Zeus decrees, from youth to old age must wind down our brutal wars to the bitter end until we drop and die, down to the last man.—ILIAD

Go beyond this way or that way, to the farther shore where the world dissolves and everything becomes clear. Beyond this shore and the farther shore, beyond the beyond where there is no beginning, no end, without fear, go.—DHAMMAPADA

CONTENTS

ILLUSTRATIONS

Tales from the Journey of the Dead

1. Traveling the Camino U.S. 380

One hundred miles downstream from Albuquerque, New Mexico, the sluggish Rio Grande slams up against a series of volcanic mesas and dark, foreboding mountains. As if to avoid the desolate place, the mighty river swings in a long, wide arc to the west.

Two parallel chains of mountains form a 120-mile-long barricade that isolates a vacant, inhospitable, 50-mile-wide jumble of black rock, dry lake beds, flesh-colored sand, and desolation.

This is the Jornada del Muerto, the Journey of the Dead. Although so named because of a particular death centuries ago, many other ill-fated travelers have wandered the Jornada; mysterious ancient people in cliff-top fortresses, Spanish conquistadores come to reap heathen souls and uncounted riches, Apache warriors, Mexican farmers, and cowboys yodeling classical poetry to their cows. Many of these died here, while other travelers, like me, wandered the Jornada while on some longer journey.

Each tale from this wild and rugged land is the story of a life, well lived or not, set under a burning desert sun.

The earliest Europeans to see this land – Spanish men and women from Mexico who came seeking domination, converts, and wealth – referred to the distance between reliable sources of water as a *jornada*, a single march, a journey. Because following the river meant traversing a series of deep canyons and sharp-edged arroyos, travelers detoured across the dry Jornada del Muerto. By the early 1600s the Spanish had established regular travel between Mexico City and Santa Fe on a road that cut across the Jornada. From then until the twentieth century, when an automobile road along the river made the old road unnecessary, much of the human history of North America marched across this wasteland.

1

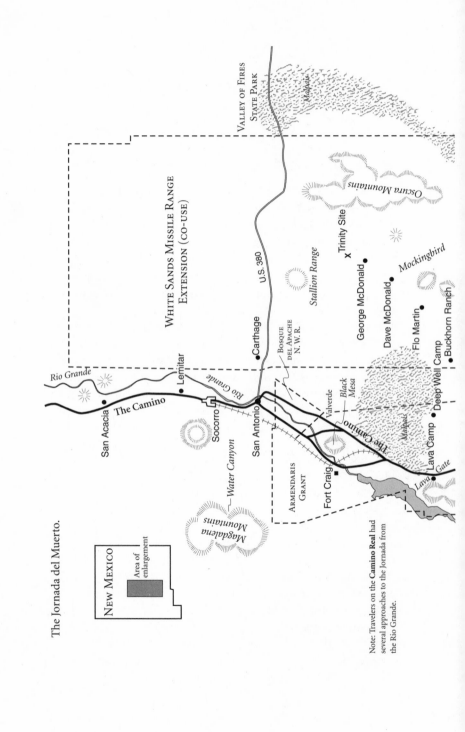

The Jornada del Muerto.

NEW MEXICO

Area of enlargement

Note: Travelers on the **Camino Real** had several approaches to the Jornada from the Rio Grande.

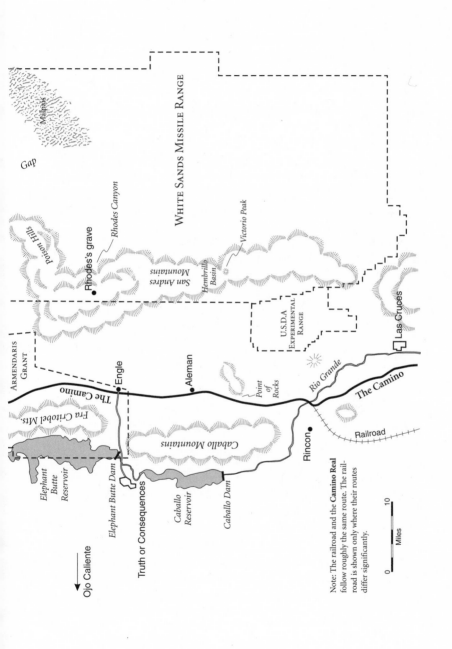

Malpaís

Gap

Poison Hills

Rhodes Canyon

Rhodes's grave

WHITE SANDS MISSILE RANGE

Victorio Peak

San Andres Mountains

Hembrillo Basin

ARMENDARIS GRANT

U.S.D.A.
EXPERIMENTAL
RANGE

Las Cruces

The Camino

Engle

Aleman

Point
of
Rocks

Rio Grande

The Camino

Fra Cristobal Mts.

Caballo Mountains

Rincon

Railroad

Elephant Butte Dam

Elephant
Butte
Reservoir

Ojo Caliente

Truth or Consequences

Caballo
Reservoir

Caballo Dam

Note: The railroad and the **Camino Real**
follow roughly the same route. The railroad is shown only where their routes
differ significantly.

0   10
Miles

Except for a few isolated wells, there is no reliable source of water on the Jornada. Even today, no one – not cowboys in pickup trucks or missile technicians in white, unmarked government cars – travels without life-giving water.

The Jornada is the northern extent of the Chihuahuan Desert, the largest arid region in North America. The Chihuahuan Desert extends for over twelve hundred miles: from the Jornada del Muerto to the Mexican state of Zacatecas. What rain there is on the Jornada falls mostly from July to September, when moist, warm air from the Gulf of Mexico piles high above the San Andres, the Caballo, and the Fra Cristobel ranges in massive clouds. Then the air turns a deathly black and dark, ominous curtains of rain hang down from the sky. Violent, widely scattered, and isolated summer storms bring brief, torrential showers. Lightning stabs the air; the dry arroyos flash to sudden flood; *playas* of sand and clay turn instantly to axle-breaking quagmires.

Then heat waves reappear and soon are shimmering across the desolation. After a summer cloudburst, you can see so far in a single glance that your mind recoils at the enormity; instead it seeks smaller details easier to comprehend: a single raven – a black ribbon in the bowl of sky – sliding down the air, leaving no trail.

The moisture during the summer "monsoon" evaporates quickly in the heat and remains only long enough to give shallow-rooted vegetation like black grama grass a quick drink before it disappears into the dry air.

The relentless sun shines on the Jornada nearly every day of the year. Once it rises above the Oscura and San Andres mountains, summer temperatures can rise above one hundred by 10 a.m. The average high in June is ninety-seven degrees, while the empty night sky in winter can chill the Jornada to below zero.

In contrast to the brief, violent storms of summer, most winter weather comes gradually from the distant Pacific Ocean and spreads wide, gray blanket of clouds over the entire sky. These storms may last for days. They don't bring much precipitation, but because of winter's lower evaporation rate they are more effective in wetting the soil. This benefits shrubs that sink deep taproots to capture moisture. Scientists say the increase in these types of plants, combined with the decline of grasslands, provides good evidence of the earth's changing climate.

Unlike the "lush" Sonora Desert, two hundred miles to the west, the nondescript plants of the northern Chihuahuan Desert seldom rise above five feet in height. Often, great sandy stretches of the Jornada have nearly nothing growing on them at all.

The plants that grow here are scrunched-up, shriveled rabbit bush, gnarled, stinking tarbush, and poisonous inkweed. The wispy leaves of low-slung mesquite trees shield thousands of razor-sharp thorns the size of darning needles. The tiny, juniper-like leaves of the creosote have a stench like the urine of rodents.

But other plants, as beautiful and delicate as their names, grow here as well: Apache-plume, chocolate flower, persimmon, desert willow, four-wing saltbrush, prickly pear.

Like a knife-cut across the top of a long finger, sparsely traveled U.S. Highway 380 slices the desolate northern tip of the Jornada. Except for it, there are no other four-season roads open to the public in an area nearly the size of Connecticut.

To get a feel for the Jornada, take U.S. 380 at a lonely exit off Interstate 25 and head east through the village of San Antonio, New Mexico. The highway ambles past the tiny village's main attraction, the Owl Bar, where Rowena Baca serves her fiery green-chile hamburgers for hungry modern travelers. At Rowena's Owl Bar the sleepy highway intersects a dusty road. That road, used today by locals in pickup trucks, is a fragment of the oldest continuously traveled road in the United States, the one the Spanish called El Camino Real de Tierra Adentro, the Royal Road to the Interior Lands.

Just beyond this intersection, U.S. 380 passes through the mosquito-haven shade of a thick, impenetrable wall of salt cedar. It crosses the blood-red Rio Grande and climbs into a series of sandy hills pock-marked with thin desert scrub, colored a pale yellow. The hills soon give way to a painted desert of bright red and purple ridges, slashed by streaks of tan and gold. This is the Jornada del Muerto. Everywhere in the far distance, dark walls of jagged, shark-toothed mountains stand black against the sky. In the emptiness above burns the furnace of a merciless sun.

A half-dozen miles beyond San Antonio, the highway passes a red-dish peak in the open expanse to the south. Out there somewhere, media mogul Ted Turner owns more than 300,000 acres encompassing one of the world's largest remaining stands of black grama grass.

The highway curls around a few low, bleak hills and comes to a marker announcing the site of a ghost town that existed here for a few brief years at the beginning of the twentieth century. The village of Carthage supplied coal for a railroad that had been completed across the Jornada. In 1906 the town's population reached its zenith at one thousand. Shortly after noon on December 31 of that year an explosion in the coal mine killed several men and injured many others. Some men who had been trapped were left to die when poisonous gasses thwarted rescue attempts.

The Jornada del Muerto has witnessed many such tales of death and destruction. On the Jornada are the bloody sites of battles of the Mexican-American War, the Civil War, and the Apache Victorio's futile fight to keep his homeland. And from the stark emptiness of the Jornada del Muerto rose the vaporized dawn of the world's first weapon of global war: the atomic bomb.

The Trinity site, as ground zero for the blast is now called, lies several miles beyond the ghost town of Carthage, beyond a series of round, high hills known now as the Stallion Range. From the relative safety of those hills, a handful of soldiers and scientists watched the explosion of the first atomic bomb.

Today, at the top of the tallest hill, a large white building sits incongruously on an otherwise featureless landscape. The building has a squat, roundish shape as if home to some giant, odd-shaped machine. This is the northern entrance to White Sands Missile Range, a ninety-mile-long area that keeps a large part of the Jornada off limits to the public. When the range was established during World War II it displaced ranchers like Florence and Frank Martin, who then spent the rest of their lives fighting an unsuccessful battle to regain their Jornada home.

Once around the bulk of the Stallion Range, the view to the south is of a single, unbroken plain that ends only at the edge of a distant, dark range of peaks. In every direction the far horizon is ringed in mountains.

Somewhere out there once lived a strange hermit known as the Wild Man. Somewhere out there Billy the Kid once crossed the isolation, fleeing his approaching death. Now, out in that barren land is an area called the Permanent High Explosive Test Site, which is used by the Defense Nuclear Agency for conducting large, above-ground explosive tests that replicate the destruction of a nuclear bomb without releasing any radioactivity. Somewhere out there too the military is currently testing strange new missiles that float on parachutes and are able to hear sounds. The devices are so sensitive they can distinguish the sound of a tank, say, from a jeep. They then release and direct several infrared guided missiles to hit the most desirable targets.

A single metal sign announces the "town" of Bingham. On one side of the highway a deserted building is plastered with fading signs: Phone Cards. Art. Park. Camping. On the other side of the road four standardized metal mailboxes are pitched in front of a tiny "Rock Shop." In the front window of the small building a faded handmade sign advertises Trinitite for sale, a greenish glass-like stone created when the heat of the atomic blast melted the sands of the Jornada.

Bingham, New Mexico, consists of this and nothing more.

Only then does U.S. 380 begin an almost imperceptible climb out of the Jornada basin and into the foothills of the Oscura Mountains toward the lava wasteland of Valley of Fires State Park. The greenspot of an occasional piñon tree appears on the hillsides. Low sand dunes dot the landscape; they are flat and featureless and the color of pennies.

Just as the highway begins to climb out of the empty bowl of the Jornada, the road passes a topless windmill; beyond it, the unbroken plain of the Jornada ends only at the edge of a distant, dark range of peaks.

Out there somewhere in the sand and dust and the ruins of war are the stories of sadistic killers, of directionless rebels, and of gun-toting cowboys. And out there somewhere too are the tales of poets and dreamers, of ordinary men and women who spent their lives under the wide and ruthless sky of the Journey of the Dead.

2. The Wild Man

He was a remnant of the Old West. Like cactus and coyote, like rattle-snake and mountain lion, he belonged to this harsh desert. A shadowy, elusive figure, the Wild Man wandered one of the most desolate wildernesses in the continental United States. For his entire adult life he lived outside in the open air of the Jornada del Muerto.

Most who remember him say he was a skinny beanpole of a man who dressed in rags and buckskins, in wool and rubber. He wore a combination of hand-me-downs and natural objects. His denim trousers were always slashed to faded, blue shreds by thorns and rocks. At the bottom of his trousers he often lashed a hunk of old automobile tire. The rubber served to add an extra sole to his ancient boots and to protect his lower legs from the multitude of stings, stabs, and poisons that his unforgiving desert home provided.

He always wore a hat.

He carried all of his belongings in a hand-fashioned pack made from materials found easily enough in cattle and goat country: a burlap bag and some rope. In the burlap pack were all of his worldly possessions: a blanket, a few shreds of extra clothing, and – if he was lucky – a couple of cans of food.

He always carried a jug of water, often tied to the end of a yucca-stalk walking stick and slung over his shoulder.

He was a tramp, a traveler. The Wild Man spent more than thirty years on the Jornada del Muerto and the rugged San Andres range of its eastern flank. He wandered from ranch to ranch, from cow camp to cow camp, from mountain to plains, from canyon to arroyo.

Only one night in his three decades of life on the Jornada did he ever sleep under a roof.

Fugitive or broken hearted, outlaw or desert rat, what turmoil of youth could have thrown a man so far from his fellow beings?

It doesn't matter which old-timer you talk to – there are dozens of eyewitnesses – just about every ranch wife, cowboy, or schoolteacher who once lived on the great open land of the Jornada remembers the San Andres hermit.

Here is what remains of his life story.

The Wild Man was born around 1890 and was last seen alive a few days before the mushroom cloud from the world's first atomic bomb sprang up from the dry desert plains he called home.

The oldest account of him is from the early 1930s, but the woman who remembered him from those days said by then he'd already been roaming the area "for many, many years."

He never talked about himself much, and when he did, the stories never seemed to match up. He wandered into Roy and Dixie Tucker's spread one day, asking for food. He had leaned against a corral and watched the rancher's horses. Then he said, "My boss used to have mares like that in Canada when I worked on a farm up there." He told them that he was from Canada, where he had worked before drifting south. Dixie was curious; she prodded the Wild Man for details. "My boss left on a two-week vacation and when he came back, I left," was all he said.

Once, when he wandered in for food at another rancher's place, he said that he had been born in Kansas and had run away from home when he was very young.

Others said he had worked ranches in Wyoming and Montana in his early years.

One story has him in trouble with the law. In the 1910s a team of two bank robbers robbed several New Mexico banks. One of the bandits had been killed, but the other was never found. Some people believe the missing man was the Wild Man.

Others speculate that he was involved in some illicit trade, smuggling *something* up from Mexico into the States. He traveled only north or south up the long spine of the Jornada and its mountains. He never moved east or west. When he was moving south, they say, he was visible to the point of distraction, but when he was traveling north he was reclusive and secretive.

Still others say that he fought in World War I, the bloody horror that left many with the profound psychological scars of the first modern war. Timid, shy to the point of nervousness, reclusive, polite, the Wild Man could well have been a shell-shocked casualty of war. Some say that what he saw so shattered him that he sought the most remote place he could find to try and hide from that fear.

A recluse. A tramp. A hermit anchored in a hermitage one third the size of New Hampshire.

Evelyn Underhill wrote about such people in her study of mysticism: "The most highly developed branches of the human family have in common one peculiar characteristic. They tend to produce – sporadically it is true, and often in the teeth of adverse external circumstances – a curious and definite type of personality; a type which refuses to be satisfied with that which other men call experience, and is inclined, in the words of its enemies, to 'deny the world in order that it may find reality.' "

To deny the world in order to find reality. No matter how often the Wild Man wandered into a dusty cowboy camp, no matter how many times he appeared at the kitchen door of startled ranch women, no matter how many dozens of people saw him, his solitary, decades-long life on the open and bleak Jornada desert remains unique in the history of the twentieth-century American West. He knew every detail of the craggy Fra Cristobels, every nook and cranny of the steep and rugged San Andres; he knew every plant and every lizard, every mudflat and every water hole in this immense and empty place. He lived here, just here, with only the most essential of elements: food and shelter.

"Old Red," seventy-two-year-old Walter Slayter called him. "He had the reddest hair you have ever seen." His long hair and untrimmed beard stood out like a bonfire on the darkest desert night. "He didn't do a thing but wander around. He'd sometimes come into your house when you weren't there – nobody minded, it was kind of expected. The Wild Man would come and fix himself something to eat. He'd wash his dishes and then turn his plate upside down over a quarter or whatever he had in his pocket. He just traveled up and down the country. He never bothered a soul."

Everyone who knew of him agreed on that point: the Wild Man never hurt a fly.

Shining through that fiery red hair, a pair of beautiful and bright turquoise eyes nearly burned you the instant you saw them. His blue eyes, his red hair, his narrow nose and broad cheekbones, and his deeply tanned skin gave him an oddly distinguished look. His mouth blossomed from his beard like a small pink flower from a briar patch of red.

It seems incongruous, but this tramp of the wastelands conversed in proper and precise English. He spoke with a slight foreign accent. No one who heard him could figure it out. Some said the accent was German, others said it was French, or Norwegian. Not only was his use of language so proper, but his range of knowledge was vast. Although no one ever saw him with a book, he was very well read. He could talk philosophy, or religion, or politics, or local gossip. He spoke in the particular, intelligent manner of an educated gentleman. He was an aimless drifter, but one who was well cultured; he was a ragged scarecrow, but one who apologized profusely for being dirty.

"He'd come up to the house and want something to eat," rancher Leonard Cain remembered. "It would be zero weather. You'd give him something to eat and you'd say, 'Come on in and stay the night.' 'No, I got to go, got to go . . .' and he'd take off." After one such encounter, Leonard watched him shuffle off in his uniquely odd but effective canter: a kind of rapid run-walk. The next morning Leonard trailed the Wild Man for about three miles until he found where the hermit had built a fire "on the windy side of himself" and spent the night.

The Wild Man slept under the stars and rain, under the heat and cold of the open air every night of his adult life – every night but one.

One afternoon in the early 1940s he appeared at Joe Pete Wood's place. The scruffy drifter told Joe Pete that earlier, somewhere out on the Jornada, a bull got him down and broke several of his ribs. The drifter ate the food that Joe Pete offered him, then spent that night curled up on Joe Pete's floor. He left the next morning. That was the only night in over thirty years he ever spent under a roof.

But eat? Now, that was a different story. Folks said he never missed an opportunity for a meal. The man was always hungry enough to eat a saddle blanket.

Leonard Cain was riding strays one season and staying in a one-room shack on the eastern edge of the lava flow. "I had been down on the flats one day. As I rode up I saw the door shut and I thought: what the dickens was that? So I got off my horse and beat it to the house right quick."

Leonard threw open the door.

The Wild Man stood at the table holding up the dishtowel that had been keeping the flies off of the sugar and hard bread. The Wild Man said, "I was just looking, looking for something to eat, something to eat."

Leonard had just cooked a large pot of beans. The pot usually lasted him a week. "I sat him down and just had that pot of beans for him. And he cleared the whole pot up," Leonard said. "He ate the whole pot of beans!"

During her years on the Jornada, Dixie Tucker fed him twice. Both times she placed plate after plate of beans and whatever else she could find in front of the Wild Man. He ate everything, washing it down with pot after pot of coffee. "I don't know how he could eat so much," she said. "When he got up to leave, well, he was just like a little quail." And like a quail, Dixie recalled, he disappeared out of sight faster than anybody she knew.

And like a coyote he appeared out of nowhere.

In November 1936, Dolly Onsrud, the sixteen-year-old bride of Art Helms, was working in her kitchen at the ranch. "I looked up and here was this great big man. He had a full beard, long hair with an old slouch felt hat."

He stood just outside the door and spoke politely to her. "Good afternoon, Ma'am," he said. "Do you think I might fix myself something to eat?"

"He wasn't filthy," Dolly recalled. "He was like you and I would be if we's out in deer camp or something. He was clean, but he wasn't dressed up," she said. "He had a rope tied around his waist, just a piece of rope. He had a long stick that he had made him a walking cane with." Since she had come to New Mexico a year earlier when her parents fled the poverty of Oklahoma, she understood the importance of sharing what she had. She sat him down at her table and fed him and then stared in amazement at how much he ate.

No matter how much he could eat, however, he always did so politely, never wolfing down his food. Leonard's brother Lewis Cain remembered how the Wild Man would leave his burlap pack a couple hundred yards from the house and then come up and ask for something to eat. "He was up on his current events and he'd ask different questions. He would talk about different things. You could tell he was a well-read man."

Joe Pete Wood Jr. claimed the Wild Man simply drifted from one day to the next, moving quickly from ranch to ranch and getting a big meal at each. "He was pretty swift," Joe Pete Jr. remembered. One day he tracked the man. "He started at Doug Cain's in the morning. Before lunch he had stopped at my Uncle Tom's place – about three miles down the road. Another six miles south of that he stopped at the Hardin ranch, and went on down to the Potter ranch--and this was by the late afternoon." According to Joe Pete Jr.'s calculations, before nightfall that day that "Ole Wild Man" covered more than twenty miles on foot and had eaten five good-sized meals. "He would come in and sit down at your table if you invited him, and he expected you to invite him."

Like the first human wanderers whose petroglyphs litter the Jornada del Muerto, the Wild Man knew how to find his own food among the plants and animals of the desert. He could throw a stone as hard and as straight "as if it were a bullet." That was how he hunted, he said. He knew too where to find shelter in the stone ruins of those ancient people, and in the heat of summer where there were cool crevasses with hidden pockets of water to quench his thirst.

The vagabond always talked. Joe Pete Jr. said that the Wild Man knew the most up-to-date world news (probably from having listened to the radio at some rancher's house). He always had the latest local news and gossip as well. Long before anyone out in the Jornada had a telephone, the Wild Man was a walking switchboard operator.

He left only footprints as evidence of his brief passing time on earth, and even those he knew how to erase.

A sheriff's posse, looking for band of cattle rustlers, once came upon the Wild Man. They wanted to check him out and to see if he knew anything about the rustlers. The men fanned out around him in a wide circle, but when they closed in he had disappeared.

As ninety-three-year-old Joe Turner told it, normally the Wild Man shouldn't have been difficult to track. No matter what, his prints were always distinctive: a long, narrow foot covered with either burlap for warmth or rubber tires for protection, or footwear made of reeds and woven like a pair of Indian moccasins in the deep heat of summer. "One time they had these boys who had just started working for the border patrol," Joe said, "and they tracked that old man around, and around until they finally decided maybe he wasn't illegal . . ."

Leonard Cain tells of the time he came upon the Wild Man at a goat camp. That day a man named Stevens from Tularosa had brought his wife out to the camp. She hadn't been feeling well and had gone into the camp cabin to rest on the bed. "When she was laying on the bed the door opened and this old guy stepped in there," Leonard said. The woman "screamed bloody murder and he hit the door and just broke and run for about a quarter mile. Well, he stopped and turned around and came back to the cabin." The Wild Man approached the door and said, "Oh, I'm so sorry, so sorry I scared you. I was just looking for something to eat." Leonard laughed, "I think she went ahead and fed him. Then he went on his merry way, but he saw that he had scared her."

Once a Hispanic woman was alone in her house taking a leisurely bath at a washtub in her kitchen when the Wild Man appeared in the door. Both of them were startled speechless. The Wild Man turned and fled.

The strange man came upon children too. Hazel Johnson lived with her parents up Bosque Canyon. She knew about him from the stories her father told. The Wild Man occasionally showed up at one of her father's goat camps. The first time Hazel ever saw him was when she was riding her horse to school one day. She knew about him well enough from her father's stories and wasn't scared.

Hazel saw him one other time. That was the last time anyone ever saw him. By then, the early summer of 1945, the government had kicked most of the ranchers off the Jornada. A few days before Hazel's family left their home in Bosque Canyon, the Wild Man appeared at her house. He had a long beard and wore old tires tied around his shoes so he'd have more of a cushion. Hazel's mother fixed him something to eat. "And that man could eat!" Hazel said. "He sat there and ate and ate and ate and ate." Hazel remembers watching him shuffle away with that strange gait of his. He was headed north.

A month later the world understood why the ranchers had been forced from their homes: at dawn on July 16, just a few miles north of Hazel Johnson's, the mushroom cloud of the world's first atomic bomb rose above the Jornada del Muerto.

For centuries Buddhist monks have been wandering the wilderness of Southeast Asia. The monks' rules require that they live entirely outside what the world calls "civilized life." They stop at small farms for food, relying on the generosity of the residents. The Wild Man was just like those monks. He ate the ranchers' food, then paid for their generosity by offering his life as an example of virtue, humility, and simplicity.

To deny the world in order to find reality.

The Wild Man's story is the spiritual story of the American West.

Verena Mahaney's mother told her not to come in contact with the Wild Man in any way, shape, or form.

Verena obeyed her mother about as well as any young teenager could. One Christmas season the Wild Man showed up at her grandmother's house across the way. Verena strung popcorn balls on a string and left them tied to a mesquite tree near where she found his trail. By morning, the popcorn balls had disappeared. She then began to leave biscuits and butter in little sacks she tied to branches. He took the food and left the little sacks.

One day near Christmas, Verena went to fill the sacks. She stood at the mesquite tree in disbelief. Instead of being empty, inside each tiny bag she found a piece of hard candy. Startled and delighted, she looked up.

The Wild Man's footprints vanished into the empty Jornada del Muerto.

3. Elements

I'm driving through the heart of Ted Turner's 360,000-acre private ranch. In the far distance a massive thunderhead billows heavenward against the blade edge of a steep mountain.

I reach an automated gate. From the window of the van I punch a combination of numbers into a keypad. In a second a motor hums and the gate rolls open. I hurry through and then watch it close through my rear-view mirror.

Just north of Red Lake Well, I see specks of black against a florescent yellow hillside. With binoculars I count five bison. I drive closer and stop. As I get out of the van, each massive beast looks up and eyes me cautiously. They are unlike any bison I've ever seen – not zoo creatures, but as rugged and as wild as the Old West. Their beards are scraggly, their eyes dark and menacing.

A few days ago, from the phone at Bosque del Apache National Wildlife Refuge, I called to get permission to hike Turner's land. The people at his Armendaris Ranch then faxed a form across the fifty miles of emptiness to where I waited for it at the opposite end of the huge ranch. A sketch of a buffalo served as a logo at the top of the form. Most of the form was fairly standard, a legal detail making sure I understood that the ranch was not responsible if I met with an untimely accident, but one question gave me pause. Had I been to Europe in the past ninety days, it wanted to know. I stared blankly at it for a moment before I remembered why I was being asked. Turner is worried about the recent spread of mad-cow disease. He has reason to be, for he has seventeen hundred bison on the Jornada alone.

"Bison on the Jornada? Ted Turner is crazy," one rancher told me. I've also heard more than a few discouraging words around here concerning Jane Fonda. At the moment, she and Turner are in the middle of a well-publicized divorce.

I take one last look at the bison and hop back in the van. I eye the sky nervously. The top of a thunderstorm ahead of me has been sheered off like an anvil. I drive further on a dusty road north along the steep wall of the Fra Cristobel Mountains.

In a few miles I stop again near a small cluster of buildings where I see three men working. I step out of the van. The men are hovering over the back of a pickup truck stacked with wire cages. In each cage is a yellowish animal the size of a small cat. I talk to Bob Wu, who wears a floppy, shady hat. "They're black-tailed prairie dogs," he says. He and the others are part of a project that is reintroducing prairie dogs on Turner's property. "We weigh them, measure them, tag them, and then take them back out and release them," he says. Several other colonies have recently been established on the ranch.

A hundred years ago the U.S. Biological Services initiated a campaign to eradicate prairie dogs from the American West in order to improve ranching prospects. Back then workers rode through the Jornada setting strychnine baits. The campaign succeeded. In one sizable Jornada colony alone, for example, 98 percent of the animals were killed in a single year. Now ranchers grumble about how Ted Turner is bringing them back. Some ranchers believe prairie dogs are competing for limited grassland. On the other hand, some recent studies suggest that since prairie dogs eat the shoots of shrubs like mesquite, they actually help keep shrubs from encroaching into grasslands. Other studies show that while the mammals increase the *quality* of the rangelands in the West, the *quantity* is often reduced. "But," Bob Wu tells me, "it takes something like one hundred prairie dogs to consume the same biomass as a single Hereford." He believes one way to maintain grasslands is to mix prairie dogs with bison. "Bison move on," he says, "they don't stay in one place and eat until it's bare like cattle." The prairie dog restoration has also attracted burrowing owls and other wildlife once common to the area.

Although none of the three men are concerned about catching bubonic plague from the animals' fleas, I'm less certain. As I turn to leave, I mention my plans to hike through Lava's Gate to the Rio

Grande. Bob informs me that prairie dogs are not the only species Turner is reintroducing. "I saw the mountain lion guy coming down from there this morning." Mountain lions? "Yeah, he had his headset on. He must have been tracking a collared lion somewhere."

I return to my car and drive away slowly.

A short while later I pull around a nondescript bend and into what I at first think is mud. Instead, a red powdery cloud of sand the consistency of flour billows up around the van. I step on the gas so as not to get stuck. I list to one side and begin to swerve. The van fishtails, hangs a fleeting second on the precipice of a deep ditch, slides around a sharp bend, and then bounces into a rut. A thick, tan cloud pours into the open window, coating everything with dust. The van nearly stalls, then finally lurches onto solid surface. I stop in the middle of the road. My heart is racing. I take a deep breath and decide that my car-luck has just about run out.

I spend a warm half hour unloading my mountain bike from the van and packing my panniers with water and gear. The thunderheads to the northeast are building. I mount up, take one last look at the my lonely automobile, and pedal off.

The road climbs an easy incline. A white, funnel-like cloud forms at the edge of the storm and then disappears. Much closer to me, and lit by a brilliant sun, a large dust devil dances across the bright land. The ground where it passes is thick with grass the color of sunlight.

More than two thirds of the Jornada looked like this in the 1880s, but today the range grass is found on less than 3 percent of the total area. Much of that is on Turner's ranch. Rainfall records for the Jornada date back more than a hundred years, but they don't offer much of an explanation for the rapid decline of grasslands. Scientists do know that a combination of drought, extreme grazing practices, and the suppression of fires contributed to the change in vegetation. Given the evidence of a warmer, drier planet, trying to understand what happened becomes more critical to scientists. The desertification of places like the Jornada, say researchers, "potentially represents a permanent loss in the productive capacity of the biosphere on which all life depends."

Because of its unique ecosystem, its remoteness, and its history as an area of scientific study, the Jornada is designated as one of a world-wide network of sites where long-term experiments are being conducted to identify and to try to solve ecological problems. Much of that research is being done in a huge protected area known as the Jornada Experimental Range, ninety miles south of Turner's ranch at the southern end of the Jornada.

I stand up on my pedals, rat-a-tat-tat across a bumpy stretch in the path, and then bog down in deep sand. I step off my bike and take a breather. Low thunder rolls from the big storm to the northeast. It hangs huge over the Poison Hills, not far from where the Wild Man was last seen alive. Almost idly, I recall the stories I've heard of cowboys who were killed by lightning while riding alone on the Jornada. I push the bike onto firmer ground and hop back on.

I've been told that the road I'm on should keep climbing until it reaches a "T" intersection on a divide between the Jornada basin and the Rio Grande valley. I'm not certain, however, because I was unable to find a topographical map of this area. Apparently, none exist.

A motion ahead distracts me. A lizard scurries from the shade of a weed and disappears behind a small, prickly cactus. I look up. I look once, twice. On the near horizon in front of me is a strange pattern of objects. Row after row of square metal frames the height of houses stand like alien soldiers against the darkening sky.

The road I'm biking up leads to a formidable iron fence where I find a sign: "U.S. Naval Space Surveillance System. U.S. Government Property. No Trespassing."

I later learn from Turner's affable ranch manager, Tom Waddell, that Elephant Butte Surveillance Station was built in secret during the Cold War. Once the Soviets began to send up satellites that were nearly impossible to track with telescopes, this and a network of four other stations were built in remote locations to form a continent-wide curtain to track them. Advances in the technology of war have relegated this station to its current function of tracking the ever-increasing clutter of space junk.

The station marks the turn in the road I was expecting. I go left. Once beyond the station's fence line I come upon a ledge of dark, menacing lava. I have reached the *malpais*, the bad place. The black, basaltic rock marks the edge of one of the Jornada's two large lava flows. This flow, the smaller of the two, stretches for twenty miles to the northeast. A part of the larger flow can be seen at Valley of Fires State Park off of U.S. Highway 380. Carved out of the black chaos of boiling lava, frozen as if just now cooled, both flows serve as bleak gateways to the Jornada del Muerto. The dark, rugged magma and the chasms of lava form a dangerous and nearly impenetrable barrier. A few years ago the U.S. Bureau of Mines studied the flows to determine if they had any economic potential. Aside from a very limited use as decorative stone, or as a crushed rock for road building, the study found no economic value to the wasteland and reported dryly that "mining the extremely rugged lava surface would be difficult and costly."

Few plants grow on the malpais, while strange black lizards, the devilish result of evolutionary adaptation, sun themselves undisturbed. Nearly no one travels the malpais. Over the centuries only a few people, like scout Captain Jack Crawford and the Apaches he trailed, knew the way through the bizarre wasteland. Everyone else steered clear of the place.

A soft crushing sound, like boots on snow, comes from the crusty black rock beneath my bicycle wheels.

I watch rain falling out on the malpais. A thick, menacing curtain hangs down like smoke: there is only darkness above it. A brilliant but ghostly sunlight illuminates a distant ridge.

Soon I'm riding downhill from the headlands of a wide arroyo. For reasons that have remained a mystery, the 1598 members of Don Juan Oñate's expedition named this gulch Dead Man's Arroyo.

I'm all alone in this forlorn place. I've come eight miles by bicycle from the van. By now the three men who had been working with the prairie dogs will have gone home, so the closest help is at ranch headquarters, twenty-eight miles beyond my van. Fifteen miles beyond that, Truth or Consequences is the nearest town. On purpose, I carry no phone or GPS device.

A jackrabbit appears at the edge of the road. Its black-tipped ears stand high. It makes a scatter-bunny run down the dirt and disappears into the underbrush. Just then the road jags left and comes to a small house. The yard is fenced, but the sandy road cuts right through it. I walk my bicycle into the yard through a gate frozen open by drifting sand.

This is Lava Camp, an old cow camp. Places like this were built on large ranches so that men who were working in distant parts of the range would have a place to stay. A run-down ramp for loading cattle leans against a wire fence. A metal frame for a windmill still stands, but there are no blades. At its base an electric pump sits near a water tank.

I walk toward the house. Another storm moves slowly across the Rio Grande valley and climbs onto the Jornada. A west wind blows. I cup my hands to the screened porch and look inside. The railing is decorated with tools, old car parts, and a mule shoe. Tacked to a wall is a 1990 license plate from the state of Nebraska. I peek into a glass window of the house itself. Several comfortable cushions that could also serve as beds line the walls of a room. Three sets of dirty work boots are arranged neatly underneath a wooden bench. Amid the sparse and utilitarian furnishings in the room is a stuffed toy bear: it must be a memento of a lost love, for there are no other signs of softness anywhere.

Back in the yard I discover that I can't stake out my tent. Everywhere I try, I strike solid lava beneath a thin covering of gravel. I consider looking for another campsite, but I'm worried about moving further with such storms forming all about me. I hesitate a moment and then take the wheels off my bike. I tie my tent to the frame of the bike and use the wheels and the rest of my gear to anchor it.

I eat a meal and watch the sunset approach behind layered, flat gray clouds. The clouds, like holy hosts of heaven, are backlit by the pale white light of the sun. Other clouds, rimmed in gold, fill the eastern sky. Directly above me a silver crescent moon hangs in the pure air. Last of birdcalls, and a distant train's lonely whistle from somewhere out on the Jornada; creosote and grass; the hot desert day exhales into the deep tan and green night. In this moment, instant by precious instant, the universe exists.

I stay up well past sunset watching the dance of moon and cloud, cloud and moon. Then, suddenly, the wind grows stronger. Soon it blasts against my heavily anchored tent, sliding it along the sand. I crawl inside, stretch out on my sleeping mat, and watch the sides of the tent billow as the wind punches at them and bends the poles. Flashes of silent lightning brighten the darkness, and then the moon disappears. Just before the storm hits in earnest, I hear the icy song of a coyote somewhere off in the desert.

Thunder: crack-whip clear and close.

The first big drops of rain sound as if someone is throwing stones on the tent: Thunk. Thunk. Thunk-thunk – then faster, until the world screams in a fury of howling wind and roaring rain.

All life is absorbed in a brilliant flash that comes unannounced.

An instant later, thunder echoes off of the mountains. I lie stunned. Breathless, I quickly try to remember the safety rules for lightning. I make myself as small as I can. I curl my body into a ball on the mat. My feet rest on a pair of rubber-soled shoes. In the tiny instants of silence between the worst of the storm's blasts I hear crickets chirping. They haven't missed a beat.

Despite it all, I am so tired that I fall asleep while the fury of the storm still rages about me. Later I wake briefly to a gentle rain and a calm wind.

In the morning I sip my coffee and eat some melon while I look around. The storm seems like an illusion; the ground is dry dust. I jump up. A truck has appeared at the side of the house. I never heard it, but someone must have driven it here during the night.

Just then the porch's screen door opens and a round-shaped man steps out. Although I'm only twenty yards away from the house, he doesn't look in my direction. He walks to the truck and begins to fill it with fuel from a silver tank suspended on a rack near the house. He still hasn't noticed me when he finishes, gets into the truck, and begins to back it up. When he finally sees me it takes him, not a double, but a triple look to make sure I exist.

I walk over and we communicate through the Morse code of our hybrid Spanglish, accented by the pantomime of our hand gestures. He tells me that he didn't see me when he drove in late last night, or even this morning when he came outside. I give him a hunk of melon. He whistles in thanks. As he eats the melon, he talks. He tells me that even this big six-wheel flatbed nearly always gets stuck in the place I had abandoned my van. He says there's another route through the edge of the malpais that he uses in order to avoid the sandy arroyo. Over and over again amid this he repeats how shocked he was to see me. We both laugh each time he retells the story in the ten minutes we are together.

After he drives away I reassemble my bike and load my gear. I leave Lava Camp headed north on a path that is a strange mix of sharp black lava and red sand. Twin peaks fill the sky to my left. Dark bands of rock form an irregular pattern on steep, pale-green slopes. This is the very northern tip of the Fra Cristobel range, named, most likely, after a friar who accompanied Oñate's 1598 expedition. From here to the south the range forms an impassable thirty-mile-long barrier between the Rio Grande and the Jornada.

The bleak landscape between the peaks and the lava flow is absolutely empty. Far to the northwest I see a distant range of dark mountains huddled under a blanket of low clouds. Directly above me two nighthawks dance in the morning air, their screech of wings on air like a call of the wild.

The cool, overcast sky keeps my tricky ride a bit easier. I glide and pedal and zigzag down the path. In places the ground is so dark it looks like melted chocolate.

About four miles beyond Lava Camp I slow through a difficult place and then entirely bog down in sandy soil. I get off the bike. I unfasten the empty day pack and load it with half of my remaining water, camera, rain jacket, and a little food. I abandon the bike and begin to walk. I trudge through the deep sand. The walls of lava close in and I come to a narrow passageway. Black columns of rock form a natural gateless gate through which I must pass. I hesitate, then walk through.

Just beyond is a small hill. Movement startles me. I stop dead.

Three large beasts stare at me. They are unlike any animal I have ever seen. Two arrow-straight horns rise from the top of their oddly shaped heads. Their color is a strange African mix of tan and black and white.

24

In an instant they are gone.

Oryx.

I take a deep breath and try to calm my racing heart. I had been warned about oryx. I knew that the state of New Mexico released thirty-eight of the large African antelopes ninety miles from here on the White Sands range in the 1960s hoping to attract wealthy or influential exotic-game hunters to the area. The beasts adapted easily to their new environment. They multiplied so rapidly that they now range free over a 150-mile-wide strip from the Texas border to the Rio Grande.

I follow the oryxes' odd tracks up a hill. A large horned lizard scurries behind a spiky, low cactus. I walk over a crest of sharp rock. It seems that everything on the Jornada either stinks or sticks or stings.

I walk in an enormous silence for the entire distance down to the lowlands along the river.

Pale-green rabbit bush dots the riverside landscape. Cottonwood trees grow amid a few feathery stands of salt cedar. Luckily, the cottonwoods here have mostly withstood the invasive plant. Salt cedars severely threaten the Rio Grande's riparian habitat. They are nearly impossible to eradicate and, once established, become so densely packed that they create a "monoculture" where no other plant life can grow. Turner is trying to restore the riverbank area in order to benefit such species as the southwestern willow flycatcher and the yellow-billed cuckoo.

I swat my first mosquito. The slap breaks the immense silence and startles me like a gunshot. A great and forlorn emptiness envelops me. I notice a disturbance on the ground. I walk to it slowly, studying it carefully. It's a big pile of tubular scat, left by a large animal. A silly little rhyme a naturalist taught me suddenly pops into my head: "If it looks like a Tootsie Roll, it's time to go."

Of the five mountain lions released on the Turner ranch, two are females. "They roam all up and down the entire length of the Fra Cristobels," ranch manager Tom Waddell told me. "They stay along the river corridor, just like people," he had said.

As I look at the fresh droppings, I take off my day pack in order to get a drink of water. Only later do I remember how oddly unfrightened I had been. I linger at the spot a long while. I think about mountain lions, and last night's storm, of oryx, prairie dogs, and of black grama grass resisting an advancing army of mesquite.

I stand at a lonely place. Before me is a dusty, dangerous path whose end no one can foretell. There isn't much I can do about it, except try to pay close attention to what is right before me.

I swing the pack onto my back and turn around.

4. Foundations

Lisa Peters jumps out of the high-centered four-wheel drive. She stands in the dust next to the car and looks up at the black butte that rises before us: a rock curtain of dark stone columns. She is wearing sturdy hiking boots and carries a water bottle. "We have earthquakes daily," she says. "We don't feel them, but they're below us in the magma chamber."

She should know. Lisa and her husband, Virgil Lueth, are geologists who live on the northern edge of the Jornada. Long-ago transplants from Wisconsin, Lisa and Virgil work at New Mexico Institute of Mining and Technology, which outgrew its original name – New Mexico School of Mines. The school is in Socorro, a small town not far from where we stand.

Lisa's short, blond hair frames the pleasing oval of her deeply tanned face. Her strong, sloping shoulders and her compact, lean frame come from the hiking and horseback riding she does.

Virgil checks for his keys and slams shut the door of the rig.

Lisa slings the day pack over her shoulder. "It was the perfect job for us," she says. Even after nearly twenty years in the desert country, a trace of her Wisconsin accent still can be heard in the soft, flat "aaah" of her round vowels. "We love this part of New Mexico," she says.

In front of us is a sturdy fence of metal poles that surrounds a lonely desert cemetery. The poles keep stray desert cattle from wandering in among the couple hundred tombstones. Although we are only a dozen yards from the Rio Grande, the ground is rocky and no shrubs grow among the graves.

We climb through the white poles and cross through the cemetery. Just beyond and across a rocky bar, we take a route down into a sandy arroyo. The butte lies just beyond us and looks like a dark tin can set on a table of golden sand.

Virgil leads, and Lisa and I walk behind him. "This butte is basalt formed from magma, and that magma is still active," Lisa says. "The earthquakes that happen here are because of that magma." She motions toward the squat, round shape in front of us. "At one time the earth's crust spread apart and this vent of lava came up from the deep rocks below."

"Snake!" Virgil says.

Ahead of us an eight-foot gray log as big around as my thigh slithers in large "S" curves, backing away. It's a bull snake, common from here east across the Great Plains.

"That's a big one," Lisa says, watching the snake disappear into a thin scattering of low shrubs.

Virgil smiles. "He sure wasn't too afraid of us," he chuckles.

"That's why I'm glad you're leading the way," Lisa says.

We reach the base of the butte and start up on a steep trail.

"That magma chamber is still quivering," Lisa says, "so there's another volcano coming sometime." Although the trail seems to climb straight up, she speaks easily and without breaking her rapid stride. "There's a lot of debate among geologists whether the next one will be more of a boomer like Mount Saint Helens or a nice, quiet basalt thing like the event that formed this butte."

Such "nice, quiet basalt things" also formed the Jornada's two massive lava flows: the malpais.

Virgil stops and in order to join our conversation. "In geological terms events like these are fairly common on the Jornada," he says. "Some of my colleagues think the next event could be a big blast, and there are others who think it could be one of the slow flows. No one really knows."

Lisa shrugs, "Once every five to ten million years, there has been a major volcano somewhere in this part of New Mexico."

"The volcanoes near Albuquerque are even younger than a million years," Virgil says, "but we don't know much about the flow you biked and hiked through out on the Jornada. It is basalt, you can see that from a distance, but we don't really know much about it. We've known about the rift that allowed the magma to reach the surface, but that part of the rift is more complex than what you find here at the northern end of the Jornada."

Lisa says, "The problem with that lava out on the Jornada is that it's not very accessible."

"That's true," Virgil says. "The White Sands Missile Range and the remoteness of the Jornada have blocked off a lot of research." He pauses, then laughs his light, warm, and frequent laugh. "But then who has wanted to go there either? This part of the country hasn't held much interest – it isn't sexy because even if a new volcano were to erupt here there aren't many people that it would affect."

We start walking again, and I catch a glimpse of the cemetery below us as I teeter over the steep edge of the trail.

We crest the top of the butte. Over ragged purple lines of mountain ranges to the west, clouds cool the late-afternoon air. To the east, across the great, empty expanse of the northern Jornada, the ragged Oscura Mountains are dark against the distant horizon. The heart of the imposing Jornada is to our south, where isolated peaks and craggy hills shimmer in the lingering heat of the day. There, the pale empty land simply disappears into the great distance beyond.

The top of the butte is perfectly flat and about the size of a vacant city block. The surface is covered with a jumble of dark, angular rocks. Most of the stones are about the size of a desk, but at the edge stand pickup-truck-size blocks the color of night.

"If you look closely," Virgil says, "you'll see that there is gravel up here. This butte was once at the river's level, but then the river eroded the upper parts and cut down through the basalt. The river cut through this entire formation," he says, and then he repeats it: "It cut right through the middle of these buttes."

We are at the edge of the butte, directly above a forlorn passageway. Two hundred feet below us, the Rio Grande punches a narrow wedge between this and a neighboring butte, then slides west and away from the harsh Jornada basin.

Lisa squints out into the expanse of the Jornada. "I can't remember if you can see the malpais from here or not," she says, searching for a glimpse. "You know, I don't know if we put a date on that older flow."

"Surely one of you guys from the lab has been out there and snagged some of it just to know how old it is," Virgil says.

"The lab" is the New Mexico Geochronology Research Laboratory where Lisa works. There she analyzes rock samples to determine their age and thermal composition. The lab is full of strange contraptions that make the room look like a laundromat on some space alien's laundry day. Among other jobs, Lisa extracts argon gas by using small but very intense furnaces (they can reach 1,750 degrees) or by blasting samples with a laser beam. Once the argon gas is extracted from the sample, its age is determined by studying the patterns it makes on a mass spectrometer – a kind of scientific tree-ring counting for rocks.

"Well," Lisa says, "the lava, and even this butte – they are relatively recent, but the other formations that are on the Jornada . . ."

". . . were forming about thirty million years ago," Virgil finishes.

Lisa smiles, "Yeah, that's when things were really popping here."

Thirty million years ago the entire western part of what is now the United States was rising up like a loaf of baking bread, the crust of the earth the yeasty-flour and the hot magma the doughy-like heat from below.

"If you keep lifting something up it eventually has to break," Virgil says. "When it breaks the middle part sort of collapses – and everything falls in."

That collapse signaled the birth of what geologists now call the Rio Grande Rift, a cleft in the earth that stretches from central Mexico to near Leadville, Colorado.

We move over a jumble of black rocks at the top of the butte, easily stepping over a thin growth of bunchgrass and shrubs.

Virgil sweeps his hand in a slow arc over the southern expanse. "The Rio Grande Rift is full of debris and sediment washed down from the surrounding areas," he says. "Eventually the river started to form by working its way down through the rubble."

Most evidence suggests that the Rio Grande began to cut into the clutter of the rift from two to five million years ago.

Many geologists think that the actual cleft of the Rio Grande Rift – the area that represents the true, the deepest basin – is in fact the Jornada itself. "When the river did form – and for whatever reasons we aren't sure – it chose to go around the Jornada. All that sand and gravelly stuff is why there's so little surface water on the Jornada and the groundwater tends to be pretty far down." Virgil looks at Lisa, who squints up at us from where she is stooped near the rocks. "Don't you think that's about right?" he asks.

"Yeaaaah," she says, her faint accent showing the strata of her Wisconsin roots, "for the last thirty million years at least. You don't get many fossils either because you have chunks of rock falling into a valley, combined with volcanic activity along the margins." The Jornada basin remains full of the alluvial wash from the surrounding mountains because it never got excavated when the river finally cut its way to the sea. Across its expanse are many dry lake beds. Before the river cut through, the low areas were frequently wet, but now it is only for brief periods after a July downpour that the playas, as they are known, hold any water.

Virgil watches Lisa stop near a small pile of rocks and then he speaks again. "When the Rio Grande cut through probably correlates to a period where the climate got wetter all of a sudden – and with all that additional water the river eventually cut through. It's mostly the climate that affects things. Trouble is, we just don't know much about how the climate changed or how it affected things. That's still very poorly understood." Much of Virgil's research involves trying to determine what the weather patterns were like millions of years ago by studying certain isotopes he finds in sedimentary and metamorphic rocks. From that information he can begin to get a small snapshot of what the climate was like during the formation of the rock.

"That's what I'm into now," he says. Virgil also serves as the state mineralogist for New Mexico, and as the curator for New Mexico Tech's Mineralogy Museum he cares for a collection of more than fifteen thousand specimens housed there. "Climate is what I'm into," he repeats, "because that's where all the money is."

"Oh hush, Virgil!" Lisa says. "You aren't doing it because of the money."

Whether the issue is scholarly or the far more complicated landscape of a long-term relationship, one quality of this couple's relationship is the deep respect and admiration they have for one another.

He pauses again, then flashes a wide smile. "The Jornada was the last frontier because it has always been so inhospitable to humans." Without the least irony he suddenly stoops to the rocks near Lisa and picks up a wedge of what appears to be a smooth, dull red stone. "Pottery," he says. He studies it a moment, and then puts it back down. "It's everywhere up here."

Virgil picks up something else. He hands me a small pink rock the size of my thumbnail. "That chipped red agate doesn't belong up here," he says. "That agate comes from the mountains west of here. The people who lived on top of this butte hauled it up here to use as tools and ornaments."

Lisa points out how the nearby stones are laid out. "Can you see how there was once a room here?" she asks, pointing to a rough square of stones. "The pueblo stood right here." She smiles. "Wait until you see the trail down," she says.

We walk to the far edge of the butte. The edge is so abrupt I feel my stomach turn.

Lisa must have noticed my look. "Don't worry," she says. "It's a steep climb down from this side, but it's worth it; just watch your step." Without another word she jumps off the edge and lands three feet below on a blocky black rock the size of a delivery truck. Virgil goes next. I follow, cautiously. Sometimes I can find my footing in tiny cracks between the rocks, and at other times I must brace my arms against the sheer sides of two boulders and try to ease myself down. I try to follow Lisa and Virgil as they negotiate the tumble of stones like mountain sheep.

They take opposite directions and for a moment I'm confused, not knowing what to do. I watch as each moves from one stone to another, carefully studying the rocks. Then I notice a figure carved into the nearest stone, then another, and another. In a moment I've lost track of my friends and am scrambling over the rocks amid hundreds of ancient drawings.

5. Glyph Time

The oldest history of the Jornada is written everywhere in messages carved on rocks: glyphs that tell the story of a great hunt, etchings of myths and mystical beasts, expressions of the ordinary, the sacred, and the profound.

On the bony spine of ridges, on the fiery fringe of brilliant rimrock canyons, on mesa top and butte, on isolated stone and fragment of pottery, the ancient people of the Jornada left their stories for the future. No Rosetta stone, no translator exists for these glyphs, yet they vibrate with the holiness of human spirit and of time's immeasurable breadth. "I don't know what it means," a modern Zuni religious leader said after silently studying an elaborate rock art site for three hours, "but I know it is important."

We are no different from the ancient ones of the Jornada: we speak, we write, we draw, we send missiles into space all in order to leave our messages for the future, in order to show that we once lived. From the gates of heaven to the science of Darwin, we try to record some proof that our life is real. We give it a name, or draw it, or trace its genetic code.

In the petroglyphs of the Jornada are preserved what theologian John S. Dunne calls the life of the human spirit. Our very self-consciousness is not an awareness of our history, or of the path we have taken in our lives, Dunne writes, but rather "merely and always the point one has reached so far in the voyage of discovery." Every epic from the literature of the ages tells the single tale of this voyage of the human spirit. Read it here in the scattered etchings that shine like bleached bones on the walls and rocks of the Jornada. It is not history captured in these glyphs, but time.

Augustine believed that the mere actuality of time accounted for the existence of God. Time gave sequence, pattern, and meaning to reality itself. He called the eternity of time God's "Today." "And how many of our years and of our fathers' years," he wrote, "have passed through this Today of yours? . . . For Thou are most high and are not changed, and this Today does not come to an end in you; and yet it does come to an end in you, since all times are in you."

Once, while on a rocky cliff high above the desert floor, I came upon a profound record of that still point in time. On a black slab, amid a scattering of symbols carved on stone a thousand years ago, someone had chiseled a circle the size of a human face. Two round holes represented eyes, and another, a mouth.

It was a simple representation of a human skull.

To the Hopis, who have a similar symbol, such glyphs represent the God of Death, a macabre stranger who wanders the desert. He leaves his footprints everywhere he travels, and he travels everywhere. I stood in the silence at this human expression of the journey we all face in death. Here some mother wept at the passing of a warrior son, here some father sat grief-stricken at the loss of a child.

We recoil at the starkness of mortality, and yet that sudden emptiness, that glimpse of eternity, fascinates us, and entices us to continue on our voyage of discovery: we explore new lands, we reach to the stars, we look deep into our own natures, we split atoms, and we chant mantras, while the God of Death continues to stare out across the empty, sun-cut flats of the Jornada beyond the incomprehensible eternity of God's Today.

Another day while hiking along a remote and isolated gravel bench on the Jornada, I came upon a panel of glyphs etched on the vertical face of a stone slab. Two masklike faces stared from the silence of the dark rock. Below them the artist had drawn a box about the size of a hand. A staircase-like line bisected the box. The zigzag line cut the space in two like the teeth of a saw. All of the area on one side of the diagonal line had been carefully chipped away to form a beautiful white design against the black rock. The other half had been left dark.

This was probably a symbol of *nan sipu*, the earth navel, the place – according to ancient belief – where we emerged from darkness to begin our journey in this life.

We materialized from the void of the nan sipu, and our time on earth began. And time, on earth, began.

"Before heaven and earth there was no time," Augustine wrote, "there was no 'then' when time was not." Only with an observer can time be measured, and "only when time is passing can it be perceived, for once it has passed it cannot, since it is not."

The trick is to keep this vision of eternity always before us, to accept what the Buddhists call the "suchness" of our small place in the great mystery. "Who will hold the heart of man, that he may stand still, and see the still-standing eternity?" Augustine cried. We catch a glimpse of the enormity of time behind us – call it what you wish, call it Eden, or Big Bang, or nan sipu – and we catch a glimpse of the enormity of time before us – call it heaven or hell, or universe never-ending. We stand empty with the sudden shock of understanding: "There is nothing there but Is; there is not Was or Will Be, because whatever was is no longer: and whatever will be is not yet: but whatever is there, simply Is."

SILENCE

Silence may be the desert's most unique quality. Few places on the planet afford such luxury as this. The polar regions must have such silence, perhaps mountaintops so high even birds shun them, and maybe there is a similar quiet in sacred chambers of meditative monks. Often the Jornada's desert winds scream, and the detonation of a July thunderstorm can shake the very air, but when nature stills the Jornada may be one of the last places where – even for days at a time – no human noise breaks the silence. Because of the restrictions surrounding neighboring White Sands Missile Range, not even the sound of a high and distant passenger jet ever disturbs the air.

I have just driven down a narrow trace until it ended at a gravel berm. I turned off the car – stilling the roar of the air conditioner –

gathered up my day pack of water, snakebite kit, film, and food, and stepped out.

The silence is immediate, absolute, and encompassing; I stand without moving and listen.

There is nothing. No wind, no insects, no voices, no automobiles, no telephone, no conversation; there is not even the soft, constant hum we hear in even the most silent of moments of our modern world. There is *NO* sound. I strain to hear something, *anything*, as if the silence itself is a kind of constant drone covering up something beyond that I'm supposed to hear, but all that is is more silence.

I step through a fence of barbed wire and walk north following a sandy cattle path. Although the space between these low, dark-green shrubs is never less than several yards, and would seem sparse to an outsider, the vegetation here is relatively thick for the Jornada.

I move around a low creosote bush. The skull of a cow stares up at me from the ground just on the other side of the bush. The bone is new enough that a hunk of hairy hide sticks to its top, and dark, fat flies buzz in and out of the eye sockets seeking the deep where dried pockets of meat still cling.

I poke the thing with my walking stick and move on.

Just beyond the skull the land slopes almost imperceptibly downhill. I walk along the upper bank of the wide, sandy plain of Tiffany Arroyo. Although I'm headed for a less ancient village, I stop and study the ground. Somewhere near here is what archaeologists call a "scatter" – a light dusting of artifacts that indicates where very old ones, ones simply called the Archaic People, had a camp.

The hunters who lived here four thousand years ago would have known about silence, for to violate it with talk, or even to allow a mindless stumbling footstep, could scare away life-sustaining prey. At camp, however, here on the edge of the wide arroyo, there would have been sound. There would have been voices. The laughter of children. The talk of men and women as they worked. And long after sunset, long after the dancers and the storytellers stopped, the calming voice of a parent soothing a child, or the whispers of a man and woman, stirred from their sleep by dreams.

I search the ground for a trace of these ancient people. I open my mouth to speak to the nothingness, but my voice forms no words.

I grow suddenly cautious. Something is different. I hear a very faint, high-pitched whine, like a metallic horde of mosquitoes. I strain to distinguish the sound. It grows more distinct, emphatic: a whirling whine from a mechanical beast. At first I decide it must be a car, or a truck; then finally it seems too obvious: a train is approaching me along a set of tracks that has been paralleling my journey across the mouth of the arroyo.

The train appears, headed south. I wave as the engines thunder past, but the engineer does not see me. The massive sound of motors fades while a long stream of empty hoppers, boxcars, and flatbed cars rumbles past.

THE FIRST HUMANS

They moved ever eastward, traveling from one camp on the mudflat coast to another further into the unknown land, a small family whose desire for life and happiness sent them further and further from the familiar. Grandmother and grandchild, mother and infant asleep in shelters of hide. They were a nomadic clan who hunted, fished, raised their children, and – small traces of red paint on hollowed earth our only proof – prayed to spirits for happiness.

They moved across a land scholars now call Berignia, the shallow land bridge that once connected Alaska and Siberia. They moved because the food supply moved, or because of some ancient rule of exile, or perhaps it was simply because of that least understood of all of human weaknesses: wanderlust.

This was the tiny trickle of human life that became Native Americans. The trace is slight, but based on a kind of an archaeogenetic study of DNA, some scholars believe nearly the entire Native population of the Western Hemisphere descended from just a handful of people who traveled in small family bands east across the land bridge from Asia.

A few campfires, a stone point, tools, fragments of the language they spoke, and the unique chemical makeup of their cells is but a faint, ancient path to their past.

At first they survived by hunting the strange creatures of the land: towering, thick-robed beasts, mammoths that floundered in the snows along the edge of the great glaciers. Over hundreds of generations they grew into larger and larger bands and spread into the North American continent. As the generations unfolded they followed the food south along the glaciers that grew and then receded.

As the climate changed, the slow trickle become an ever-widening stream of humanity. The river moved, and human culture flowed across the Western Hemisphere leaving evidence of its passing: arrowheads and bones, temples, cities of gold, and tepee rings. Trace that evidence down the face of the continent, and see how like a river it widens and splits, spins into quiet eddies or rushes onward. Branches sweep to the east, others to the south; centuries later some reunite as a single stream, while others curl their way deep into South America.

One of the oldest traces of this stream of humans in North America is just a couple dozen miles southeast of the Jornada. There, in a cave near the small town of Orogrande, archaeologists found stone tools, charcoal with a fingerprint, and a single human hair. The charcoal was radiocarbon tested and found to be about twenty-eight thousand years old.

While the ancient date of this site remains debated, most archaeologists agree that humans first arrived in the Jornada area about twelve thousand years ago. The Clovis people, as this group is called, lived in small family bands and frequently moved from place to place following herds of mammoths, camels, small ancestors of the modern horse, and a now-extinct large-horned bison.

The remains of one significant Clovis site were discovered on the low, barren divide known as Mockingbird Gap on the Jornada's eastern edge. A concentration of artifacts marked what was probably a winter camp where several family bands gathered together.

Mockingbird Gap is a wide, gently sloping shoulder between the dark Oscuras and the rugged San Andres Mountains. It is difficult to imagine how any landscape could be more forlorn. For a hundred miles to the southeast a flat, featureless expanse of gypsum sand the very shade of snow shines desolate white in the desert heat. To the northwest lie fifty miles of yellow, barren gravel. Nearly no one visits

Mockingbird Gap. The politics of secrecy have isolated this Clovis site since that morning in 1945 when humankind detonated its first atomic bomb a dozen miles to the northeast. Today the spot is protected by virtue of its location deep in the military security of White Sands Missile Range.

Long before the invention of the bow, and longer still before the dawn of the atomic age, the men at Mockingbird Gap used what archaeologists say was then the world's most advanced weapon. Men hunted with the aid of an *atlatl*, a long, slender stick with a handgrip. At the end opposite the handgrip was a notch. That notch fit into the back end of a short spear tipped with a grooved stone point. When the hunter swung his arm in a wide arc, the missile-like spear would fly toward the target with far greater speed and accuracy than if it had simply been tossed by hand. According to Carroll Riley's history of the earliest New Mexicans, the atlatl was deadly to within 150 feet.

Stone and wood served the Clovis people in other ways as well. They shaped stone into tools and wood into dishes and packs and baby cradles. In winter camps like Mockingbird Gap they hoped that the strength of community would carry them safely through the hard times. In these camps friends and acquaintances caught up on one another's lives, and people gossiped, found a partner, and made tools for the next season. Stories were told, secrets were shared, and survival was ensured through cooperation and trust.

Then: change. The climate – always the unknown card in fate's hand – shifted. For thousands of years the Jornada region had been cool and moist, but starting around seventy-five hundred years ago, a very different weather pattern emerged in the Northern Hemisphere. Instead of cool and wet, the weather became exceedingly hot and dry – much warmer, in fact, than even the modern climate of the Jornada. A period some call "the long drought" lasted for the next thirty-five hundred years. The melting of the glaciers, combined perhaps with the human tendency to overhunt, caused most of the Pleistocene animals to disappear and be replaced by the more familiar animals of the American West.

Now too the people evolved. Over the centuries it took for the glaciers to recede back to the far north, the great stream of human culture divided again, as if around an island of time. To survive, humans gathered in small, mobile bands and fanned out across the land.

About ninety-five hundred years ago the Clovis culture evolved into a group most archaeologists call Folsom. In the Jornada area the Folsom people hunted a now-extinct species of bison as well as rabbit, antelope, wolf, and coyote. Little is known of these people, but due east of the Jornada about two hundred miles, archaeologists uncovered a Folsom shrine of some sort. On a small hill they found the long, white bones of a bison's legs carefully arranged around several jawbones. These were placed in a small hole in the ground. Most likely it was a shaman's shrine, a holy place on the landscape.

The remains of Folsom-era camps are scattered lightly across the Jornada, usually a hundred yards or so from playas or arroyos, usually on a slight rise, and usually on the downwind side from where game would come to graze and to water. As is the case with the older Clovis people, most of the details of the life of the Folsom people are based on the scant evidence of their tools. The Jornada's Folsom people still used the atlatl as the weapon of choice, but they had improved in the art of killing. Razor-sharp points with thin, pointed barbs at each base were attached to weighted spears that increased both the speed and accuracy of the atlatl.

Folsom people sewed their clothing with eyed needles fashioned from bone. They used hammers and knives made from obsidian obtained from quarries hundreds of miles distant. The small family bands that typify the Folsom people probably traveled light in easily moved camps of brush shelters or hide tents.

What happened next in the human history of the Jornada is not clear. The record is cloudy, but it is possible that for a while no humans lived anywhere in all of what is now New Mexico. When humans returned to the area, about eight thousand years ago, the Jornada became the location of a vague and constantly shifting border between distinct cultural traditions. Initially there may have been only two cultures, while a third arrived later. One of the initial cultures, sometimes called the Cochise culture (named after the great Apache warrior of the 1800s), spread in from what now is Arizona. At about the same time, the Chihuahua culture moved up from the south. Later, a third tradition, the Oshara, appeared along the northern edges of the Jornada. One researcher believes this last group moved into the region sometime between 5500 and 4800 BCE.

For several thousand years the Jornada served as a shifting, natural border between these groups who intermingled, traded, and fought.

THE HOLY LANDSCAPE

I follow a faint path from the cow skull. Whether the path was created by tire treads or moccasins I cannot be certain, but it leads to a low gravel bench hunched up against a slightly higher ridge. Every once in a while I splat at the snakeweed with my walking stick just in case a rattler might be lazing about.

At the top of the low bench is a scar. At some point a bulldozer has been here and scratched a jagged ditch in the earth. A twenty-yard-long line of rocks, dirt, and gravel borders the trench, the debris of the scourge of the West: pothunters. Just beyond their destruction I see the other rubble that marks the remains of two freestanding room blocks. Tiffany Pueblo was small – there are only forty rooms here divided among the three buildings. Through the feathery filter of creosote bushes I can make out a circular indentation at the center of plaza area. While the oldest part of this pueblo – a tiny, four-room structure – dates to 1300, the bulk of the village was built around 1530, about the time of the first European contact. There aren't many artifacts in this area, since the site was never occupied for a long period of time. This means that, despite their destruction, pothunters have never found much to steal.

The destruction angers and saddens me, but in a way I don't mind the barely discernible rubble of the room blocks, for I haven't come here to find walls, or pottery, or flint, but to seek artifacts of the spirit.

According to Alfonso Ortiz's brilliant study of his native San Juan Pueblo's rituals and beliefs, to the modern-day Tewas of northern New Mexico the physical world serves as a symbolic counterpoint to the spiritual. Each mesa, mountain, and lake is as holy as a mosque, temple, or cathedral. Great mystery is present in the very nature around us.

A circular underground chamber found at most modern and ancient pueblos, known as a *kiva*, is the symbolic representation of nan sipu, the earth navel from which we emerged. The kiva represents our birth, our emergence, into the troubled, profane world we think of as real, and it represents our end. We came from darkness, and to that darkness we shall return. A kiva serves both as a symbol of our spiritual and physical birth and – round and squat and dug deep into the earth – as an actual nan sipu – the sacred center. A sacred geography radiates from the plaza and kiva in a perfect alignment of mountains, lakes, hills, and shrines that are understood to be endowed with holiness.

At many pueblos, when you stand at the kiva and turn in a great circle, the landmarks of mesa and mountain of the real world are seamlessly juxtaposed upon the spiritual realm. At each of the cardinal directions, a coincidence of geology has placed other sacred landmarks in perfect, symmetrical juxtaposition to the village. Four holy mountains – themselves nan sipus – are aligned with the kiva. Nearby hills and clusters of rock further the spiritual geometry. It is as if the kiva stands at the center of a gigantic natural petroglyph – village and mountain, plaza and hills not only create a symbol for life's journey but provide a constant, inescapable presences of time made manifest on the land.

I have come to see if such a landscape marks this ancient pueblo as well. I turn my back to the ruins and scramble a little higher along the northern edge of the wide arroyo. In five minutes of hot, slow climbing I am standing on a point of land twenty feet directly above the pueblo site. Considering the low elevation, the view is expansive. I slowly turn in a circle, and the universe itself is revealed.

The sky first: endless blue, endless black, it is so immense that for a moment I'm lost in the enormity of distance, universe without beginning, universe without end colored the blue of robin's eggs.

To the north, a golden, pale-yellow plain burns in the blistering heat of an unsheltered sun.

To the south I can trace the arc of the Rio Grande in the curve of the vegetation along its banks. A green so light it seems nearly white sweeps out and away from where I stand and disappears from view behind the distant ridge. Beyond it, massive Black Mesa sits like a fortress of rock in the expansive mouth of the yawning Jornada.

I have yet to even glimpse it, to leave alone whatever comes to the eye. Augustine said that what distinguishes eternity from time is that time moves. Eternity, by its very definition, is without change. But it still isn't clear to me yet. As long as I insist on seeing the landscape as *separate* from me, even a glimpse of that still point of eternity remains elusive. I stand on the hot ridge trying to silence the part of me that insists on a past, the part of me that projects myself into the future.

According to Alfonso Ortiz, the transition from the mythical time before people emerged from the nan sipu to historic time is not unlike the change a squash might make from a flower to a hardened, ripe fruit or the subtle shift an innocent child might make evolving into a knowing adult. The shift from holy eternity to an existence shackled by time has been gradual. According to Ortiz, that transition embodies the distinction between sacred and profane. "What occurred . . . prior to emergence is sacred. What has been occurring since is profane, because illness, death and evil were introduced only after emergence."

But emerge we did. And to that unknowing place we shall return.

"An earth navel is like an airport," one informant told Ortiz. "You notice how airplanes, no matter where they go, always return to an airport. In the same way all things – game, people, and spirits – always return to the earth navel."

The heat is oppressive, and I still have the two-mile hike back to the car. I turn away from all of this and scramble back down the hillside.

I walk like a man possessed; I seek the exorcism of shade and the thin comfort of the sound of the ticking of clocks. Near the cow's skull I come across more bones: the delta shape of a single backbone, and through a bleached hipbone, an oval of sky shining. I am suddenly captivated. Like a madman I scurry around trying to decide how long the bones have lain here. A year? A decade? I scoop up the backbone in order to determine its deterioration. Like sandpaper, the surface of the bone brushes the thin skin at the tips of my fingers. I gasp and throw it down.

I gulp down the last of my water, shaking like a leaf. I wait a moment for my head to clear. Like phantoms, half a dozen wild cattle suddenly appear from the brush. Most of them scurry away like frightened deer, but a big bull stops short a few feet from me. He stares at me a moment, then turns and thunders away.

I stop and listen: the hoofbeats disappear and then the Jornada del Muerto is once again as silent as eternity.

SEEING THE SPIRAL

The sun is about as bad as it gets on the desert. When we started hiking away from Dan Perry's truck at 11 a.m., it had already reached ninety-eight. Now we're walking across a level gravel bench just below a squat, red butte. Dan, a naturalist for the Bosque del Apache National Wildlife Refuge, agreed to escort me to this restricted area of the Jornada. A tall, friendly man with an ever so faintly graying, close-cropped beard, he wears a National Park Service hat, a western-style straw affair with a wide, shady brim. We carry plenty in our day packs, so there is little chance that Dan and I, with throats parched dry, will have to search for cool, clear water.

"The bulk of the Jornada is on the other side of the butte," Dan says, walking across the broad, hot plain. "There're no roads anywhere in here."

Because of the significance of this remote area, the U.S. government protects it, and coming here without an official escort is normally a federal offense. I don't mind the company. Dan is the most pleasant kind of fellow you'd ever want for a companion. He laughs easily, knows his bush penstemon from his pyrrhuloxia, and makes a trusty guide.

We reach a flat area about the size of a baseball field. Except for the high metallic whine of an insect, our voices are the only sound.

"We should be seeing lots of pottery," Dan says.

Instantly I distinguish a round, flat piece from among the stones at our feet. Nearly the same color as the earth, the smooth brown wedge is painted with a single black line across it.

Then artifacts are everywhere. From the shape of sand and rock and gravel the singularity of pottery appears. Brown or pale white,

smooth or curled, painted in the geometric exactness of skilled mathe-
maticians.

Dan looks around and then spies an object. He stoops near a clump
of rabbit bush and gently picks up an oval stone. He hands me the
reddish-tan disk of sandstone. It is the size of my hand and is neatly
bisected by a groove worn in the stone. I run my finger down the
length of the arrow-straight furrow.

"It's a shaft straightener," Dan says. "This was a very important
object to someone long ago. Isn't it lovely?" he asks. Indeed. I have
never seen one outside a museum. I tip it one way and then the other
until the stone fits easily in my hand. The groove parallels my fingers.
I hold it to my eye and sight down the notch back toward the red-
rimmed butte behind us. I hand it back, and Dan replaces it in the
same spot near the rabbit bush. "I like to keep it here to show the
tourists," he says smiling.

A few mounds of what appear to be gravel and clay are in the low
open space before us. Dan moves slowly and decisively, turning first
one way and then the other. He walks in a straight line toward one of
the mounds of gravel. I follow a few feet behind him, searching in vain
for a ghost I have yet to see.

"This is the largest known pueblo on the Jornada," he says, his voice
now as soft and reverent as if in church.

"Largest *known*?" I ask.

Dan shrugs, but instead of answering me he indicates a small rise
directly ahead of us. A crumbling wall outlines a single small room on
the gravel.

"Ah," I say, "the pueblo!"

"Not quite," Dan says. "Sometime long after this pueblo was in
ruins, a shepherd built a cabin here." He points out a few small scraps
of metal, two white ceramic shards, and – mostly covered by sand –
the gnarled, dark turd of a boot heel. "Whoever it was most likely used
adobe bricks from the pueblo in order to build his cabin."

Dan understands my question before I ask it. "No," he says in his
easygoing southern drawl, "I believe it was all right for him to have
used the bricks. He wasn't here to steal or plunder the place. Instead,
this guy lived in a kind of symbolic harmony with the ruin."

Then Dan falls deeply silent and does not move. Several seconds pass before I realize why he has stopped. The long, low rise of gravel before us runs for nearly fifty yards in either direction. I look. Look again. As if slowly emerging from a fog, the massive pueblo appears out of the desert. The remains of the puny shepherd's cabin are dwarfed the instant I see the shape of the enormous city outlined by hundreds of low gravel ridges that were once towering walls.

"This pueblo has over 750 rooms," Dan says. "We are standing in the center of the main plaza. If you look carefully over there . . . ," he points, and points again, "you can see three other plazas."

In the final three hundred years before the arrival of the Spanish, the Native population of the Jornada increased sevenfold. For centuries this village stood as the southern outpost of the great pueblo cities far to the north. The foremost authorities of the Piros, Michael Marshall and Henry Walt, estimated that this pueblo was home to at least two thousand people. This pueblo was a kind of frontier metropolis where Native people from all over the Southwest gathered. Bustling and busy with commerce and the mix of cultures, it was likely both a dangerous and an exotic place to live.

The day grows ever hotter, and although our brains are shutting down some, we drift around ruins chatting. Dan speculates on the function of some of the rooms. He points to where he thinks the people of this lost city grew squash and corn.

Corn, the great pacifier of civilization, has made its own long journey to the Jornada. *Zea mays*, a small plant with gnarly pods of popcorn-like kernels, had been domesticated from a wild plant seven thousand years ago in central Mexico. It is not known whether the plant was a trade good or came north into the Jornada with the migration of people, but when it arrived here five thousand years ago, people who had depended for centuries largely on weapons for survival turned to cultivation of the earth. These groups evolved into what most archaeologists call the golden age of precontact history, distinct traditions known now as Hohokam, Anasazi, and Mogollon. From these came the Piros, the last permanent Native American residents of the Jornada.

The ancient desert varieties of maize need far less moisture than our modern hybrids, and they thrive in the blazing sun of the desert. But growing corn meant staying in one place and tilling the land. Around the year 200 CE, large agricultural-based pueblos like this one began to appear along the wet seeps and damp arroyos.

Dan tells me too that – given access to the Rio Grande – the Piros' diet was based on considerably more fish than was that of most other desert cultures.

We talk softly of the old ones as we move around their ancient town. We imagine children, teenagers, women and men. Fields and fishing, life and life no longer. Dark-haired men from the north in their cotton shirts and loose-fitting leggings mingle with the blanketed desert people from the south. Others, like the master potters the Mogollons and Mimbres from the mountains to the west, come and go on the well-traveled footpaths that lead out from the plaza. Strangers from as far away as the Mississippi, dressed in eagle feathers and robes of bison, linger at the edge of the plaza bearing their bundles of trade goods. A solitary Apache drifts like smoke across the busy plaza.

What happened to all of these people?

It's not an idle question. Many of the largest cities in the desert Southwest were already abandoned when the Spanish arrived. By 1500 this great pueblo on the Jornada was but a shadow of its glory days.

Theories abound to explain it.

Some scientists think that climate shifts once again played a roll. Tree-ring data indicate that a severe century-long drought caused the population to revert to smaller groups. Such a drought would cause people who had become dependent on agriculture to revert to hunting. The effects of famine over the course of one hundred years would be significant.

War too might have caused the Piros to abandon this city. About this time, newcomers from the north – Athapascan or Shoshonean – arrived in the area, and the resulting clash of cultures may have resulted in widespread war. Unprotected cities like this one would have made easy targets. The theory is that war and the threat of war forced people to move to safer locations or to live in places that could be easily fortified.

Some theories about why the great cities were abandoned are macabre: at a site in northern New Mexico, human bones that had marks
consistent with cannibalism were recently unearthed. Some theorize
that invaders might have introduced the practice from the south,
where cannibalism was more common. Like cattle and other animals
that have been fed ill-processed animal proteins, transmittable spongi-
form encephalopathies – a human form of mad-cow disease – could
have swept like a plague across the population.

Plague. Famine. War. We step from the nan sipu into a troubled,
profane world. But perhaps a more spiritual reason accounts for the
abandonment of so many great pueblo cities. Ed Ladd, an authority
on Zuni religion, says they "moved because they were looking for
the center place. And where they found the center place, that's where
they settled."

Dan and I have circled the entire pueblo site and have returned to
the central plaza. When I ask him, he points out the round indentation where the kiva once stood. I dig around the waistband of my day
pack to grab the compass in my pocket. I hold it flat in my hand and
watch the black needle swing into position. I squint my good eye and
sight as carefully as possible. The blood-red monolith of the butte rises
from the Jornada like a wound; it is due east of the kiva. I turn to
stammer something at Dan, but he has already noticed. "You think
you've discovered something?" he says. "Well, shall we go find out?"
I nod and together we turn away from the ruins of the pueblo and
begin walking toward the high butte.

Half an hour later Dan and I stand at the base of the brownish-red
mesa. The sandstone stands in stark contrast to the dark lava rocks
near its base.

I follow Dan across a slope of red rock and yellow sand. We reach
the base of the imposing rock and stop for a drink of water. Before us,
a sandstone wall rises perpendicularly. High above, the rugged top of
the mesa seems only a few feet beneath the burning sun.

Dan speaks. "The only way up is steep and dangerous," he says. We
both take another deep drink of water and without another word start
up the trail. It is questionable whether either of us is thinking too
clearly, for the sun burns a dry furnace heat right through our hats.

We trudge up the sudden steepness of the hidden path, moving silently, working our way through the rocks.

After a few minutes of climbing, Dan stops and points. Deeply etched into stone as red as human blood, a petroglyph shines in the blistering sunlight. Two spirals, connected by an angular line, form a figure shaped like an ornate letter "E." Similar glyphs are found all over the Southwest and represent the movement of the people. From the center of the top spiral, the glyph says, human beings emerged. A series of concentric circles spiral from that still point. Each loop of the spiral represents a single jornada, a single journey away from the place before birth. An angular line connects the top and bottom spiral. It represents the present moment, here, now. Then every loop of the lower spiral represents another jornada back toward what Ed Ladd called "the center place" that awaits us all in death.

At every instant of our lives we stand just here on the angular center between the twin spirals of birth and death.

Dan begins to climb higher into the blazing sun of noon. He stops, almost as an afterthought, and turns to glance back at me. "I don't think we'll see any because of the time of day," he says softly, "but this is the area where I see the most rattlesnakes, so keep on a look out."

We climb until Dan reaches a sheer cliff of stone. Carefully he lifts himself up the rock face. I take a deep breath and press my palms against the chest-high ledge. I hoist myself straight up and squeeze through a narrow crevasse in the stone. I look back down. I fumble for my water.

"Look," Dan says. For an instant I think the heat has driven him impossibly insane, for he leans back out over the abyss, then leans back in. "Look," he says again.

I slowly lean out. A cliff face hangs above open air. On it are carved a half-dozen petroglyphs. They are of corn plants, stick figures shown roots and all – tall, thin-leafed stalks in full summer.

"How did people get out there to carve those?" I stammer.

Dan simply shrugs. "Beats me," he says. "How would *you* get out there to carve those?"

I study the corn glyphs as they glow in the golden sunlight.

When asked why he thought there were so few center places on earth, Hopi cultural preservation officer Leigh Jenkins responded with a story. When the Hopi guardian spirit emerged, the only material possessions that the spirit carried were a planting stick, a patch of corn, and a jug of water. "That's really the message that the Hopi bring to everyone," Jenkins said. "If there is yet a chance for all of us, it should be through the recognition of some of the basic elements of life." What the ancient ones left is that simple wisdom: to survive we need hard work, food, and water. The Hopis believe that technology and science have caused that simple spirit to grow dim, but they also say that in the future, short little ears of corn will save the world.

I am still leaning over the brink of the rock when I turn to study the opposite wall.

The snake's open mouth is inches from my face. I gasp and stumble backward.

"Pretty authentic-looking petroglyph," Dan says.

I lean back out for another look. The carving of an uncoiled rattlesnake moves directly toward my eyes. I shudder and seek the thin comfort of the faint trail.

Dan turns starts to climb toward the top of the mesa up a somewhat easier route. "The funny thing," he says, pointing, "is that the last time I was here I saw a fat old rattlesnake right over there in that four-wing saltbrush."

We scramble up a jumble of soft stones and soon are standing against an open sky high above the earth.

We walk through the ruins of a very small pueblo. Dan stops at the circle of stones that marks the kiva. He looks at me. "Go on," he says, "what do you see?"

I almost forgot. I dig my compass out of my pocket. I stand at the center of the kiva and try to steady my hand. The needles swivel, and then points.

It would be a mistake to make too great a parallel between Ortiz's explanation of the Tewa belief systems and this place. The cosmology of the Tewa Indians is as intricate and comprehensive as any philo-sophical or metaphysical system in the world. But still, it *is* possible that the people at this Jornada pueblo were the keepers of similar beliefs. Could they have stood where I now stand and seen, not mesa and plain and mountain, but a sacred drawing that gave proof to and replicated the central mysteries of the world?

Due north a conical-shaped mountain rises in the distance.

Carefully, I align myself to the west. Thirty miles away a grassy peak rises from the San Mateo Mountains. Directly below us on the gravel plain lie the ruins of the large pueblo.

I spin around and use my arm to point due east. "Do you see that?" I ask. Dan is watching me closely; he mumbles something in reply, but he too is staring. Straight as an arrow from where we stand, the lone peak of a distant black mountain marks the eastern nan sipu.

The people who once lived on the Jornada del Muerto knew that we came forth from eternal mystery, and that after our journey through time our death would return us there. They saw it in the very land around them, in butte and mountain and stone where sacred eternity dwells.

Death awaits, but from the fear of its snakelike fangs, charity comes forth.

From nourishing corn, hope.

And amid the spiral reminders of our life's journeying from darkness to darkness again, faith is born.

Every civilization, every history, every stone-pecked story on rock has simply been the record of a journey of the spirit. Oh Lord, the stories of our existence pray, *let something remain!* We shout and listen to it echo across the ruins.

I turn to the south, but there is nothing on the landscape, only the flat and featureless plain of the Jornada del Muerto. At first I think the time-glyph has failed, but then Dan speaks. His voice is very quiet. "Out there on a day in 1581 the first Europeans appeared," he says.

6. Artifacts

Last night I parked the van on the edge of a gravel road near an isolated pocket of rock that snugged up against a hillside. I flopped a blue tarp onto the ground, threw down my sleeping bag, and was asleep before I'd even seen the stars.

I awoke well before dawn. I fired up some coffee and now sit on my comfortable bag having breakfast. I munch on dried fruit and watch the dark eastern sky slowly reveal the outline of mountains. An owl who-hoos the night away. A line appears, dark blue in the dark cloth of the eastern horizon. One by one the eternity of stars disappears.

I study the dust of the road. I thought maybe I had slept too soundly to notice, but there are no vehicle tracks except mine from nine hours ago. In a pale light I pour the rest of my coffee into a big cup, then throw my gear into the van. I take a last look at my roadside camp near the bleak, southern entrance to the Jornada and jump into the driver's seat. In my rearview mirror the Hershey Kiss tip of Robledo Peak turns silver in the coming dawn. I creep north on a skinny road into isolation.

I'm driving along the oldest continuously traveled road in the continental United States. This forty-mile-long remnant of the old Spanish Royal Road, the Camino Real, is frequently washed out, undependable, and barren, but on this route for thousands of years, parrots, shells, masks, and spiritual knowledge traveled back and forth between the Native peoples of Mexico and the Pacific and the Native peoples of New Mexico. Along this jornada, too, the New World first came face-to-face with the Old.

I drive slowly on the rough road. I cover only a few miles before the rosy-fingered dawn slices the dark horizon. An instant later the glare of white sunlight causes me to switch to sunglasses.

The first people from the Old World to get anywhere close to the Jornada were castaways. In 1534 a handful of Spaniards who survived a shipwreck on the Texas coast slowly made their way across the interior of the North American continent to become the first non-Natives to see what is now the southwestern United States. Carrying buckskin packs, traveling or trading with the Indians as they went, they struggled west hoping to find their way to the Spanish capital at Mexico City. By some scholars' reckoning, Cabeza de Vaca, a Spaniard, and Estaban, a black man, passed within a few miles of the southern end of the Jornada.

Somewhere around here they crossed "some desperate sierras, in great hunger" thanks to "the poverty of the country." After three more days of difficult travel they came to a river where they "found people and houses and stopped and had beans and squashes to eat." They ate a flatbread made with mesquite bean flour, as well as a nut from a pine tree that was "as good as those of Castile, or better because they have a shell that is eaten with the nut." They saw corn, and along the edges of the wasteland the village medicine men performed rituals with rattles made of gourds.

After three years of wandering the deserts of North America, the ragtag wanderers reached Mexico City. Hailed as evidence of God's power, the men's mere survival in the Catholic capital was deemed a miracle.

At 5:45 a.m. I pull the van to the side of the dusty road and stop. I step out into the early sunlight and open my carefully folded topographical map and hold it taut against a light but warm breeze. No green on this map, only a wild mix of brown lines bunched up against the sharp escarpment of the Caballo Mountains. The map encompasses nearly seventy square miles and shows not a single human habitation. It doesn't matter. I know there's not much more on any of more than forty such maps that encompass the Jornada.

I load the day pack with two quarts of water, find my walking stick and notebook, and turn to study the desert. I set a course for a point in the barren yellow mountains to the west. I walk slowly, since snakes are very active at this time of morning, but also so I can study the ground for any trace of former travelers across the Journey of the Dead. For good or for evil, whatever change we humans have brought to this place on earth, it has come to the Jornada upon the Camino Real.

Wild tales of de Vaca and Estaban's miraculous journey spread across Spanish Mexico. People soon believed that the men had found cities basking in gold. If such wealth existed, the Spanish viceroy in Mexico City wanted it. In 1538 he appointed a Franciscan monk to explore the uncharted lands to the north of Mexico City. The monk could gain souls for God while at the same time claiming all of the land and its wealth for the Crown.

Historian Marc Simmons writes eloquently of the missionary zeal the Spanish brought with them to the New World. He notes that the Catholic Spanish believed God had *given* Spain the New World not just to gather the wealth of gold and silver but "for the harvesting of Indian souls." He writes that the Spanish saw the riches of the New World as God's "heavenly lures" to draw Spanish expeditions into the wilderness and thereby provide a way for priests to reach heathens in need of conversion.

Fray Marcos de Niza, the first missionary in the Southwest, had the best of all possible guides: Estaban himself. Although they did not reach the Jornada, the 1539 de Niza expedition set off an ongoing rush for wealth that continues to affect the American West today, because de Niza returned to Mexico City proclaiming that he had seen a city "bigger than the city of Mexico." He said it had been only the smallest of seven great, golden cities.

I walk slowly in a zigzag pattern, my eyes looking for something, anything that might be from the old days. Except for the high, winding pitch of an insect, like an electronic alarm clock left unattended, there is silence. I see a rusted can, then a smaller scrap of rusted metal. Since nearly nothing was thrown away and nearly nothing ever lost its usefulness, the Spanish who first traveled the Camino Real left few items behind. By the 1800s, however, the tin can had gained its position as our nation's first true road trash. Food could be preserved and carried in tidy, disposable containers. The dry desert preserves the artifacts well. Soon I'm following the route of the old road by walking from one tin can to the next.

When I turn back toward the car, the full force of the morning's sunlight hits me. It is not yet 8 a.m., but the glare from the sunlight burns against the reddish sand. I hear only the blood humming in my inner ear.

I return to the van, take a long swig of water, hop back in and slowly drive further north.

De Niza's talk of golden cities ignited the viceroy's desire for the riches of northern New Spain. The next expedition north was large and well financed.

On a cool afternoon in February 1540, a grand army paraded past the viceroy. The ruthless and determined Francisco Vaquez de Coronado led three hundred mounted men north out of Mexico City. Many of the horsemen carried lances and the West's first firearms: cumbersome matchlock harquebuses. Behind the horsemen marched three hundred foot soldiers carrying crossbows, swords, and shields. Some of these men wore chain-mail coats. To the rear as many as a thousand slaves and servants brought up the pack animals or herded cattle, horses, and oxen.

According to historian Frederick Hodge, Coronado's voyage was "the most pretentious and spectacular exploratory expedition that has ever set foot within the limits of the United States." That appearance would mark the true meeting of the Old and New Worlds on the Jornada.

For the next two years the army from New Spain ranged as far east as the buffalo plains of Kansas and Nebraska, as far north as the pueblos of New Mexico and Colorado, and as far south as the northern edge of the Jornada.

By late summer 1540 Coronado had reached the Zuni basin near what is now the central New Mexico/Arizona border. He moved eastward to what we now call the Rio Grande, where he found pueblo villages clustered along the large river. The Native people of the Rio Grande greeted Coronado and his men hospitably, but shortages of food and shelter soon led to trouble.

In the second year of Coronado's conquest, a captain led a group of men several hundred miles south down the Rio Grande to become the first non-Natives on record to see the Jornada. According to the best eyewitness account, "the captain . . . found four large villages which he left at peace." One of these villages was probably the pueblo that once stood on top of the stark mesa I climbed with geologists Lisa Peters and Virgil Lueth.

The captain reported that to the south, in the hot, empty land beyond these pueblos, the river simply disappeared into a sandy desert. Although the Native people assured him that the river eventually reappeared, the captain and his men traveled no further into the Jornada and soon returned to join the rest of the conquistadores to the north.

By now the tensions between the invaders and the Natives had escalated. Food shortages led to a regionwide famine. In search of food, Coronado's men seized an entire pueblo. Almost instantly the Native people up and down the Rio Grande valley reacted.

Then came war, with all of its ancient and attendant horrors.

Once hostilities began, the Spanish attacked every pueblo that resisted them. The results were often deadly. The people of one mesa-top pueblo survived a two-month-long attack and finally surrendered under a flag of peace. Once the Indians were down off of the mesa, the Spanish massacred all of them.

One day, nearly three years after entering the Southwest, Coronado injured his head when he fell from his horse. "Whereafter," wrote an eyewitness, "he gave evidence of a ruined disposition."

A ruined disposition.

Shortly after this accident, empty-handed and destitute, Coronado returned south.

I have driven only a few miles when I stop the van to look at a low, mean range of sharp-edged hills that comes down from the mountains. This is Point of Rocks, a dangerous place where Apaches often hid in order to raid travelers on the Camino Real.

I hike the area for an hour, find nothing, and then drive slowly for a few miles. The white sunlight glares on the dark road.

I pull the van to a stop at the barely perceptible bottom of a wide valley. I click off the engine and step from the air-conditioning into a furnace of hot, still air. I stand on the bumper and study the area with binoculars.

The draw is no more than a faint suggestion on the flat desert. It climbs slowly toward the barricade of a wide hill. Distant mountains rise above the hill like a black rope flung wide on the cloudless sky. The land is scattered everywhere with creosote bushes and shrubs.

One of the best archaeologists of the Camino Real, Michael Marshall, claims that the earliest traces of the ancient road form an obvious swale here as they climb up that distant hill. I rest my elbows on the roof of the van in order to steady my view. I slowly scan the hillside from left to right. From a distance the mesquite trees on the fiery pale desert seem as green and plump as Christmas trees. I stop. Something glistened in the high sunlight. I steady my arms and squint through the glasses at an object on the far hill. Just below the crest of the isolated hill and on the sandy side of a lonely ridge, a cross stands highlighted against the sky.

I don't think about it twice. I step off the van's bumper, collect my water, and once again head across the desert.

I beg to differ with the eminent historian Marshall, but if there is an "obvious swale" to be seen on this godforsaken two miles of waterless furnace, it certainly has escaped my roving eye.

Hiking on sand is not easy. Each step requires the use of many more muscles than walking on a hard surface. Usually I can walk around the shrubs, but at other times I have to push straight through them and endure the vicious scrapes from barbed thorns.

It takes an hour of this kind of struggle for me to reach the hillside.

The distant western mountains give birth to radiating disks of storm clouds. East, above the jagged line of the San Andres Mountains, smoke-like thunderheads rise high into the cobalt blue dome. A lone bird, a crow, caws up the sky; all around me is a thick scattering of yucca in full bloom.

Before me, painted a weather-weary white, is the metal cross.

In 1581, almost forty years after Coronado, three Catholic missionaries under a small military escort plotted a difficult route from Mexico across the desolate Chihuahuan Desert. They followed the rivers and draws until they eventually reached the Rio Grande somewhere near what is now Big Bend National Park in Texas. They followed that river northward until they reached the Jornada. Here they met the native Piro people of the Jornada.

Marc Simmons writes: "The Franciscans were elated by what they found. On both sides of the river appeared a scattering of Indian towns whose adobe buildings resembled the half of a multi-layered wedding cake, rising to five or six stories with upper terraces reached by pine log ladders."

A soldier's report described the elaborate dress of the people: sewn cotton shirts, pants, and skirts. They wore shoes and covered their shoulders with gorgeous cotton blankets decorated with beautiful geometric designs of spirals and shapes and animals.

I study the metal cross at the top of the hot hill and decide it is of recent vintage – perhaps mid-twentieth century. There is no name or date, nothing but the cross to mark this lonely grave. My van is a speck in the great distance, the only other human object in the entire expanse of wilderness.

I cannot think. I turn from the metal cross and start back across the desert to my car. Instead of causing a sharp awareness, the high sun burns my mind to a dull stupor. Despite the shade of my wide-brimmed straw hat, I trudge mechanically, not aware of anything but the motion of my own legs. Lift foot, step, lift foot, step, in little puffs of sand and dust.

I spend an hour hiking back across the wide, bone-dry draw. The day grows blistering hot. I find only a single cartridge from a vintage twentieth-century weapon: the 30.06. Except for a few glimpses of the van from time to time, the shell casing is the only bit of humanity I see. It is noon when I step back to the road a little south of my car. I walk up the lonely road back to my van. I fumble for my keys and get in.

The missionaries never made it back south. Ignoring the soldiers' warnings that they not stay behind, the three missionaries remained along the Rio Grande in the zealous belief that divine providence would allow them to convert the Indians and then return.

After the soldiers made it back south, a rescue mission was hurriedly organized in the slim hope of finding the missing missionaries alive. At the head of that expedition rode the first of the Jornada's long history of bloody killers, Antonio de Espejo. Espejo had recently escaped punishment for assisting in the murder of two men at his brother's ranch. He had fled to the Chihuahuan Desert and then heard talk about the silver that could be found in the north. He immediately offered his services as a guide to the expedition about to set off in search of the stranded missionaries.

By early 1583, Espejo, one priest, and fourteen soldiers reached the western edge of the Jornada. They camped on the Rio Grande at the base of a towering black mesa. On the northern flank of the mesa the men found a ideal place for their horses, a small, green pasture – a *valverde*. For the next four hundred years Valverde would be at center stage for much of the Jornada's history.

Indian residents met the small party at Valverde. Soon the Spanish learned that two missionaries from the previous expedition had been killed. Despite this, the Natives treated these invaders with generosity. "As we were going through this province," Espejo later wrote, "the people came out to receive us, taking us to their pueblos and giving us a great quantity of turkeys, corn, beans, tortillas and other kinds of bread." He especially noted the baked bread, "which they make more nicely" than the people of Mexico.

He observed the round, basement-like kivas of the pueblos and mistook them for winter shelters instead of religious and social centers. He saw how the fields of corn were irrigated by an elaborate system of ditches to utilize the waters of the Rio Grande.

He noticed how the pueblo people used "ores of different colors" for decoration. Now convinced that immeasurable wealth was at his fingertips, Espejo began a campaign to find it. He began to slash a bloody swath through the pueblo villages.

For the better part of a year Espejo roamed from present-day Arizona to northern New Mexico. He visited more than seventy pueblos. At one point he killed sixteen puebloans by tightening a rope around each man's neck until he suffocated. "A strange deed," one of the soldiers wrote, "in the midst of so many enemies."

Contrary to what previous Spanish expeditions had believed, Espejo discovered that the pueblo Indians were not a single empire but divided by language and differences in culture. He noted that such divisions would make the people much easier to conquer than if they had been united in single large "empire."

When he returned to Mexico, Espejo's observation that the pueblos could be conquered, along with his glowing report of fertile valleys ripe for settlements, signaled the ultimate colonization of New Mexico.

The Spanish brought to the Southwest more than just gunpowder and crucifixes. Tens of thousands of years of isolation in the Western Hemisphere had left the immune system of Native peoples defenseless against diseases the Spaniards unknowingly introduced. In the first century following contact with the Spanish, even the largest pueblo cities that ringed the Jornada were virtually empty.

Seven years passed on the Jornada with no sign of the Spanish intruders. Then, in July 1590 the lieutenant governor of a northern Mexico province led a group of 170 men and women northward into New Mexico. Although he had not yet been given official sanction for his expedition, whenever Gaspar Castaño de Sosa arrived at a new pueblo he announced he had come to rule them in the name of a distant king and that all people must all pledge allegiance to him. At each of the twenty-two pueblos he visited, he appointed Native leaders as his governors, judges, and sheriffs. Many of the different pueblo cultures soon adapted these positions into their existing governmental and spiritual systems, where they remain today. Likewise, the missionaries' tales of a Christ risen from the dark underworld blended with the traditional beliefs of the Pueblo people.

According to most historians, Castaño de Sosa was an ethical ruler. When some of his men wanted to seize Indians for the slave market and to take what wealth they could find, Castaño de Sosa prohibited it, citing Spanish laws against such inhumane action. According to historian Robert Silverberg, such laws "were being ignored almost everywhere else in the empire." Castaño de Sosa's soldiers were so annoyed by his insistence on the law they plotted to kill him. He survived the plot but was arrested by soldiers sent from the south for having entered New Mexico without permission. The same wagons and carts used to haul his belongings to the north now took him south. These *carretas*, the Spanish name for the covered, wooden wagons of the caravan, were the first wheeled vehicles to cross the Jornada.

I steer my own gas-guzzling *carreta* over a very rough and deeply rutted stretch of that same road. I take a drink of warm, precious water from the sweet rim of a plastic bottle and check again to make sure the air conditioner is on high.

After Castaño de Sosa, only one group of non-Natives crossed the Jornada before Oñate's great conquest. In 1593 a small expedition came up the Rio Grande and traveled east onto the buffalo plains, where they were killed by Indians. Almost nothing else is known about these men except that they died in a lonely place, far from their homes.

DUST

It's late afternoon. I'm a half-dozen miles south of Ben and Jane Cain's ranch at Aleman. Because I made so many stops, I've driven only thirty miles in the nearly nine hours since breaking camp. I've got bluegrass music playing in the van's stereo, and the air conditioner is cranked up to high. I hold a topographical map between my hands and steer down the gravel road. I crest a small hill; to the right I see what I'm looking for. In the desert scrub are two faint lines: an old road trace. I swing the van onto the desert and stop. Ahead of me the old road trace fades as it disappears down into a small desert valley. The old Royal Road, the Camino Real, should be about three miles due east.

The air conditioner roars, and Ralph Stanley's angelic voice rises above heavenly mandolins. It's time to stop for the night. I pull the van further off the road but leave it running while I collect my gear. For a moment the CD is nothing but background music, but then the pure, sweet harmony of the brothers' bluegrass singing fills the air: "Are you afraid to die?" they sing, "Are you a-fraaaaid to die?"

I was all right until I heard that song.

I snap the motor off. The air fills with the immediate silence of the hot desert afternoon. A blast of dry heat slams against me as I step out of the van. No one in the world knows where I am right now, and I've parked far enough from the road that even if a car passed, the van would be invisible. I grab the big backpack and double-check my gear. I plan to hike to where the Camino Real once crossed an arroyo and then camp there for the night. If something happens to me out there . . . I shake my head to clear it and hoist the big pack onto my back.

I know enough about solo wilderness travel to understand that I must not give in to fear, but it's hard to stop the first faint whispers in my ear.

Twenty yards ahead I see a clutter of white stones against the nearly gray sand. Lighter-colored rocks form a rough circle. Inside the circle a scattering of smaller black rocks litters the ground. The small dark pieces are coal. Until motorized times, many desert travelers carried coal in their wagons and carts in order to fuel makeshift roadside forges where a man, handy as a blacksmith, could form a needed horseshoe or wagon piece. The desert climate has left these remains untouched for years. The coal, which centuries ago burned red hot, looks as if scattered only yesterday.

I turn from the ghost of the nameless man who briefly tended this fire and walk deeper into the desert.

In *The Wisdom of the Desert*, Thomas Merton compares the "colonizers of the Renaissance" with a handful of fourth-century monks who sought religious solitude in the deserts of the Middle East. In contrast to the hermits, the conquistadores' motivation was a result of being alienated from their true selves. "In subjugating primitive worlds," Merton writes, "they only imposed on them, with the force of cannons, their own confusion and their own alienation."

It would be several more years before an officially sanctioned colonization expedition would arrive and the Spanish conquest would be nearly complete. By 1598 the government had received a stampede of petitions from wealth-crazed men for the official right to colonize the area. The viceroy eventually awarded the official *entrada* (the formal right to enter a new land) to one of the richest men in the entire New World: Juan de Oñate.

According to Robert Silverberg, Oñate's bloodlines went to the very heart of the Spanish history of North American. Oñate's family "had been prominent in the conquest of Mexico. His father had been governor of a Mexican Province." His wife came from the heart of a new nation: Mexico. She was "the granddaughter of the famed conqueror Cortez, and the great-grand daughter of Montezuma, the Aztec King."

According to his official instructions, Oñate was to colonize the area and to convert "many large settlements of heathen Indians who live in ignorance of God and of the Holy Catholic faith . . . so that they might have an orderly and decent Christian life."

Oñate began the long, frustrating process of putting together a group of properly outfitted colonizers. Marc Simmons points out that the "most seductive" reason why a commoner might risk such a dangerous voyage was that it automatically made him eligible for a low rank in Spanish royalty. With this status also came "the right to use the title Don before one's name (an acronym formed from the first letters of the phrase *de origin nobel*), exemption from taxes and freedom from arrest for debt."

In February 1598 the two-mile-long colonization caravan finally set off for New Mexico. Six weeks later the colonizers reached the Rio Grande where the city of Juarez now stands. They forded the river at what Oñate described as "a heavily used Indian trail."

Following that trail at five to ten miles a day, they moved slowly upriver. Where the modern-day village of Rincon, New Mexico, now hugs the river, they stopped. Oñate's scouts warned him of a brutal jornada they must now cross. They rested at the river for two days, preparing to cross the long, waterless stretch. On the morning of the second day, a Sunday, well-respected Pedro Robledo died. The exact origins of the name *Jornada del Muerto* are unknown, but ever since Robledo's death the name has appeared in the written record.

Enraged because his advance scouts had been seen by the pueblo people living on the far end of the Jornada, and worried that those Indians now would form a strong defense, Oñate selected a small party of about sixty to ride quickly out ahead of the rest of the slow-moving caravan. He wanted to find provisions for his people and to try to assure the Indians they did not mean any harm. He selected two friars, several soldiers, and some of the soldiers' wives. He led the advance party himself.

I've been following the route Oñate took in my travels today. Unlike him, however, I have plenty of water. For two days Oñate's party trudged northward without a trace of it. "We all fared badly from thirst," Oñate wrote. By the time they reached this arroyo, their search for water had become nearly desperate.

I walk for a long while along the upper edge of the arroyo. Following nothing but my compass, I snake a route east around an occasional tarbush.

The arroyo widens and deepens. I stop a moment and unclip the water bottle from the belt of my backpack. The splash of water in my dry mouth heightens my awareness. The burning sun, a cloudless sky, and the desert are full before me. Even the smell awakens me. It penetrates my consciousness like ammonia, although not as toxic, and nowhere near as deep. The scent of the Jornada is that of a warm garden hose on the hottest day of summer – just before the water comes out. The smell is sweet and sour: poison plants and the sugary smell of tiny desert rosebushes that grow just at the bottom of the arroyo. Gunpowdery, Fourth of July odor arrives suddenly on a slight wind – the gentle smell of creosote bush.

I walk further and further from the van, hoping to find some trace of the Camino. A sudden squawking startles me. A large flock of crows rises from a mesquite tree. They circle me until I'm well past their tree and then descend again like a giant black net. The long, hot day of hiking has gotten to me. I stare at the hot sand, my eyes barely focused on the monotonous paleness. The paleness suddenly moves. A horned lizard, its spiky crown pulled close against its sides, slides from the top of a hill of red ants.

I stop and take another drink of water to clear my head. A rattle-snake bite out here could prove fatal. If I made it back to the van, the long hike will have caused the poison to spread, and I still would have a couple of hours' drive to get medical help.

To shake the fear, I stop and take stock of my surroundings. The desert's beauty shines everywhere before me. I breathe, and in my breath I find peace. I begin to walk again.

The sandy bed of the arroyo is as wide as a road. I follow it for another mile and then stop. There is a gap in the high bank on the south side of the arroyo. I study the opening. Although not even the faintest of trails blemishes the veneer of sand and brush, this must be where the old Camino crossed the arroyo. The route through here is obvious: a gentle slope climbs the embankment. I follow it and soon am on open desert, walking south toward a pass between low hills a mile away.

I trudge through the deep sand. With each step forward my foot seems to slide a half step back. After twenty yards I stop; I need more water. I take a big drink and for a moment don't mind the heavy weight of the backpack with its sloshing supply of water.

When Oñate and his party reached this spot neither human nor beast had tasted water for two days. On May 23, 1598, they were descending the hills and approaching the dry arroyo when a miracle of sorts happened.

"On this day, a dog appeared with muddy paws and hind feet," Oñate wrote. "We searched for some water holes. Captain Villagran found one and Cristobal Sanchez another." Quenched for the time being by the stagnant and tepid water, they named this camp Perrillo, meaning little dog.

I stand on a small rise that allows me to see the way south from here. Across a low bench of tan and green, a higher pass shows where they descended out of the hills. I study the way with binoculars. I see no trace of the old road. I walk another half mile before I turn and retrace my tracks back to the north. I keep searching the sand for artifacts but find none. At least the sun no longer burns. Judging by the warmth of the air, today's heat has peaked.

In a half hour I'm back at the arroyo. The lower angle of the sun has changed everything. Where before the high, hot desert sun cast few shadows, now the landscape has softened. Bushes, rocks, and cactus smear cool, dark shadows across the burning sand.

Several miles to my north is a small clump of tall Lombardy poplars that marks the headquarters of Ben and Jane Cain's ranch. When travelers on the old Camino came over the pass to my rear they would have made straight for Aleman, where later travelers knew water could often be found. I head for the distant trees, hoping to stumble on some evidence of the old road.

I try to follow what I think is a line of mesquite trees. One way to find an old road in the Spanish Southwest is to look for the alignment of mesquite trees. Travelers like Oñate had discovered that oxen and other cattle would eat mesquite beans if other food were not available. The light, dry pods were easy to pack. The seeds passed through the animals' digestive tract, and soon mesquite trees, which had not yet invaded this far north, lined the road. Even today you can often trace an old road by simply following a line of mesquite trees.

In ten minutes I come upon a large and very old mesquite. The bark on the gnarled trunk hangs like shredded wisps of gray hair. I study how the mesquite's small, feather-like leaves cast long shadows on the cracked red earth. It is just then that I see the glass, and, an instant later, the pottery.

A piece of dark glass about the size of my thumb pokes up from its tomb in the hard, sandy soil near the tree. As I stoop to pick it up, I see a light object a little further away. A shard of pottery sits on the ground as if placed there yesterday.

I hold both artifacts in the palm of my hand.

The glass shimmers like a bubble in the lowering sunlight. I know from my study that this dark, handblown specimen is a rare piece of Colonial-era glass. The first settlers to cross the Jornada never carried much glass, for it was far too delicate and expensive. Sacramental wine and oil, the two most common liquids, were carried in heavy but durable crockery. The glass I hold is exceedingly rare. The only glass that came north would have either been an expensive luxury or some priceless family heirloom.

I inspect the small piece of history in my hand. Sometime during the hundreds of years since this glass broke, something dinged against its surface, for a brighter, more recent concave wedge of it is missing. In that tiny crater I see the reflection of a nearly full moon, which has just risen into the still sunny sky.

Like the fragment of glass, the light-brown shard of Indian pottery is extremely old. One tiny part of the broken edge is smooth, like the outer edge of a bowl. Except for a small white stripe, it is the color of the sun.

I drop my pack to the ground. I will camp here.

On their third night on the Jornada, Oñate and his advance party camped somewhere near this place. They had come about twelve miles that day. In the evening someone discovered a grinding stone – an artifact from the ancient inhabitants of the Jornada. Now, more than four hundred years later, I prepare my own camp, carefully glancing at the Indian pottery and the Spanish glass where I have replaced them on the earth. The humanity of their history binds me to their shape.

I set up my tiny single-person tent, leaving my footprints in the dust as I work. I could easily sleep on the open ground, and I try to deny a vague, uneasy fear by telling myself I'll be glad I'm in the tent if it rains tonight.

Oñate himself experienced a monumental storm while on the Jornada. No one in his party had ever witnessed such a torrent. "The elements clashed in terrible combat . . . [as] the entire earth shook and trembled [beneath] a veritable downpour of rain, accompanied by such mighty claps of thunder that we were terrified." The gigantic storm passed directly over them with such fury that the priests knelt and prayed to heaven chanting litanies amid the thunder. "God took compassion on us . . . for the skies emptied as suddenly as they had become clouded, and the sun shone forth bright and clear." Marc Simmons says that after the storm "the clean, ozone-scented air proved downright exhilarating and helped restore spirits."

After crossing the arroyo, one of Oñate's people noticed a low split in the wall of mountains to the west. In the morning, Oñate ordered a march toward that gap. Although the eventual route of the Camino Real would avoid that treacherous exit and continue across the Jornada for another fifty miles, Oñate's party left the basin and reached the Rio Grande about where Elephant Butte Dam now holds back its wealth of water.

Traveling upriver, Oñate soon reached a large Pueblo village. All of the villagers had withdrawn to some nearby rocks. When Oñate moved further north, he found other villages deserted as well until he came to an occupied village on the river near the far northern entrance to the Jornada. The village leader stepped forward and made it known that he intended to help the mysterious men. He gave the travelers food, and in return the Spanish named the place Socorro, meaning succor or assistance. The next day Oñate climbed a nearby mesa. He had hoped the sacred kivas held goods he could plunder.

I bend over my small stove, cooking dinner. I pour boiling water into the pouch of freeze-dried food, seal the bag, check my watch, and wait as it cooks. The sun is well to the west, and the evening shadows soothe my soul.

I jerk up from the steaming aroma of my food, keenly aware. I do not face attacks by Indians or Spanish, but since my scare at Lava Gate I'm worried about mountain lions. At least a dozen are known to roam the ranges of this part of the Jornada. I study a canyon-like crevasse along the wall of the arroyo. The breaks in the wall would be an ideal place for a lion. Evening's shadows darken the interior. My fear flames quickly. I struggle to put it out.

I have a sudden, nearly uncontrollable urge to jump up and start running away from the enormity of my isolation. I fight the strange urge until I recognize it as simply a deep fear of my own mortality.

Thomas Merton believed that in order to realize the nature of the divine we must first face the reality of our own death. Solitude was essential for such a realization. The isolation of a desert was the best solitude because it was "where evil and curse prevail, where nothing grows, where the very existence of man is constantly threatened."

Few places like this are left in the world, places where I can be completely alone, where I can be "constantly threatened." Solitude is wilderness, and losing even the harshest, most inhospitable lands endangers our ability to confront our true place in the universe. Merton understood that only when we confront such desolation could we come face-to-face with the true nature of time and being.

I sit cross-legged on the gravel and eat my meal. I calm my breath and force my heart to slow. I look around at the simple beauty of the approaching dusk. The arroyo lies sheltered from the setting sun. In the blue shadows small animals scurry around; I can hear them moving in the scrub and grass. A small bird flies across my view. Silhouetted against the sky, it passes but leaves no artifact of its passing.

I ride the crest of a wave of time. In each purple shadow, on every distant mountain peak, bathed in gold, there is peace. Every instant, the world around me is in the simple act of becoming. The moment I try to stop things and say, *right here*: *this* is what life is, the wave of time has moved.

According to Merton, the desert hermits of fourth-century Egypt said little about God "because they know that when one has been somewhere close to His dwelling, silence makes more sense than a lot of words."

In the solitude of the deep desert, I have no choice but silence.

It took Oñate's expedition five months of hard travel to reach northern New Mexico. Once there they set up their colony not far from present-day Espanola. Later voyagers on the Camino would make the same journey in half the time, but Oñate had blazed the trail all others would follow. The route north through the Jornada became known as El Camino del Real de Tierra Adentro – the Royal Road to the Lands of the North.

For the next several years Oñate explored the Southwest from the Arkansas River to the Gulf of California. Some of the colonists charged that these needless explorations threatened the colony's safety and that Oñate angered the Indians to the point of revolt. Many of the settlers began to abandon New Mexico. By 1609 the Spanish government determined that the missionaries were bringing Christ to the Indians, and that it was important for the colony to stay, but that Oñate was becoming a liability and had to be removed.

"The expenses of the project had devoured his once considerable fortune," Robert Silverberg wrote of Oñate, "and the dispute over his capacity to govern the colony had clouded his high reputation." Broke and disillusioned, he returned south in disgrace. Somewhere out on the Jornada – most likely at Point of Rocks – a band of what probably were Apaches attacked the caravan.

The single casualty was Oñate's only son.

7. Rowena

The Owl Bar sits perched at the intersection of U.S. Highway 380 and the dusty country lane that is a part of the original Camino Real. Housed for the last sixty years in the same low-slung adobe building in San Antonio, New Mexico, the Owl Bar is famous for having served the world's first green-chile hamburger.

Owner Rowena Baca sits at a back booth in the cool, dark room. It is early afternoon, and the Owl Bar is not crowded but busy enough for Rowena to keep an eye out for work that needs to be done.

"My dad started chile burgers," she says, watching a waitress move across the room. "This was way early on, maybe 1948." At that time her father, who served as a cook during the day and a bartender at night, always served his burgers the way he knew his customers would like them, with a side dish of locally grown green chile.

Rowena shakes her head. "We kids worked waiting on tables, or if we had a break we had to go to wash the dishes," she says, her strong hands gently working the air before her as she speaks. "Well, one day I was mad about something and there were no clean dishes," she stops and smiles, "and I wasn't about to do any." Someone placed an order for a burger, and her father grew nervous; he knew better than to push her too far. "So instead of asking me to wash more dishes, he just put the green chile right on the burger."

Rowena chuckles and looks around the busy room. A steady stream of customers frequents the isolated Owl Bar. Two men and a woman dressed in military fatigues are having lunch in another booth. Nearby a table of older local women laugh and chat.

Rowena sits in the booth and spreads her hands out flat on the table before she tells the story she has repeated so many times. "In the middle 1940s all of these 'prospectors' started showing up here. They called them 'prospectors,' but it was Oppenheimer and all the other scientists working on the atomic bomb. My grandpa rented some of his cabins to them and he had the only telephone in town." She looks toward the front corner of the room as if the ancient phone were still there. "They'd come back and forth from Los Alamos and they'd use the phone and all that.

"Those men told my grandfather if he wanted to see something he'd never see again in his life to stand out in front of the store that morning." She pauses then says, "Grandma told me it looked like the world was coming to an end; everything was just red in the sky – the clouds were red, the sky was red, the world was red . . ."

Three women who had been seated at a rear table stand to leave, and Rowena says good-bye to them with a "You be careful!" The tallest one, a woman with thick graying hair, replies, "Why?"

We watch them leave. "My mother was furious with our government," Rowena says matter-of-factly. "She was so mad because even though they didn't know what might happen, they didn't evacuate the town of San Antonio. They didn't know if everybody here in town was going to die or if people would get sick because of the radiation. San Antonio could have disappeared and they didn't protect this town."

The wild winds of the Jornada would have blown the tiny town of San Antonio clean off the map long ago if it hadn't been for the Owl Bar. And while the age of the tiny village is not clear, one thing is for certain: the dry dust that twirls in the parking lot of the Owl Bar has seen a long parade of human history. Ever since Oñate's colonization expedition in 1598, almost every human to cross the Jornada del Muerto has passed by this spot.

Long ago the Spanish government understood that without women no place could be settled successfully. As a result, they recruited both women and men for colonization expeditions. They believed that without women and families the land of New Mexico would never become self-supporting. According to historian Salome Hernandez, the Spanish promoted having women recruits because the men would take wives and "thus have more love for the land."

Women native to Mexico constituted the bulk of the women who came up the Camino. Others included the Southwest's first black women – who most often were freed slaves from the Caribbean Islands. Single women came. Widows came. Women heads of household often led extended families for the entire fifteen-hundred-mile trek.

Caravans traveled from two to ten miles a day. After the months-long journey from Mexico, most caravans tried to hurry across the Jornada in from three to five days. Usually each man was rationed a horse, while one women and one child shared a single mount. To accommodate such an arrangement, women were issued a special saddle that was designed so that an adult or older child could comfortably carry one or even two smaller children. Later expeditions would include saddles that seated three children and came complete with armrests.

The women endured what one expedition leader described as "untold agony." Some leaders would not stop to allow mothers time to grieve the loss of a child. Often people went without food or water for days at a time. When there was food, it was limited. Normally women made chocolate for their families in the morning, and then did not eat again until an evening meal of *posole*, tortillas and pinto beans. On the Jornada, however, the lack of firewood meant that even these meager rations could not be prepared.

Today, most customers at the Owl Bar get an order of pinto beans to go with their green-chile burgers. Rowena watches a waitress deliver a steaming bowl of the beans to a nearby table. She waits until the customer has taken a spoonful of them before she speaks again.

"My husband, Adolph, is a good cook," she says. She met him when they both were attending high school in Socorro. "Back then San Antonio had its own school, but it only went from kindergarten through eighth grade," Rowena says. After her marriage, Rowena continued to run the Owl Bar with Adolph's help. The couple's two children helped too when they were growing up. She hesitates a moment before she comments on what might happen next to the Owl Bar, then says, "I don't know if my kids will take it over the way I had to when I was a kid; they have their own homes now away from here." Her son is a mechanical engineer at the labs in Los Alamos, and her daughter is a schoolteacher in Socorro. "If I retire, I'll probably have to close the place down," she says.

Rowena gets up from the booth for a moment in order to help deliver a large order to a crowded table. In a few minutes she slides back into her seat. She points to the rear of the building. "My grandparents used to live in a tiny house behind here," she says. "My grandfather started his store in that house because it was right on the old road. He started there, then in 1939 he built this building."

Rowena remembers her grandfather telling her how he used to trade groceries for fur with the Indians. "When my grandpa was young, he worked for Mr. Gus Hilton," she says, leading up to a mention of San Antonio's most famous native. "My grandpa and Conrad Hilton were boyhood friends. They were the fur buyers for the old Hilton store."

In addition to a store, the elder Hilton ran a bar for the coal miners who populated nearby Carthage in the years before the mine explosion. Hilton owned the first saloon, store, and rooming house in San Antonio. When his son Conrad Hilton eventually left San Antonio he created a worldwide network of hotels that still bears his name.

Rowena nods to the long, dark, and shiny bar that fills one wall of the room. "That bar there is the one from Mr. Hilton's saloon," she says. "Conrad Hilton came back to town for a visit when he was famous. My grandfather and Mr. Hilton were both old men then." Soon after that visit, Rowena's grandfather died. By then Rowena was working full time at the Owl Bar.

When Rowena's father came back from the navy after World War II, he opened a bar in a small corner of the store to provide for all the military people who had come as a part of the bombing range that was being hacked out of the ranches of the Jornada. "He noticed how everyone would come in from the desert all thirsty and hungry," Rowena says. "At first the bar was in the small space where I have the kitchen." She swings her arms. "All of this big space was the grocery store." She stops again to laugh. "Then pretty soon the bar got too busy and big so he moved it in here, and my grandpa moved the grocery store into the small space at the back."

She waves toward the front door. "The Hiltons lived just across the way there," she says. "Now there is nothing but some old adobes melting away."

A block south of the Owl Bar, the artifacts of the world's first Hilton hotel are baking in the midday heat. Across from them are the remains of the old mission church, which was destroyed by the 1906 earthquake.

But even when traffic patterns shifted in the second half of the twentieth century with the construction of U.S. 380, and later, with Interstate 25, customers continued to find the Owl Bar. While the old storefront still faces the dusty remains of the four-hundred-year-old Camino Real, the café part of the building fronts the modern asphalt of U.S. 380. For a sign, someone has painted a colorful, stylized owl on the side of the building. Strangers have no trouble finding the place, while locals gather here to eat and meet.

The door of the Owl Bar swings open, and the white sunlight momentarily floods the cool room. A young woman and a young man step inside and stand a moment, letting their eyes adjust to the darkness. Their awkwardness suggests that they have never been here before. They could be college students on a summer adventure. The strong young woman turns and notices that the walls are covered in one-dollar bills. Rowena watches the couple move to a table.

"The dollars started four or five years ago," she says. "People used to put their business cards on the wall. Well, one day this guy comes in and he said, 'I'm gonna make sure people look at my card.' He stuck his card to a two-dollar bill. That started it." Once the walls get too full of bills, Rowena collects the money and donates it to a local charity. She has raised more than eighty-five hundred dollars for charities. "Now it's kind of like a superstition," she says. "People always leave dollars on my wall."

Superstitions have always haunted the history of the Jornada. Many of the Mexican women who came up the Camino brought their folktales and beliefs with them, but holding onto those beliefs left them vulnerable to charges of witchcraft. Often their "crimes" were that they had concocted love potions to keep philandering husbands home.

Women weren't the only ones who suffered at the hands of the Inquisition.

A San Juan Indian man named Pope was arrested in 1678 for witchcraft and idolatry for refusing to give up his Native beliefs. Four of the men arrested with him were hanged for the crime. Pope served many months in jail; then, after he was released he organized and led a massive revolt against the Spanish interlopers. The uprising would become the greatest revolt of Native Americans in the history of the continent.

Precisely at dawn on August 10, 1680, hundreds of Indians made coordinated attacks on dozens of Spanish villages in the populated regions 150 miles north of the Jornada. From the Rio Grande to Zuni and Hopi towns far to the west, the Pueblo people fought for their freedom. Churches were burned; men and woman who ran from their houses were slashed to pieces, while missionaries lay dead on their altars. Estimates were that more than four hundred Spaniards were killed.

Within days the entire surviving Spanish population of New Mexico fled the area in two large groups. One group escaped south from Santa Fe "without a crust of bread or a grain of wheat or maize," as one witness recorded. As they moved south toward the Jornada, they came upon bodies of men, women, and children. Every single Spanish ranchero and village on the river had been attacked.

Unaware of the fate of their countrymen, the second large group of survivors gathered near the village of Albuquerque and then moved south. In early September these survivors of the Pueblo Revolt reached Lava Gate, twenty miles south of the Owl Bar. On what little ground existed between the mountains and the malpais lava flow, one thousand human beings – devastated, starving, and bemoaning the fate of loved ones – came to a stop. Clearly, there were not enough provisions to sustain a march of so many suffering people across the Jornada. Everyone knew that many would die crossing the desert. They set up a large and sorrowful camp at Fra Cristobel.

A few days later the other large group of refugees from around Santa Fe arrived at Lava Gate. The sweeping success of the Pueblo Revolt became painfully apparent: more than two thousand people were now gathered at a site one historian described as "incapable of supporting more than a few dozen souls." The hungry, homeless, bereaved, and underequipped survivors had no choice but to enter the lava-jagged gates and cross the Jornada. Some say that it was the suffering of these refugees that truly christened the Jornada the "Journey of the Dead."

The leader of the Santa Fe refugees, Governor Antonio de Otermin, rode with an advance party ahead of the main body of survivors. On September 18, 1680, they reached the southern end of the Jornada. Quite by accident, they found forty mounted soldiers leading a small caravan of provisions up the Camino Real. The small caravan itself was in trouble. Despite being led by six pairs of mules and several men who could swim, the first wagon across had swamped in the flooded river. The mules made it out, but the wagon and its driver, a friar named Ayeta, were stuck in the raging waters. Despite having just crossed the Jornada, Otermin's weary men dashed to the river in order to save the friar and his wagon.

Once the small caravan was on the east bank of the river, the men created a pack train in order to take the meager supplies to the thousands who were struggling across the Jornada. A witness from the relief caravan later wrote, "There was no heart that was not moved by compassion" after seeing two thousand people "on foot and unshod, of such a hue that they looked like dead people." Over the course of the next several weeks the survivors built several villages near what would one day become the modern cities of El Paso and Juarez.

The Pueblo Revolt shook the entire Spanish empire. Futile attempts were made to retake the territory, but for nearly two decades there was not a single Spaniard resident north of El Paso. In 1980, on the three hundredth anniversary of the victory, a Pueblo man claimed that it was because of the revolt that his people survived. When the Spanish finally reconquered the area they were much more cautious about interfering with Native culture.

In 1692, twelve years after the Pueblo Revolt, Diego de Vargas, who had recently assumed the office of governor of New Mexico, organized a reconquest expedition and led it northward. More than two hundred men left El Paso in late summer. When they reached the Jornada they found that all of the remaining pueblos there had been destroyed.

The first de Vargas expedition seemed to address many complaints of the Pueblo people and to cause little bloodshed. Within months he returned south and reached the Jornada in a blinding snowstorm. A chilly wind whipped the sands into a wall of gray. De Vargas hesitated and then gave the order to move into the storm.

Out of that gray storm rode a new tempest on the Jornada: Apaches. There followed a short but intense battle. There were no Spanish casualties.

A year later de Vargas was back, but this time at the head of a large resettlement caravan of over eight hundred people. They moved up and onto the dry Jornada near Robledo Peak, trying to follow the old road that had all but disappeared after years of disuse. De Vargas ordered that the sheep and cattle be sent ahead to try to smooth the path for the carts and wagons. Men and women had to dig their way through drifts of sand and then help the animals push and pull the wagons out of the shifting dunes. The carretas were made of a simple square box body that was mounted over a single axle made from a cottonwood trunk. The wheels had no spokes but were solid disks of wood. Very little metal was used in their construction. Wheels and axles wore out, and loose fittings made many of these wagons wobbly and difficult to pull. Little if any grease was used to ease the friction, so the bulky wooden wagons gave out a piercing screech as they moved. One witness to this journey across the Jornada said that they had no fuel and so little food that they were forced to eat "sweat soaked leather, horse meat, and even worse, dogs and cats." Thirty women and children died on that journey across the Jornada del Muerto.

This second of de Vargas's reconquests was not so peaceful. For the next several years the Spanish waged a nearly continuous war with the Pueblo Indians. By 1694 de Vargas had destroyed Taos Pueblo, executed hundreds of Indians, and fought off several new revolts.

From de Vargas's reconquest in the 1690s until Mexico gained independence from Spain in 1821, Spanish caravans crossed the Jornada with clockwork regularity. New settlers and supply trains struggled across the Jornada from the south, carrying fabric, clothes, chocolate, paper, and ink, while trade wagons full of apples, grain, chile, brandy, raw wool, piñon nuts, and furs came from the north.

Before they entered the Jornada from either direction, caravans were inspected to ensure they carried enough firearms and provisions. Caravans sometimes numbered as many as five hundred people. To ease the dangers of the Jornada, emergency water was often carried in heavy casks across the wasteland.

Salome Hernandez says that the numbers of widows increased with nearly every expedition. These widowed women took over extended families, became the managers of large haciendas, and assumed all of the responsibilities of their husbands. However, even a woman's most common bravery – giving birth – was often praised in official records as exemplifying and glorifying the courage of the expedition's leader, not the woman herself.

Most caravans crossed the Jornada in late summer to take advantage of the surface water provided by the seasonal rains. Others were timed to match the annual trade fair at Taos. During the Spanish colonial era, caravans frequently included a number of armed men and a small core of regular army troops.

The Spanish had a right to be nervous. In addition to the threat of more Indian uprisings, the French were establishing a foothold to the east of the area. French goods from Louisiana, traded to the Pawnees, then traded to the Comanches, were finding their way to the Jornada. The first Frenchman to cross the Jornada, a trader, was arrested and sent to Mexico City in 1751.

To protect their claim on New Mexico, the Spanish encouraged even more settlement. By the 1700s privately contracted freight caravans replaced the government led supply and settlement caravans. By 1766 regular traffic crossed the Jornada on a well-worn and easy-to-follow roadway. Mail from El Paso to Santa Fe began crossing the Jornada in 1783. The present village of San Antonio dates to around 1800, when the nervous Spanish government ordered the resettlement of many of the old mission villages on the northern border of the Jornada. The railroad was completed in the 1880s.

From about 1650 until around 1800, however, almost all human contact with the Jornada was transitory. During those 150 years only seven small *estancias* (ranches) clung intermittently to the edge of the Jornada. Pedro Armendaris, whose grant would one day constitute

Ted Turner's ranch, owned one such estancia. San Antonio served briefly as the location of another. Eventually all seven estancias were abandoned because of the Apache threat.

The faint murmur of country music floats into the booth. Rowena is silent a moment, as if listening to the mournful chords. "My sisters live in Albuquerque and my brother lives in Las Cruces," she says. Rowena says she bought her siblings' shares of the Owl Bar just before they left San Antonio. She slowly shakes her head. "I wouldn't live in any of those places," she says, as if those towns – each a little over one hundred miles distant – were in another universe.

Both of Rowena's parents died when they were only in their fifties. "My mother died of a stroke," she says. "I had to grow up in a hurry. I had to take over the next day – and if I hadn't had come and opened the door . . ." She pauses. "It was after the funeral – the funeral was on a Saturday. If I hadn't come and opened the door on that next Monday this place would have stayed closed. It was hard, very, very hard."

Rowena has never lived anywhere but San Antonio. She grew up just behind the Owl Bar in an apartment her grandfather built from adobes from an older building. Now she lives just twenty yards away from that place in a pretty house on the Camino Real.

She seldom leaves the village, not even for the twelve-mile drive to Socorro. "I was taught to work since I was twelve years old. I started in the grocery store when I was little and I've worked here ever since. I'm usually here day and night. I work fourteen hours a day, six days a week. We don't go very many places – we aren't sociable: we don't go nightclubbing, we don't go to movies. We go to work and come home. I don't do any thing for relaxation."

She pauses. "Well – whenever I get three days off in a row – I'm gone! I go to Las Vegas . . ."

8. The Coming of the *Ingles*

Lieutenant Facundo Malgares sat on his fine horse on the high butte at the northern edge of the Jornada del Muerto. The medicine he had ingested last night at camp eased his fever, yet it did nothing to calm his concern for what lay ahead.

For six days he had escorted the captive *Ingles*, the English-speaking people, down the easiest stretch of the river from Santa Fe. From here to Chihuahua, he knew, would be the most difficult part of the journey. The open, immense Jornada stood now before them.

Malgares was an intelligent, wealthy, well-educated, and well-trusted soldier under the command of a nervous Spanish government in Santa Fe. Fearful of the Mexican people's growing sentiment for rebellion, Spain now also had to contend with both French and American incursions into their immense territory.

At Malgares's side rode the leader of the *Ingles* captives, the dauntless explorer Zebulon Montgomery Pike.

It was midday, March 11, 1807. Several dozen Spanish dragoons under Malgares's command were taking Pike and fifteen or sixteen other men from the United States to Chihuahua City. Malgares was given the delicate task of enforcing a kind of polite house arrest, while allowing Pike and his men to have at least the illusion of free will.

Pike had recently gained fame when he led an expedition north from St. Louis in an attempt to discover the source of the Mississippi River and to try to establish control of the area's Native populations for the United States government.

After his return and a two-month rest period in St. Louis, soon-to-be-Captain Pike was ordered to command another expedition for the United States, this time to explore the source of the Red and Arkansas rivers. He had orders to make contact with the Indians and to "approximate" the Spanish territory. The exact intent of Pike's expedition has forever been clouded in mystery and speculation, but some historians suspect he was allied with the conspirator Aaron Burr, who had plans to create a new country from large tracts of Louisiana and Mexico.

When the Spanish government in Santa Fe learned of Pike's movements, and probably as a counter to it, they organized their own expedition east into Louisiana Territory. By one of the odd coincidences that seem to litter the Jornada like bones, as Pike and his men were moving west toward the Rockies the previous fall, it was Malgares and his men who moved east out of New Mexico and onto the plains into what is now Kansas. Each came upon the other's tracks at least once.

The late-season start to the uncharted Rockies caused Pike's expedition to reach the eastern foothills just as winter was coming on. Although snow had already fallen in the mountains, the expedition entered the Rockies climbing over the shoulder of a tall, triangular mountain we still call Pike's Peak. After barely surviving three harrowing months in the mountains west of Pike's Peak, Pike led his men south. In February they entered Spanish territory on the upper Rio Grande and were soon met by Spanish soldiers. Pike would later claim he was lost and had thought he was still in Louisiana Territory.

The ragged captives straggled into Santa Fe. "When we presented ourselves in Santa Fe," Pike recorded, "I was dressed in a pair of blue trousers, moccasins, blanket, coats and there was not a hat in the whole party."

In Santa Fe, Pike was taken to meet the Spanish governor. World politics then, as now, teetered constantly between the desire for possession and the blackness of war; then as now, men of power stood on slippery foundations of mistrust and suspicion and faced a world full of aggression.

The governor bowed slightly and, speaking in French, asked Pike if he too spoke French.

"Yes sir," Pike said.

"You come to reconnoiter our country, do you?"

Pike shook his head. "I marched to reconnoiter our own," he shot back.

The governor pressed on. "In what character are you?"

"In my proper character," Pike snuffed, "an officer of the United States army."

The conversation shifted to something resembling a formal inquisition. "When did you leave St. Louis?" the governor asked.

"July 15th."

"I think you marched in June."

"No sir!" Pike snapped back.

Soon the governor told Pike that he was to be taken to Chihuahua City for questioning.

"If we go to Chihuahua," Pike asked, "we must be considered prisoners of war."

"By no means," the governor said.

"But sir," Pike said, "I cannot consent to be led three or four hundred leagues out of my route, without its being by force of arms."

The governor understood the delicate propriety of the situation. "I know you do not go voluntarily," he said. "But I will give you a certificate from under my hand of having obliged you to march."

Placed at the command of that delicate march on the brink of war was a man of honor. Lieutenant Malgares treated Pike and his men with respect and as equals, and they responded as gentlemen and soldiers. The strange collection of men made their way south in a relaxed, congenial fashion.

As they neared the Jornada del Muerto, Malgares stopped at Rio Salado Arroyo and led Pike to the top of the neighboring mesa.

That day Zebulon Pike and his men became the first *Ingles* to see the Jornada del Muerto. That night Pike wrote about it in his journal. "Here we entered the wilderness and the road became rough." Far to the east, night-blue mountains formed the horizon: a serrated tear as dark and ragged as blackened teeth. Closer still, islands of isolated peaks – the Black Mountains – rose from a sea of yellow desert.

Two days later, March 12, Pike recorded that they broke camp at dawn and followed the Rio Grande toward where the Camino Real crossed the river and entered the hundred-mile Journey of the Dead.

The flat, parched, yellow, black, and red land of the Jornada stretched to distant mountain ranges. At one point Malgares pointed off at a side canyon. "He showed me the place where he had been in two affairs with the Apaches," Pike wrote. A recent battle with the always-troublesome Apaches had left one Spaniard dead. Malgares had led soldiers in the attack of retribution. The Spanish had surprised the Apaches at night. Malgares said that fifty-two Apaches were wounded and seventeen had been killed. Malgares had killed two of the Apaches himself.

Just before they stopped for the night, Pike and Malgares "passed the encampment of a caravan going out." Three hundred men and women, escorted by their own military protection of forty troops, and a stockyard of animals that included fifteen thousand sheep, had just completed their journey across the Jornada. "A similar expedition goes out in autumn, but during the other parts of the year no citizen travels the road," Pike wrote.

Pike and Malgares camped that night in the cottonwood *bosque* along the river. They camped amid thousands of migratory birds that flocked in the spring wetlands along the river. Geese and ducks and cranes flew amid the strange cacti and tough desert grasses. An hour before sunset the clouds were lit gold by the setting sun. Somewhere out on the Jornada, low gray clouds touched the ground and a gentle rain fell. At dawn the next morning, Pike saw several deer amid the cottonwoods.

They traveled south and then stopped at midday to rest. They started moving again at four. The stop-and-go travel allowed them to siesta during the hottest parts of the day, which – even in spring – wear down the hardiest of travelers.

Before they stopped that night one of the horses threw a young woman and ran off. "Many of the dragoons and Malgares pursued him," Pike wrote. "Being mounted on an elegant horse of Malgares', I joined the chase. Notwithstanding their superior horsemanship I overtook the horse, caught his bridle and stopped him, when both of the horses were nearly at full speed." Not only did his accomplishment gain him a round of applause, but it also brought him the goodwill and admiration of the Spanish soldiers.

The next day the caravan reached Black Mesa, and they grazed their animals at the incongruously bright valley known as Valverde, where in a few years Pedro Armendaris would build his estancia.

They began to march at ten o'clock the next morning, and by early afternoon had reached Lava Gate. Instead of keeping to the road and crossing the dry Jornada, Malgares chose to keep to the river along the more precipitous route. That route, which roughly parallels Interstate 25 through the area, is bisected with steep, jagged canyons that tumble to the river from the surrounding mountains. Following the Rio Grande ensures adequate water, but the rugged canyons were difficult and time consuming to cross, and their rocky outcrops added the danger of attacks by the Apaches as well.

Almost immediately they ran into trouble. On their first ford of the river, two mules fell into the water. "Unfortunately," Pike commented, "by which means we lost all our bread, and an elegant assortment of biscuits."

In the late afternoon, sunlight danced on the rugged Fra Cristobel range. With almost no vegetation, the mountains shone white in the flat, high light of the bright and broken sunshine. Deeply rutted slopes gave the peaks the appearance of bleak triangles with their tops sliced flat.

It took them days to traverse the deep arroyos that bisected the river. They struggled across the precipitous Canyon de Alamosa; they passed the aptly named Elephant Butte and came to the dark crack in the wall of mountains that signaled the Canyon del Muerto, the difficult ascent to the Jornada that Oñate had used to reach the river in 1598. Beyond that, the horse mountains, the Caballos, shut them off from the Jornada.

"Marched down the river 26 miles. . . . Came on a trail of 200 horses," Pike wrote one evening. Another day he found "the trail of a large party of horses . . . fresh signs of Indians." Another time they saw "several fresh Indians tracks." Apaches seemed to be everywhere; other tracks led them to conclude that a large party of Spanish troops was also in the area in pursuit of the Indians.

It took them five days of rough travel to struggle down the rugged river route, but by March 20 they had rejoined the Camino at the southern end of the Jornada.

Once Malgares delivered Pike to the authorities in Chihuahua City, the United States soldier was questioned at length. Zebulon Pike was allowed to return to the United States under a military escort. He was killed in Canada during the War of 1812.

Don Facundo Malgares, his duty finished, returned northward. He would come to affect the Jornada one more time before his life ended.

9. The *Viejo*

Because of his service and his knowledge of New Mexico, Facundo Malgares was appointed governor of Spain's northern frontier. In 1819, a dozen years after the incident with Pike, Governor Malgares received a request for a land grant from a tax collector living in the village of San Elizario, eighty miles south of the Jornada. Recently retired from his position as a first lieutenant in the town's garrison, Pedro Ascue de Armendaris was asking to be honored for his years of service fighting Apaches by being given a large tract of land on the Jornada del Muerto. Such petitions were customary, and Malgares granted the request. A few months later Armendaris was given an additional tract so that by 1820 he owned nearly half a million acres. In his petition Armendaris promised to build an estancia that would service travelers along the Camino Real.

The land grant skirted both sides of the Rio Grande and included the Jornada's richest grasslands as well as an entire mountain range. Armendaris built his combination home, ranch headquarters, hostel, and stage stop near one of the Jornada's most dominate features, Black Mesa, a low but massive flat-topped mountain that rises from the floodplain of the Rio Grande.

Subtler and far more imposing in its own way is the perfectly concave bowl at the mesa's eastern side where Armendaris chose to build his home. Even in winter the emerald tinge of vegetation colors the valley, setting it in stark contrast to the desert surrounding it. Cut into the same broad plateau from which Black Mesa rises, Valverde seems the mirror opposite of the neighboring mesa. It is as if a ragged knife had cut the rough circle of the valley and the remains had been flung down at its side to form the mesa.

All traces of Armendaris's original rancho at Valverde are gone, as are most of the remnants of a late-nineteenth-century ranching village that grew up nearby. The spot, which lies hidden in the cool shadows of Black Mesa, is now chiefly known as the location of a vicious Civil War battle.

For several years Armendaris managed his land from his hacienda on the banks of the Rio Grande. During those years his home also served as a station for caravans moving in or out of the Jornada. He tended a large flock of sheep and improved the land by irrigating his fields with water from the Rio Grande. His family likely harvested local berries and grapes to make wine and *aguardiente* (brandy). Those and other improvements have strengthened Mexico's claim to priority rights to water from the Rio Grande.

Soon after Mexico won its independence from Spain, repeated attacks by Apaches forced Armendaris and his family to abandon Valverde. Armendaris died without returning to Valverde.

His land was unoccupied when the United States acquired jurisdiction over the area as a result of the Mexican-American War. Because of the difficulty in trying to superimpose an Anglo-American system of land law upon a Spanish and Mexican system, problems regarding the ownership of the land arose. The troubles began when the man who had married Pedro Armendaris's only daughter claimed to be the single heir. The Spanish custom was that the oldest *son* inherited his father's land, while the daughter – and far worse, the daughter's husband – should not do so. All of this was complicated by the fact that the United States had already built and occupied Fort Craig – a strategic military base in the rising war against the Apaches – on the Armendaris grant. Throw into the mix a couple of shady lawyers from Santa Fe, and add the fact that there were new settlers – members of Colorado volunteers who held claims on the land grant as compensation for *their* military service – and you get a rough idea of the complexity of the problem.

By the late nineteenth century the Armendaris grant became a part of the Bell Ranch holdings – a cattle operation so huge that its "southern pastures" encompassed nearly all of the massive "boot heel" of the state of New Mexico. The Armendaris grant was used as that ranch's "summer pasture," and cattle occasionally grazed on the grasslands of the grant. From then until the early 1990s, when businessman Ted Turner took possession of it, several different individuals and corporations have owned and managed the massive territory.

The dust rises from behind my car like smoke. I'm bouncing down a road through the heart of the Pedro Armendaris Land Grant. Except for a handful of minuscule parcels of land called "in-holdings," the huge grant is still intact; it constitutes a single piece of real estate one-third the size of Rhode Island. The black grama grass that fed Pedro Armendaris's sheep, cattle, and horses, and which first attracted him to the Jornada, now provides range for Ted Turner's bison.

A distant cloud of billowing dust rises far ahead on the road. In a few minutes I see sunlight glint off a windshield. It is the first vehicle I've seen all day. I stop the van in the middle of the road and step out of the car to wait.

A well-used pickup truck appears. It slows and then stops alongside me. The windows are both open: the truck has no air-conditioning. Inside, wearing an Americorps T-shirt and sweating, sits a young man of about twenty-five. His has a deep tan and a muscular frame. "My name's Myles Traphagen," he says, extending his hand for a strong western handshake. I soon learn that he is a scientist. "I study grasses," he says. "I am on the Armendaris to study the effects of fire on a range that has never been grazed," he says.

Never?

"Well, we know places where it hasn't been grazed for at least several decades," he says. "There are places here where the black grama grass . . ." he searches for the right words. "This is among the best black grama grasslands in the world," he says flatly.

We chat like that – Myles in the cab and me leaning against my van – smack dab in the middle of the deserted road. The land beside the road is not black so much as a shade of vibrant yellow-green. Black grama grows in widely spreading bunches, like islands of nourishment in a sea of barren soil. Close up, the wiry, short leaves of grass spiral upward from a swollen base.

Myles nods off toward the malpais. He says he's been holed up in an old cowboy bunkhouse twenty miles or better out that way, doing research. He says he's been preparing for a prescribed burn he hopes to ignite in a few days.

Myles's research is being done in order to better understand how the climate is changing and how to best meet that challenge. "Anything about predicting climate is questionable," he says, "but rainfall records – they are indisputable." Those records indicate that a dramatic shift in the weather pattern is occurring. During the last fifty to one hundred years, the *rate* of precipitation hasn't changed so much as its distribution. Instead of summer's flash floods, more moisture now comes in winter. "So you get to a situation where grasses just can't compete with shrubs; they're just not getting adequate moisture," he says.

Myles takes a pull at his water bottle. "The Armendaris land is good for grass because the water resources have never been overdeveloped," he says between swallows. Then he comments on the biggest threat to the area's grassland. "Trouble is, once you lose that ground cover, it erodes easily. And sand dunes form."

Each dune, called a coppice dune, is roughly the size of a small garage. Coppice dunes look like scrub-topped mushrooms growing on a desert of sand. Once shrubs like creosote are established, their roots penetrate deep and hold the sandy soil in place. Soon the desert winds erode the land not held down by roots. Other than the dunes themselves, nothing but blood-red sand remains in some areas of the Jornada.

Our conversation drifts on in the slow, easy way of strangers passing on a bleak frontier, but finally Myles reaches for the keys to restart his truck. He has work to do.

The truck's metallic rumble startles the silence. I wish him luck on getting the right "prescription" for his burn. Myles nods, drops the truck into gear, but still does not move. We debate the chances of rain later in the day. Myles thinks the air has that sticky feeling like its building toward rain, but he notes that the clouds are kind of scattered. "What I'm finding is that precipitation is the driving force here no matter what," Myles says and nods to me. I step back from the truck and he drives away.

I get back inside my car. At first the air-conditioning blasts from the vents with the heat of a blowtorch. In a short while I drive over the crest of a barely discernible hill. I think I am witnessing the most miraculous mirage, but it is true: acres of grapevines cover a flat expanse in the sea of prairie-like grass. This is one of the small "inholdings" that barely blemish the massive Armendaris grant. Rows and rows of dark grapevines wrap their wooden arms around invisible strands of wire. Sometime around the mid-1980s the previous owners of the Armendaris, the Oppenheimer Estate, sold around 10 percent of the land for vineyards. "Own a vineyard and pay American taxes in the European economy" was the way current Armendaris manager Tom Waddell described the sales pitch.

Today, peppered along a barely discernible valley near the heart of the Armendaris, only a small number of viable vineyards remain.

I pull off the gravel road at a small sign announcing a winery and swing the van up a long, sandy path. I drive past a pleasant-looking winery building and head instead to a large, garage-like steel building. I stop the car under the shade of a lone tree.

In the building five men are working and talking. Their shadows move about as I step out of the van. The men are standing near a tractor. One man fades into the shadows. The rest turn toward me.

Three come to greet me. One is a strong boy about seventeen. He walks with a white-haired man, who moves much slower. The third is a pleasant-looking man of about thirty. I tell them I'm here to learn about the Jornada. The thirty-year-old turns to the other two men and translates my words into Spanish for them.

The old man stops in the shaded cool of the doorway and half-leans, half-sits upon an oil barrel. My Spanish is meager, but I offer what I can. "Buenas dias, *Viejo*," I say to the older man, using the title of respect.

The viejo's voice is as gentle as an evening's breeze. "Buenas dias," he says. He has thick, strong hands, and eyes like pools of sky. He turns and introduces me to the young man at his side. Nervously, the teenager smiles at me. The viejo speaks and the other man translates. "He is new here," the old man says of the teenager, "but he works hard."

The viejo motions to the rows of grapes soaking in the July heat. He says they pick over twelve thousand pounds of grapes by hand here. It takes more than fifty workers to harvest the crop each fall. He says he has worked here for more than a decade.

The men laugh when I ask the viejo if he is considered an old-timer by virtue of his decade-long work here.

"Si," he says. He figures he is kind of a permanent fixture on this part of the Armendaris.

I laugh and nod. "Like that old tractor," I say.

As soon as my words are translated, all three men speak at once, agreeing on the quality of the tractor and of its longevity. The two younger men fall silent, and the viejo speaks.

"It is important to fix things when they break," he tells me in Spanish. He smiles and stands upright. It is time to get back to work. We shake hands all around.

I walk back to the van contemplating how men like this viejo materialize out of the harshest of deserts like blessings. Just as I'm about to get in the van, a dark roar splits the sky. I squint and then see a strange, dark military jet fly low through Rhodes Pass and disappear.

10. The Captains of Death and the Young Missouri Bride

JAMES KIRKER

It's a simple matter, really, to scalp a human being. Place the sharpened tip of the knife on the forehead just where the skin meets the hair. A single, quick slice of flesh: trace the hairline, now the bone lies exposed. Slip the fingers into that slit of skin. A quick snap peels the scalp: the human pelt is freed.

His given name was James Kirker, and he was one of this continent's most notorious murderers. By the time he was being described in newspapers as "heroic and kind-hearted" he had probably killed no fewer than 487 people.

He always rode – heavily armed – on the fastest and most lively of horses.

Thick muscles enhanced his stocky frame, and a wide Mexican hat usually shaded his bearded face. He dressed in the ragtag and practical clothing of men who hunt for pelts: fringed buckskin, rabbit fur, and, in deep cold, bear and buffalo skin. He was said to carry a Jake Hawkins rifle with a stock of inlaid silver.

Kirker was born in Ireland in 1793 and came to New York when he was seventeen. Two years later, during the War of 1812, he sailed on the privateer *Black Jake*. He resurfaced three years later at the furthest edge of the American frontier, working as a grocer in St. Louis. Then, in 1822 he ventured up the Missouri as far as Fort Henry. When he returned to St. Louis a year later, he stayed only long enough to outfit himself for a life in the West and then left for Santa Fe.

In 1826 he drifted south from Santa Fe, across the Jornada del Muerto, to El Paso. With Kirker on that initial voyage was a young

Christopher Carson, not yet well known as "Kit," a man who one day would leave his own mark on the Jornada.

For the next several years Kirker never stayed in one place for very long, but moved about illegally trapping furs and running guns during the Mexican-Apache Wars.

In 1837 that long and sorrowful conflict grew bloodier when the government of Chihuahua first offered a bounty for human scalps. The brilliant scholar of Apache history Dan Thrapp said that in the moral history of the world this official sanctioning of scalping was unprecedented. "The policy frankly sought extermination," he wrote. The scalping laws are "evidence that genocide has widespread roots and was not the modern invention of a single nation."

For its own financial protection the government set a strict range of prices: one hundred pesos for a man's scalp, fifty if the scalp was determined to be a woman's, and twenty-five for a child's. The law provided for a duly appointed citizens' board whose job it was to judge the gender, age and ethnicity of each scalp. To help them at their task, the committee required that each scalp be presented with ears still attached.

At forty-four, James Kirker had found his life's calling. For what he would need lucky months of trapping and hunting to earn, he could now make with a single pelt. Human life reduced to simplest form: a market economy. Now accompanied by a small, ragtag band of Shawnee and Delaware Indians, Kirker began to roam the Chihuahuan Desert, attacking small bands of Apaches who were easy prey for his henchmen and their guns.

"My people were invited to a feast," said an Apache chief named Mangas regarding one of Kirker's slaughters. "*Aquardiente* was there; my people drank and became intoxicated, and were lying asleep when a party of Mexicans came in and beat their brains out with clubs."

Kirker would one day claim that in all of his scalping he lost only three of his own men. When one of those – a Mexican guide – was killed, Kirker simply scalped the man and threw the skin into the pouch with the others. The scalp of an Apache did not look much different from that of a Mexican. That helps explain the rumors that soon spread among the region's poorest that if you were so misfortunate as to look up from your work to see Querque, death was certain.

For some in that dark-skinned Catholic stronghold, the white, Protestant *Ingles hombre* came to represent all whites. In El Paso a priest used Kirker's name to inflame the already strong anti-American sentiment. His name came to be used as a common, fearful, and derogatory label for men who killed without passion, men who killed merely for the money placed on a human life. They were all *quirky*; they were all *querque*.

Still, the Chihuahuan government recognized efficiency when it saw it. In 1839 they contracted Kirker for another scalping expedition among the Apaches and Comanches, hoping to produce a decisive end to the Indian "problem." As Thrapp points out, not only was scalping abhorrent, but it inflamed hatred. "The bounty system had about it the smell of vengeance and was no more truly effective than a bounty system on any wild game. It served to cancel out any tendency on the part of the Apaches to become tame, and drove the wilder spirits deeper into the mountains, where, if anything, they became more implacably hostile."

CHULY

In 1838 a group of about thirty men from the United States headed west from Missouri, each hell-bent on riches, or adventure, or anonymity. A written account of this journey by a participant became a best-selling book. Josiah Gregg's 1844 *Commerce of the Prairies* helped fuel the United States' interest in the territory of northern Mexico. There were riches to be made in New Mexico, the book promised, but it took hard work and guts. That idea soon provided an economic justification for what would become known as the Mexican-American War.

Several months into their journey, Gregg and the other men were camped at a Creek Indian village near present-day Oklahoma City. They had been huddled about their campfires when an Indian emerged from the shadows. The man spoke no English but made it known that he had quarreled with his wife. "He proposed to join us," Gregg wrote. The next morning, despite what Gregg claimed was "a most dismal weeping" from the Creek man's wife, the man, "to our great surprise, carried his proposal into execution."

The Wild Man at the Jornada
Experimental Range Headquarters in 1934.
Courtesy Jornada Experimental Range.

Above: An oryx. Photograph by Jim Eckles, White
Sands Missile Range.

Top right: Geologists Virgil Lueth and Lisa Peters on the
Jornada in 2001. Author photo.

Bottom right: The snake petroglyph from the cliff trail
on the way to the mesa-top ruins. Author photo.

Above: Susan Magoffin. Courtesy Yale University Press.

Below: James Kirker. Easterly Collection, Missouri
Historical Society, St. Louis.

Above: Rafael Chacón. Reprinted from *Historia Illustrada de Nueva Mexico*, circa 1896.

Below: Alfred Peticolas's self-portrait, sketched a few weeks after the Battle of Valverde. Arizona Historical Society, Tucson, Peticolas diary.

Above: Victorio. Arizona Historical Society, Tucson.

Below: Dismounted Buffalo Soldier. Courtesy Frederic
Remington Art Museum, Ogensburg, New York.

His name was Echu-eleh-hadjo, or Crazy Deer Foot. The men just called him Chuly for short.

Chuly joined the caravan. Once in Santa Fe he "took another freak and joined a volunteer corps organized by one James Kirker to fight the Navajo and Apache Indians."

Gregg recorded dryly that Chuly "was somewhat disposed to commit excess."

Chuly would ride with Kirker for the next six years until just before Christmas Day 1846, when he disappeared from history on the eve of the Mexican-American War.

Gregg's party headed south from Santa Fe without Chuly. They traveled along the old Camino Real for several weeks until they reached the stark plain of the Journey of the Dead. As they approached the Jornada, Gregg noticed how Mexican traders on the route slowed down, and began to linger, "on account of the hostile savages which infest most of the country through which we had to pass."

Gregg and his men camped within sight of the ruins of Pedro Armendaris's old ranchero at Valverde.

The next day they climbed into Lava Gate and entered the Jornada. They camped under the sawtooth shadow of black mountains at a place called Fra Cristobel, which, like many other named places on the route across the Jornada, "is neither town nor village, but a simple, isolated point . . . a mere camping ground." Gregg wrote that dozens of other places – with names like San Pascual, Aleman's Well, and Robledo – "led the stranger to imagine that the route was lined with flourishing villages."

Instead, of course, they found only a bleak and empty wasteland.

THE REPORTER AND EL CAPITÁN DE MUERTO

In late spring of 1841, a twenty-eight-year-old newspaperman named George Wilkins Kendall joined an expedition headed west from the newly declared Republic of Texas. It is a matter of ongoing debate just what intentions the Texans had, but it seems likely that they believed the Native population of northern Mexico would welcome annexation to their newly created republic. Other men saw the expedition as a business venture. They hoped the trip would establish a lucrative trading route. What they found instead was sorrow and horror.

During that hot, dry summer, more than three hundred men, twenty-four wagons, and a small band of fifes, trumpets, and drums struggled wearily toward Santa Fe. Exhausted, sick, and close to mutiny, Kendall and the entire Texas expedition were captured by Mexican soldiers the instant they set foot on the Mexican frontier.

The man who captured the hapless Texans was the maniacal Captain Damasio Salazar. As soon as he surrounded Kendall and the dozen others who had been scouting ahead, Salazar turned to the soldiers standing behind him. "Detail, forward," he barked in Spanish. A dozen Mexican soldiers stepped forward. Some were armed with old muskets, others with new, automated carbines.

"They're going to shoot us boys," said one of the Texan prisoners. "Let's die hot-blooded, it's much easier."

The Mexican soldiers took aim.

Writer George Kendall later recorded his thoughts at that instant: "A man lives almost an age in a single moment of immense danger," he wrote. "His thoughts crowd upon each other with such lightning rapidity, that his past life, its promises and hopes, are reviewed at a glance."

A Mexican man stepped up to Captain Salazar and argued for the men's lives. After much debate, Salazar finally put his men at ease.

Later that night, Salazar stood in front of Kendall and the other starving men. He tossed a single tortilla in among them and then watched them fight over it. A moment later he tossed a second tortilla to them, and then tossed a few others, one at a time.

The entire Texas expedition was taken briefly to Santa Fe before Salazar was ordered to take the nearly two hundred prisoners south to Chihuahua.

The sorrowful caravan left Santa Fe on October 18, 1842. The soldiers jeered the Texans, telling them that they were being taken to work in mines. Salazar led the captive Texans on a forced march.

Those who could not walk traded whatever few possessions they had for a few hours' ride on a Mexican mount. Other men were tied together in pairs at their waists by ropes. A guard would occasionally tie the rope to his pommel and then spur his horse into a gallop, dragging the two men behind.

At the rear of the sorry band of prisoners Captain Salazar placed a brute of a man. According to Kendall, the man "sought every occasion to insult, ride over and strike the sick and the lame, and the weary."

They reached the Jornada at San Acacia on October 26 and the tiny village of Socorro the next day. A prisoner named Thomas Falconer wrote in his journal that bands of well-armed Apaches roamed the Socorro plaza. He also noted that the houses in Socorro had thin, broad sheets of mica instead of glass for windows. A day later the macabre march passed through the bosque south of Socorro. The cottonwood trees sheltered "blue and black birds" – sandhill cranes.

On the night of October 28 the prisoners camped at Valverde, a place Kendall called "one of the best camping grounds" of their miserable journey. At Pedro Armendaris's pretty valley was a trading caravan from the United States. Kendall met the as-yet-unmarried Samuel Magoffin, "a native of the United States, but by this time a merchant of Chihuahua." Five years later, swept up in an unpredictable war, Magoffin himself, along with his new and pregnant young bride, Susan, would themselves face starvation and violence on the Jornada.

The prisoners slept on the open ground at Valverde. During the night it snowed. "I drew my blanket entirely over my head, thought of home and its comforts," Kendall wrote.

The next morning Captain Salazar advised the captives to fill their canteens, as there would be no water for the next several days' journey. It was the only time he would show a glimmer of kindness. Kendall filled a water gourd with close to two gallons of water, but he lost it all when he accidentally broke the gourd while climbing over the black lava of the malpais.

The Texans crossed through Lava Gate at noon on October 31. They were led through the gloomy entrance to the place their Mexican captors called the Journey of the Dead Man. "It is a level, sterile and desolate plain," Kendall wrote of the Jornada, "a desert with no vegetation save here and there a few stunted thorns, different species of cactus of dwarf-like proportions."

They marched through a bitterly cold night. To keep warm the soldiers lit branches of the soapweed, *lehuguilla*, and the captives ran from plant to plant following this train of short-lived roadside fires. Kendall recalled the night: "The sufferings, the horrors of that dreadful night upon the Dead Man's Journey cannot soon be effaced from the memory of those who endured them. Although my sore and blistered feet, and lame ankle pained me excessively, it was nothing to the biting cold and the helpless drowsiness which cold begets. No halt was called – had any of us fallen asleep by the roadside it would have been the sleep of death."

On the morning of November 1 they reached one of the Jornada's dry lake beds. At sunrise they rested without food or water, waiting for the stragglers to catch up. They began again at midmorning and marched all day.

At sunset on that horrible day Kendall was startled by the report of a gunshot. He turned to see that "a poor unfortunate man named Golpin, a merchant, had been shot by the rear guard." Golpin had broken his arm and could not walk without great discomfort. He had made it this far by bartering rides. He had apparently bargained his shirt for a ride with a guard. "While in the act of taking it off," wrote Kendall, "Salazar ordered a soldier to shoot him. The first ball only wounded the wretched man, but the second one killed him instantly, and he fell with the shirt about his face." The man's ears were cut off and saved so that Salazar could claim his bounty by delivering the proper number of prisoners.

They marched on.

By nightfall both the mounts and the Texans were so exhausted that the caravan was forced to stop. Out of sympathy, some of the women who accompanied the soldiers gave the prisoners food. Shortly after midnight they were ordered to march again.

Just before daylight another prisoner collapsed. A man named Griffith was "too weak and too lame to travel," Kendall reported. "He sank to the ground. A soldier told him to rise, or he would obey the orders given by Salazar to kill anyone who could not keep up." The man made a feeble attempt to rise but could not. "He cast an imploring look at the soldier, and . . . the brutal miscreant *knocked his brains out with a musket!*" His ears were cut off, and the soldier took the dead man's blanket. "He was thrown by the roadside, another feast for the buzzards and prairie wolves!"

With a ghastly mixture of horror and humor, Kendall describes the torture of yet another man. "For some trifling cause Salazar drew his sword and with the flat of it struck one of the prisoners a violent blow across the shoulders." Begging for mercy, the man used the only Spanish expression he knew. "Muchas gracias," he whimpered. Salazar was infuriated, thinking the man was mocking him. Over and over again Salazar slapped the flat of his sword across the man's shoulders. "Muchas gracias," the man screamed. "The Captain was now more infuriated than ever. He looked upon [this] as a defiance and accordingly redoubled the blows." The incident ended when the man finally stopped speaking.

Before they left the Jornada, Salazar killed another man. The prisoners stood by and silently watched. "Callous too we had become," Kendall wrote, "and although we could not look upon the horrible butchery of our comrades with indifference, we knew that any interference on our part would bring certain death."

Once they reached El Paso the prisoners were handed over to a far more humane commander for their remaining journey south. During that journey Kendall heard talk of the notorious scalp hunter James Kirker. It was "suspected that he was in the practice of bringing in counterfeit scalps. He did not scruple to kill any of the lower order of Mexicans he might meet with, where there was slight chance of being discovered, and pass off their topknots for those of true Apache."

After lengthy legal maneuvers in Mexico, Kendall and the Texans were eventually allowed to return home.

Soon after the Texans were released, Mexican papers reported that Salazar – "this barbarous captain" – was being held by his own government "for the cruel and brutal action" and for "atrocious acts peculiar only to savages."

INTERLUDE: DON SANTIAGO QUERQUE

The reasons for the Mexican-American War boil down to nothing more complex than the reasons for any war: a slathering of greed spread on a foundation of racial mistrust and human ignorance.

Mexico had barely recovered from its own war of independence against Spain and was struggling to build a democracy when it had to turn its attention to its aggressive neighbor. When the fledgling Republic of Texas was annexed by the United States in 1845, Mexico took it as an act of war. Early in 1846, President James Polk ordered American troops to the mouth of the Rio Grande River at the heart of the disputed land. Mexico's leader, Santa Anna, responded by amassing an army of his own. Two days later the United States declared war on Mexico. The three-year-long war would claim the lives of fourteen thousand Americans and more than twenty thousand Mexicans. It would cost the United States more than one hundred million dollars. As had happened in the past, the barren sands of the Jornada became a stage for this war as well.

On a July morning six months after war was declared, a strange group of men rode into Chihuahua City. They led a string of burros loaded with bulging packs of "green" human pelts. At the front of the group, already pulling at a bottle of aguardiente, was Don Santiago Querque himself. His moccasin-clad henchmen rode at his side, their knives glimmering in the sun. One man, probably Chuly, carried a slender pole with several pelts dangling from the top, each with a set of human ears.

George Ruxton, a young British adventurer who was visiting the city, reported that Kirker entered the plaza under state escort. Ruxton said that a local musical band accompanied the killers and that a parade of dignitaries and priests followed close behind. Ruxton watched as dozens of human scalps were strung on a rope and then dangled in front of the cathedral.

The town's bull ring served as the offices of the government's "Council of Honorary Rewards." The citizens' board counted and recounted the pelts and then wrote out the proper vouchers. The 160 scalps came from two raids Kirker had made recently on Apache villages northwest of the city.

The fact that the government never paid up on the money it owed the men from this raid, combined with Mexico's distrust of Querque, set off a series of events that would soon sweep Kirker northward to the Jornada del Muerto just at the moment hostilities between Mexico and the United States flared into war.

SUSAN MAGOFFIN

Early on Friday morning, July 31, 1846, the day after her nineteenth birthday, Susan Shelby Magoffin's contractions began. "My pains commenced and continued till 12 o'clock," Magoffin wrote a week later in her diary. Then, "after much agony and severest pains," she gave birth to a premature baby. A little while later, it died.

"In a few short months I should have been a happy mother, and made the heart of a father glad, but the ruling hand of a mighty Providence has interposed and deprived us of hope, the fond hope of mortals!"

She sat writing at the single table in a mudroom at Bent's Fort on the high, open plains of eastern Colorado. On the table a lamp's sputter and deep oily smell filled the room with a greasy light. In that improbable place, "the mysteries of a new world" opened before her eyes: the depth of sorrow, the strength of women, the frankness of death.

Sitting in the dark, cool room at Bent's Fort, Magoffin wrote of her despair at the loss of her baby, and then added: "My situation was very different from that of an Indian woman in the room below me. She gave birth to a fine healthy baby at about the same time. In half an hour she went to the River and bathed herself and it."

Despite the privileges her southern aristocratic upbringing provided, the death of her own child and the birth to this Indian woman added to her growing understanding of the demands and the strengths of women. "Never could I have believed such a thing if I had not been here. It is truly astonishing to see what customs will do. No doubt many ladies in civilized life are ruined by too careful treatments during childbirth."

As if to illustrate, and in stark contrast to the robust Indian woman, after she gave birth to her premature baby, Magoffin had been forbidden to rise from her bed. A white doctor assigned to troops hurrying west for the coming war with Mexico gave her strict orders even though she herself felt strong.

It had taken Magoffin and her considerably older husband, Samuel, seven weeks to push across five hundred miles of Kansas plains just to reach Bent's Fort. Most of the time she traveled in proper attire, prudently covering her neck, shielding herself from the stares and catcalls of the men, but when the hot, relentless sun bore down she would strip down to a cotton chemise.

To the seldom-sober, curse-throwing men who drove the oxen of her husband's trade caravan, Susan Magoffin traveled in unimaginable luxury. Born into one of the richest families of pre–Civil War Kentucky, she let her wealthy forty-five-year-old husband spare no expense for her comfort. At night she slept in a house-like canvas tent, waited on by a servant girl. Others prepared her fireside dinners, and her thoughtful husband made certain a good wine accompanied the trailside meal.

Now she sat in the dark room at the edge of the Mexican frontier, brooding on her loss and the loss around her. Two soldiers had died that day as well "and have been buried in the sand hills, the common fate of man."

Fifteen hundred men from the United States had marched past the Magoffin caravan in the past several days. Like any soldiers during the world's weary pathway through time, these men came as offerings to the god of war. They came as patriots, under a righteous banner, marching for freedom. They came – these sons of veterans of the War of 1812 – from parents who were strapped to the bone by poverty and need. They came as innocent heroes and criminals; they came as brave men and as killers.

Instead of a gory battle in the Sangre de Cristo Mountains, however, Santa Fe fell to the invading U.S. Army without a shot. As Colonel George Stephen Watts Kearny and his army approached the capital, the Mexican governor and his strong-armed military adviser simply abandoned the city.

The Magoffin caravan moved westward from Bent's Fort a few days later. They reached Santa Fe, now occupied by the U.S. Army, and stayed there for about six weeks until Samuel decided the time was right to move the caravan south toward Chihuahua City. In her coming travels Susan likely became the first Anglo woman to see much of what today are the states of New Mexico and Chihuahua. They left Santa Fe following the old Camino Real. Several days later they reached the Jornada.

"A memorable day this," she wrote in her diary on November 25, 1846, "the anniversary of our wedding. Yes, we have been married a whole year today!" She sat in an adobe house in the shade of the dark volcanic mesa at the northern end of the Jornada. Despite the great tension and fear she felt, she tried to keep a happy face. Apaches had been raiding other encampments regularly and driving off stock. Men had been killed. On top of that, rumors had recently reached them that a large Mexican force was coming from the south to take them captive.

Because of the war, very few of the season's caravans had ventured south across the Jornada, and now, along with the Magoffin caravan, close to five hundred carts and wagons, thousands of animals, and hundreds of men were trapped at the northern entrance of the Jornada. There was a great deal of money to be made in the coming uncertain times, yet no one dared to go any further south. Stalled at the gates of the Jornada, the many traders were "corralling together and sinking their wagon wheels to the hubs for a breast-work in case of an attack."

During the long encampment at the entrance to the Jornada, Susan became a local sensation. People from great distances came to see the fair-skinned woman. She wore her long hair pulled behind her ears, wrapped in a tight and efficient bun. The style exposed her wide, angular forehead and framed her deep-set, bright, oval eyes. She had a curious, ageless beauty, a faint Mona Lisa smile, and an adventuresome tomboy glint in her eyes. "As usual the villagers collected to see the curiosity," she told her diary after one such incident. "They whispered among themselves and picked at my dress. I did think the Mexicans were as void of refinement and judgments as the dumb animals till I heard one of them say '*bonita muchacha!*' And now I have reason and certainly a good one for changing my opinion; they are certainly very *quick and intelligent people.*"

After their initial curiosity wore off, Susan engaged many of the local people in lively discussions, learning their customs as well as their opinions on a wide range of subjects. "The wife and daughter of the owner of this house came by today with their *mola* stone and corn to show me how to make tortillas!" she wrote. The women taught her how to grind corn into a paste. Then they "divided the paste into little pieces the size of a biscuit," which she "patted out and into tortillas." Susan helped the women put them onto an iron griddle to cook. Sitting in the warm adobe house while the cold wind of winter whipped across the empty land, the three women stuffed the cooked tortillas with frijoles and green chiles and then ate. She ate Mexican food as well as the local eggs, apples, goat cheese, and grapes. She learned to love the taste of roasted sandhill crane, served with the always-present green chiles and tortillas.

"The old lady also brought over her knitting, which like the tortillas is done in a way tedious enough. I learned how she did it. On showing her the much easier mode of the U.S. she seemed much surprised and delighted."

Even with her growing sense of humanity, Susan could never quite escape her royal southern roots. She had grown up in the culture of slavery, and it is likely that the black women servants who accompanied her were the first African Americans from the United States to see the Jornada. "Nothing hurts me more than to have a cross, ill-tempered servant about me," she wrote one morning. "The only way to treat a turbulent domestic is to look above them too much to answer back, or even hear their impudence, till it becomes correctable by the rod."

But even as she wrote of using force on her maid, Susan was using the legality of slavery in order to improve the life of another human being. One morning "a little Mexican boy of nine or ten years" approached Susan's husband and asked to be purchased. The Apaches had murdered his father and carried him off as a prisoner. "After three years of hard servile among them, the little fellow ran off and found his way to the house of an old Mexican who resides here on the banks of the river in a lone hut the picture of misery. Here the boy has been for two months under the fostering care of the old *compadre*, but growing weary of his life, which was not better than that with the Indians. He now wishes to be brought with the sum of $7.00 which he owes the old man for his protection. Tomorrow the money is to be paid and hence forth Francisco is our servant."

Susan also befriended an older half-Indian, half-Mexican woman. The two had much in common. "We talked of all family concerns from the children down to the dogs," she told her diary. The woman asked Susan if she had a mother and a father. When she explained to the woman that she had left her parents to marry her beloved Samuel, the woman incredulously asked if she had run off from them "just for a husband." "But I laughed and said *perces es mejor nos* which means 'Well, isn't it better?' and with a hearty laugh she assented."

GEORGE RUXTON

"The news," Susan Magoffin wrote on December 1, 1846, a week after her wedding anniversary, "comes in very ugly today. An Englishman from Chihuahua direct says that the three traders who went on ahead to Chihuahua had been taken prisoners."

The "Englishman from Chihuahua" was the young adventurer George Ruxton. He had left Chihuahua City headed northward toward the Jornada shortly after witnessing Kirker's grotesque parade of scalps.

The tale of George Augustus Frederick Ruxton's brief life shames any "extreme sports" story of the twenty-first century. Born in England in 1821, he enrolled at a military academy at age fourteen, then dropped out and made his way to Spain, where a vicious civil war was unfolding. He joined the army of Queen Isabella II. After his courageous action in one battle, Ruxton became a knight of the Spanish royalty. He was seventeen.

Ruxton returned to England for a brief stay and then moved to Ireland. There his wanderlust took full hold of him, and his true life's journeying began. He soon caught a ship for Canada. In Ontario the twenty-one-year-old befriended a Chippewa Indian and lived in the Canadian wilderness with him through a long, bitter, and dark winter.

From Canada Ruxton twice sailed to Africa. On his second visit he plotted a walk across the continent. He planned to follow the Tropic of Capricorn across the Namib and Kalahari deserts, then travel down the headwaters of the wild, unexplored Limpopo River to the Indian Ocean. After several months and encounters with "African Bushmen," distrustful merchants, and missionaries who held a questionable regard for human life, Ruxton abandoned his African quest. He was twenty-four years old. At the time he scribbled a letter to the Royal Geographical Society that "my movements are uncertain, for I am trying to get up a voyage to Borneo and the Indian Archipelago; [I] have volunteered to explore Central Africa; and the Aborigines Protection Society wish[es] me to go out to Canada and organize the Indian tribes; whilst, for my own part and inclination, I wish to go to all parts of the world at once."

Instead, he chose to sail to Mexico. For the next year and a half he explored much of Mexico on horseback with a small group of Mexican guides. By 1846 his travels had taken him to Chihuahua and the northern territories.

About a week before he met Susan Magoffin, Ruxton and his small party reached the southern end of the Jornada. "We saw more Indian signs," he wrote nearly a year later in his book *Adventures in Mexico and the Rocky Mountains*. Fearful of an Apache attack, and aware of the tense situation between the United States and Mexico, all but two of his guides left him and turned south. "I was now at the edge of this formidable desert," he wrote, "where along the road the bleaching bones of mules testify to the dangers to be apprehended from the want of water and pasture and many human bones likewise tell their tale of Indian slaughter and assault."

Ruxton rode up from the Rio Grande onto the Jornada's plain on a hard-packed road "bounded by sierras." He noted that yucca and rabbit bush were scattered here and there over the level plain, but "the mesquite is now becoming scarce . . . the screw-wood taking its place: farther on the wood ceases, and there is then no fuel to be met with of any description."

He came to the dark outline of Point of Rocks, the series of abrupt hills adjacent to the road. "Behind these rocks," Ruxton wrote, the Indians "frequently lie in ambush, shooting down the unwary traveler, whose first intimation of their presence is the puff of smoke from the rocks, or the whiz of an arrow through the air." Ruxton reported that the Apaches had recently killed several Americans here.

He made it to the dry playa of Lake of the Dead at midnight. Shaken by cold, he set fire to every soapweed plant he could find, but "the dry twigs blazed brightly for a minute and were instantly consumed." By the temporary light of one such fire Ruxton "discovered that a large party of Indians had passed the very spot but a few hours, and were probably not far off at that moment." He moved on quickly and lit no more fires.

"The mules and horses, which had traveled at a very quick pace, were suffering – even this early – from want of water." The horse Ruxton rode was so thirsty that it "bit off the neck of a gourd, which I had placed on the ground, and which the poor beast by his nose knew to contain water."

At dawn they stopped for a few hours at a place where there was grass for the animals. The rest gave Ruxton time to look around. "The plain through which the dead man's journey passes is one of a system, or series, which stretch along the table land between the Sierra Madre on the west and the small mountain-chain of the Sierra Blanca."

From the two local men who were with him, the British adventurer learned that the mountains that ringed the desolate Jornada were the stronghold of the Apaches. He also learned that the mountains of the Jornada were said to "abound in minerals" and that the surrounding mountains were "also celebrated for medicinal herbs of great value, which the Apaches, when at peace . . . sometimes bring for sale."

Ruxton noted that the Jornada was "in many places strewn with volcanic substances, and exhibit the bluffs of tabular form, composed of basaltic lava, known by the name of mesas."

He spent the night of November 30 at the campsite Fra Cristobel, near Lava Gate. The next morning "I pushed on to the ruins at Valverde. Here, encamped on the banks of the river in heavy timber, I found a great portion of the caravan which I have before mentioned as being en route to Chihuahua."

Ruxton met Susan Magoffin and told her of the traders who had been captured. He also got a good, long look at the other Missouri merchants idling at Valverde, men caught between war and revolt, disaster and great riches. "The traders had been lying here many weeks and the bottom where they were encamped presented quite a picturesque appearance," he wrote. Among the trees of the bosque and in the open spaces of the edges of the Jornada, wagons were drawn up to form corrals. The wagons were so close together that "the whole made a most formidable fort. When filled with some hundred rifles, it could defy the attacks of Indians or Mexicans," he wrote.

"Scattered about were tents and shanties of logs and branches of every conceivable form, round which lounged wild looking Missourians, some cooking at the camp fires, some cleaning their rifles or firing at targets – blazes cut in the trees with a bull's eye made with wet powder on the wet bark." He complained that from morning until night the air resounded with the pop of the rifles as idle men with guns shot at nearly everything.

Ruxton pushed northward. A few days later he met the U.S. troops who were marching southward. Because of his crisp British military training, he was horrified at what he saw. "The camp was strewn with the bones and offal of the cattle slaughtered for its supply, and not the slightest attention was paid to keeping it clear from other accumulations of filth." As if he needed any further proof of the U.S. Army's lack of preparation, Ruxton noted with disgust the fact that no sentries were posted, even after the recent Apache attacks.

After spending several days with the army, Ruxton moved northward alone.

As the war between Mexico and the United States began in earnest, Ruxton arrived in southern Colorado. There he re-outfitted himself from desert gear to that better suited for mountain terrain and then rode into the Rockies just as a savage winter began. He survived, and in the spring he was exploring the headwaters of the upper Arkansas River. That summer he rode down out of the mountains and made a final visit to England before returning to the United States. A month after his twenty-seventh birthday, as he was outfitting for another solo journey into the American West, he died of epidemic dysentery in St. Louis.

DEATH WAITS

Death stalked Susan Magoffin daily.

While the Magoffin party waited for the arrival of the U.S. Army from the north for protection, a force of more than twelve hundred Mexicans was marching rapidly toward the Jornada from the south. As Christmas approached, Susan worried that at any minute the local Mexican people who had so recently befriended her might "murder us without regard."

It was obvious that the coming battle would be fought somewhere close by. Susan wrote that the Jornada was "the enemy's breastwork" and that she sat in "the very jaws of the enemy." Bands of Apaches continued to raid the outlying encampments. Any traders who ventured into the Jornada would surely be "cut to pieces."

Susan eased the stress and her tedium by turning to the few books she had brought with her from her Missouri home. She read her Bible daily and found comfort in a collection of Methodist sermons, "plain in speech and beautiful."

Despite the imminent danger, however, the traders at Valverde were "on fire" for the arrival of the U.S. soldiers from Santa Fe. None of the traders were willing to abandon the quest for wealth that the coming war promised.

Colonel Alexander Doniphan and his 856 men reached the Jornada at Valverde on the afternoon of December 14. That afternoon the weather turned colder and a bleak snow began to fall. Doniphan immediately ordered three hundred soldiers across the Jornada. Two days later he sent two hundred more. On the following day he took the balance of his men and set out on the Journey of the Dead. He kept his soldiers moving at a fast clip and allowed them only short stops during the two sixteen-hour days he needed to cross.

Like the adventurer Ruxton and the hapless Texas prisoners before him, the soldiers tried to keep warm by burning *lehuguilla*, soapweed. A soldier named John Hughes wrote in his diary that soldiers marching through the night often set the bushes on fire simply for fun. The plants "would blaze up like a flash of powder. For miles the road was most brilliantly illuminated by sudden flashes of light, which lasted but for a moment, and then again all was dark."

The U.S. soldiers reached the southern end of the Jornada on the longest night of the year, winter solstice, 1846. The Mexican force was at El Paso, less than sixty miles distant.

IN CELEBRATION OF THE BIRTH OF THE PRINCE OF PEACE

Doniphan's men celebrated Christmas morning by shooting rifles and singing. At three in the afternoon they set up an early camp at Brazito, a "little arm" of the Rio Grande just south of the Jornada.

Colonel Ponce de León and his twelve hundred Mexican troops were just a few miles to the south. They approached the United States' camp undetected. When they were directly across the river from the enemy, de León ordered his soldiers into battle formation.

The men in Doniphan's camp were relaxing after their easy Christmas Day. Doniphan himself was playing cards. He looked up from the blanket where he was sitting to see a large cloud of dust rising from across the river. He jumped to his feet and grabbed his saber. At that same moment, his scouts galloped into camp shouting that the Mexican army was about to attack.

The Mexican cavalry pranced across the river. They were regal, dressed in their bright-red coats and white belts. Doniphan held a short, fruitless parley with the Mexicans in order to stall for time.

The large, well-disciplined Mexican infantry marched up from the river, halted, and took aim.

Just as the Mexicans opened fire, Doniphan ordered several of his men to lie flat. Many Mexican soldiers believed that the sudden disappearance of so many of the enemy troops had meant their shots had hit home. They cheered as they reloaded their muskets and marched forward. With each Mexican's volley Doniphan ordered more men to hit the ground.

When the Mexican army moved to flank the U.S. Army, Doniphan's men stood up from where they had fallen and fired. Several Mexicans fell. The advancing line faltered. One shot had wounded the Mexican commander. The Mexican line broke and retreated back toward El Paso.

Christmas Day's Battle of Brazito injured seven of Doniphan's men, none fatally. The United States claimed it killed thirty to sixty Mexicans; de León said he lost eleven.

SUNSET

About an hour after the Battle of Brazito, a strange group of riders approached the United States' camp from the west. From the parched, yellow land across the river, seven men stood in the glare of the blood-red Christmas sunset. These men bore no gifts; nor were they wise men come to seek a savior. Armed better than an entire company of the U.S. Army, they seemed more like the murderous horsemen of an apocalypse.

Some soldiers called to the small group of oddly clad riders who lingered on the far side of the river.

A man answered, speaking in English. He said his name was James Kirker. He told them that he was a trapper who had come from Mexico and was headed north. The soldiers allowed the men to cross the river. The strange men rode the best horses anyone had seen since leaving Missouri. The soldiers took Kirker to see Colonel Doniphan. Kirker told Doniphan that he had come to help the Americans fight the Mexicans.

Doniphan did not trust this man who apparently got along in life "having nothing but arms and the disposition to use them." On the other hand, he also understood how a man like Kirker might be of great use to the army. Kirker spoke fluent Spanish; he had extensive knowledge of the territory ahead; and he had no hesitancy to kill. Doniphan decided to allow Kirker and his men to stay, but he placed them under careful scrutiny.

At camp that night Kirker mounted his beautiful horse and galloped in a wide circle around a fire. As the young soldiers watched, this fifty-four-year-old man lowered himself down the side of the racing horse's saddle. At full speed he rode nearly upside down, his long hair sweeping the ground beneath him. Afterward he drank whatever he was offered of the men's plentiful supply of *aguardiente.*

In the morning Kirker was alone. His Indian companions had disappeared.

Kirker remained with the troops. During the first weeks of January 1847, Doniphan sent Kirker and a small group of soldiers around the area in order to round up stock. While Kirker was away on one of these trips, Doniphan learned that a gang of Delawares and local Indians had killed the new United States governor of New Mexico, Charles Bent, at the northern town of Taos.

According to historian George Bird Grinnell, on January 19, 1847, a number of Indians attacked the village. They killed one local official, and then another, "the latter having infuriated them by calling them all thieves. They chopped his body up into small bits." The murderers approached the house where the newly appointed Governor Bent was staying. Along with the governor and his family, inside the house was the wife of the well-known Taos scout Kit Carson.

The women and children escaped, but not Bent. First "they climbed upon the roof and dug a hole into it," and then "the Indians broke into the house, shot him with their arrows and his own pistols, took his scalp, stretched it on a board with brass-headed tacks and paraded it all over the town."

Although Kirker himself was probably somewhere near the Jornada raiding ranches and stealing horses for the army at the time of the Taos Rebellion, rumors persist that he helped his former henchmen precipitate the murders.

THE CAPTAIN OF DEATH AND THE YOUNG MISSOURI BRIDE

Once they learned of Doniphan's victory at Brazito, most of the remaining caravans rushed south across the Jornada. Shortly after Christmas, however, Susan Magoffin become ill, causing her husband's caravan to linger behind. She soon recovered, but they now had to wait for a military escort to lead them safely across the Jornada.

Susan used the time to explore her surroundings. In her diary she carefully noted details that no man's journal of the same period ever mentions: the way the local women breastfed their babies wrapped in long, colorful scarves where the infants would "take care of Number One." She described how women smoked little *cigarittas*, made from local tobacco and wrapped in corn husks. And when they danced – which was always with pure joy and delight – she noticed how the women twirled fans about their faces and peeked out at the handsome men who always gathered to watch.

Susan never confined herself to the circle of wagons. Despite the dangers of the war and marauding Apaches, she hiked alone up into the barren Jornada wilderness, exhilarated by life in that great, empty land. "There is such independence, so much free uncontaminated air, which impregnates the mind, the feelings, nay every thought, with purity," she wrote. "I breathe free without that oppression and uneasiness felt in a settled home." She was always alert to whatever she saw, whether it was "a curious little pebble, a shell, a new flower, or the quill of a strange bird." Once she climbed to the precipice on a rocky cliff and stopped. "Everything is perfectly still and quiet," she wrote of the experience, "scarcely a breath of air, or the flitting of a feathered warbler has appeared to disturb the solemn stillness. Ever and anon the sharp whistle of a partridge, the chirp of a lark, or the croaking of a raven in the distance is heard."

When weather or her disposition temporarily prevented her from exploring, she found joy in solitude. One of the "varieties of life," she said, was to be shut up in her tent all day with a buffalo robe rolled around her and a violent storm pounding down against the entire desert world. And then, in the peace following the storm, "to be quietly without any trouble, by one's self, in the middle of a bed in a nice, dry tent, with writing materials around you and full privilege to write anything and every thing that may chance to enter one's head." So she wrote, and then, after lunch, "laid down with *mi alma* on a buffalo skin with the carriage seat for pillows and took what few ladies have done: a siesta in the sun."

Still, there was much to be feared. "We also had a rattlesnake fracas," she wrote one night. "Two or three were killed in the road . . . these were quite enough to make me sick." While in camp at Valverde she reported that "Last night I had a wolfish kind of a serenade." Just as she had begun to prepare herself for bed the "music" began. "Bak! Ba! Gnow, gnow, in such quick succession, it was almost a mixture of cat, dog, sheep, wolf and dear knows what else. It was enough to frighten off sleep and everything else."

But even when she confessed her fears that "some wily savage or hungry wolf might be lurking," she steadfastly refused to let her husband know of her fright, for "it would be torture for him to know my fears."

In late January she sat at a small fire in the open bowl of Valverde, the dark bulk of Black Mesa at her side. For the past three days fear for her life had kept her from writing in her diary, and she wrote quickly to catch up. "We are on the road again. The news is that the Taos people have risen and murdered every American citizen in Taos including the Governor," she wrote. "Within our little tent we have 12 sure rounds, a double-barreled shot gun, a pair of holsters and belt pistols, with one of Colt's six-barreled revolvers."

That day, January 26, 1847, a strange group of men rode down from the north and approached the trade wagons.

In her diary, Magoffin recorded the horror she felt at seeing these men. "Without a doubt 'tis the intention of nearly every one of them to murder without distinction every American in the country, if the least thing should turn in their favor." She watched the strange group of men whispering as they moved about. They observed her husband's every move, "always peeping out after him to see if he was near or far off, on which occasions they talked more and faster. Everything was said in a whisper."

One particular man, she declared, was among "the greatest villains and smooth-faced assassins in the world." The next day the men disappeared.

Two days after this incident at the Magoffin caravan, James Kirker reappeared at El Paso, where he turned over to Colonel Doniphan the livestock he had captured. Because Doniphan suspected that Kirker had been involved in the insurrection at Taos, he immediately placed him under guard and gave orders to kill him if he made any false moves. However, over the coming weeks Kirker slowly regained Doniphan's trust. Eventually his knowledge of the territory and his advice became critical to the colonel's success. Kirker accompanied the U.S. Army on their long and bloody march through Mexico. In the summer of 1847 he sailed from Mexico to St. Louis, but soon he returned to New Mexico. When he did, the *Santa Fe Republican* praised him as a "free and kind-hearted man" who was "highly intelligent." For a time he resumed killing Apaches for their scalps. Eventually he migrated to California, where he died at age sixty.

The ethical paradox at the center of existence is that to endure, human life requires the taking of other life. Humanity's attempt to unravel that moral contradiction has given birth to philosophy and religion and has fueled terror and war.

Long ago at pueblo ruins scattered like stones on the Jornada, the ancient ones held sacred dances so that men wielding deadly atlatl might be blessed in hunting and in war. Since time began, shamans and popes, presidents and dictators, kings and philosophers proclaim: kill or be killed.

Black, ruthless evil appears, wielding a bloodied knife, inflicting wounds so deep we doubt we can survive.

But from whence does evil come, and to what end does it announce itself?

SUSAN ON THE JOURNEY OF THE DEAD

On the day she began her voyage across the Jornada del Muerto, Susan Magoffin wondered if she would live to see her home in Missouri. "But 'tis all the same if I do or do not; I must learn to look farther ahead than to earthly things. The two great rewards are laid before me, with the command to chose the 'evil or the good.' What must I do?"

Within hours of passing Lava Gate, the Magoffin caravan came upon a ghastly phantom. "We observed a wagon standing near a little woods," Susan wrote. The animals were "broken down." The deserted wagon sat like a ghost ship drifting in a barren ocean.

Later that night, by the light of a cold but beautiful moon, she came to the shallow and bone-dry Laguna del Muerto – the Lake of the Dead. "I should fully say the name it bears is not too solitary for it." She described the bleak, flat terrain and, in the great, dark distance, the jagged teeth of mountains. "The whole area puts on a gloomy aspect," she wrote.

She resented the confinement of traveling at night. "I have to be shut up in the carriage on a road I know nothing of," she fumed, "and the driver nodding all the time and letting the reins drop from his hands to the entire will of the mules." Her anger kept her steaming all night long, she said, "though everyone else complained bitterly of the cold."

The Magoffins rested for only a few hours, then started on again at dawn. They traveled without stopping until late afternoon, when they finally rested at a place with grass for the fatigued animals. She took time to write a precise description of black grama grass: the joints in its blades, the texture and color of its roots, and how, "at all seasons the taller portion has a white and harvest-like appearance, larger fields of it are like hay."

On the move again, at midnight they reached the southern end of the Jornada and the steep descent to the Rio Grande at Rincon. They rested for a few days at the tiny village of Doña Anna, where she finally revolted against being confined to camp. "Notwithstanding the many reports of Indians stealing animals and murdering people about here, I have been bold enough to climb up and down these beautiful and rugged cliffs both yesterday and today."

On the Sabbath she took a few hours of to catch up with her diary. She confided her disappointment with her husband, who at that very moment was doing business with the residents of the village. "I wish he would observe the Sabbath more," she wrote, "and shut his store. It hurts me more than I can tell that he does not find six days of the week sufficient to gain the goods of this poor world, but is also constrained to devote the day that God himself has appointed us to keep holy, to business. . . . As for myself I must first remove the beam from mine own eye, and then shall I see clearly to pull out the moat from my brother's eye. At times my sins and transgressions are heavy on my head. In my weakness, I will endeavor to walk according to God's laws, as my own understanding points them out to me. At all times, I have his help in the light and darkness."

The Magoffin trade caravan crossed the Jornada and followed Doniphan south into Mexico. Susan's diary ends on September 8, 1847. Shortly thereafter she contracted yellow fever and then gave birth to her second child, a son, who died a short time later. After the war she sailed from Mexico to New Orleans. She and her husband then settled in eastern Missouri. Her third child, Jane, was born in 1851. Another daughter, Susan, was born in 1855. Susan Shelby Magoffin died shortly after the birth of this daughter. She was twenty-seven.

While she was at the southern end of the Jornada, Susan had befriended a local Mexican family. "The more I see of this family, the more I like them," she wrote. Warmly hospitable in a time of much want, polite and respectful of others, the family welcomed everyone into their home and judged no one.

Their conversations often dwelled on the great mysteries. One breakfast the grandfather said that life had taught him many lessons. Time and sympathy, he said, were the best healers.

Susan pointed out to him that sympathy did little to help her with the "troubles, dangers and difficulties I have been in, those I am now in, and those I may be in."

Yes, he said, but she was learning a lesson nobody could teach her.

"Tis true, what he says," she wrote. "No one else could ever have made me sensible of what I have seen and felt since I left home to travel."

The old man smiled and nodded his head.

"He is quite philosophical and fine," she wrote. "I can't help but loving them all."

11. Coffee on the Porch of the Bar Cross Ranch

I step through the heavy steel bars of the gate and into the main yard of the Bar Cross Ranch. Ben and Jane Cain's two scruffy ranch dogs charge at me from the shade of the long, low adobe ranch house. I stop to scratch the ears of the light-colored one while the other barks one last time and then disappears back into the shade of the porch.

I'm setting out in the late afternoon in order to hike a few miles south across the open Jornada. The Cains are gone for a few days visiting relatives on the far side of the Jornada. They were kind enough to let me use their ranch yard as a base camp.

Once inside the gate, I walk across the open yard between the low-slung house and a large metal shed. Inside the shed are a tractor and several pieces of large equipment.

The Bar Cross Ranch headquarters lies a dozen miles south of the vineyards on Pedro Armendaris's land grant. It is located at an original campsite of the Camino Real. Travelers from the earliest times have stopped here in hopes of finding water. The Spanish called this place La Cruz de Alemán, the Cross of the German, after a fugitive who died here. In 1880 the Apache Victorio and his people rested at Aleman just hours after an intense battle against Buffalo Soldiers. Six miles south of here, the small dog with muddy feet led Oñate's 1598 expedition to water.

I cross the yard and step through the rear gate. A few small, irregular clouds dart in front of the sun and soften its light. Just west of the ranch buildings Ben's new well and pump house stands at the spot where the first well on the Jornada was dug in the mid-nineteenth century. Behind his pump house, a stout, working windmill remains motionless in the still air. Beyond the windmill a clump of skinny Lombardy poplars flare like green flames against the desert sky.

I walk down the steep bank of an arroyo, following an ancient road cut. The descent is so steep that I'm instantly shut off from the expansive view of the Jornada and am confined by the embankments. Late last night a brief rain fell, and parts of the surface of Aleman Draw are still damp.

I cross the draw and climb up a low place on the opposite bank until I face an open plain that is peppered with tarbush and an occasional rabbit bush. I check my compass and head due south. I make my way across the hard-packed pale-pink sand that typifies this part of the Jornada. I hike along the edge of the sparse vegetation, occasionally weaving my way around shrubs.

After nearly two hours I am several miles south of the ranch. I look back and find the green of the poplars standing above the plain. I squint until I make out the windmill and, finally, the adobe ranch buildings.

I'm just about to start back to the ranch when I notice a bulky shape just beyond a nearby mesquite tree. I walk toward it. Amid gray clumps of dry weeds are the recently decomposed remains of a cow. A rotting blanket of dark hide clings to an arch of bones. Leg bones stretch out from the carcass as if this specter cow had only moments before lain down to sleep.

In 1670, near where Ben and Jane's home now stands, a party of travelers making their way across the Jornada came upon a dead horse still tethered to a mesquite. Nearby they found scraps of clothing. They searched the area and soon found bits of human hair, and "in very widely separated places, the skull, three ribs and two long bones." These were the remains of a man named Bernard Gruber. He had been a trader in the area. One night, in a drunken stupor, Gruber told anyone who would listen that he could cast spells. When the authorities tried to arrest him for witchcraft he escaped and fled south. About a month later, in mid-July, the travelers found his bones. They buried the remains and marked the spot with a cross.

Gruber was the Alemán, the German.

As I walk back toward the ranch the sun is darting between clouds hanging over the Sierra Caballo. In another hour I make it back to the steep embankment that marks the edge of Aleman Draw and start down the embankment. At first I assume the hoofprints I spy on the mudflat before me are from a cow, but then I notice their odd shape. They are unlike any prints I've ever seen. Each hoof faintly resembles a cartoon mouse. Two oval "ears" extend from a round circle.

Oryx again.

When the New Mexico State Game Commission imported the thirty-eight gemsbok oryx from Africa's Kalahari Desert in the 1960s, the plan was to attract high-spending and influential big-game hunters to the area. Instead, the experiment went awry. The Jornada must have seemed like a Garden of Eden to beasts that evolved on one of the planet's harshest deserts. The oryx can survive without drinking *any* water, getting enough moisture solely from foraging. They can detect sounds at great distances. In Africa the antelope-like creatures use their long, very straight horns to impale their only natural enemy: lions. Compared to African lions, the mountain lions of the Jornada are like mosquitoes to the strange creatures. Now the ever-expanding herd competes with bison, sheep, and cattle for the Jornada's limited forage. There are currently more than four thousand oryx in the Jornada area.

The oryx has not been the only "experiment" with exotic animals on the Jornada. In the 1850s the U.S. military was considering the strategic value of using camels for freighting the weapons of warfare in the West. In 1853, Jefferson Davis, then the secretary of war, pushed legislation through Congress to fund a trial run. In 1857, seventy-seven camels, along with several men who were to serve as their handlers, arrived at Galveston, Texas, from the Middle East.

In June, Lieutenant Edward F. Beale led a caravan of twenty-one of these camels westward. His mission was to test their strength and endurance and to scout a new wagon route to the Pacific Ocean. Their route eventually took them up the Rio Grande, through El Paso, across the Jornada, and then westward from Albuquerque to California.

Beale's journal included his meticulous weather records as well as his personal observations. He was the first to propose "to supply a deficiency of water by a system of dams along the Rio Grande and across ravines and canons such as are used in Mexico." He stressed that in the dry country, water was the most valuable commodity.

Needless to say, the caravan of camels attracted crowds all along its route.

After being nearly mobbed by a curious crowd in El Paso, and a night camped at Fort Bliss, the camel caravan moved north toward the Jornada. The beasts moved slowly under the weight of their nearly two-ton loads, but Beale praised the camels for being "exceedingly docile, and easily managed. . . . I am very much encouraged to see how eagerly they seek the bushes for food instead of the grass, which certainly indicates their ability to subsist much easier than horses and mules in countries where forage is scarce."

Beale noted how the camels preferred the bean pods from mesquite trees to almost any other forage. "Although the branches are covered with sharp thorns which are larger and stronger than those which grow on a rosebush, the camel seizes the branches in his mouth and draws the limbs through his teeth, rapidly stripping off the leaves and briars and eating both greedily."

On the evening of July 30, 1857, they left the Rio Grande to enter "the much dreaded *Jornada del Muerto*." They trekked through a driving thunderstorm and "traveled on cheerfully" until they set up a camp and fell to an exhausted sleep.

At dawn they saw the Jornada for the first time. "Nothing exceeds the beauty of the country we have traveled over this morning," Beale wrote. That day they traveled twenty-four miles and made a dry camp just about where I had seen the rotting cow carcass. "The night was passed watchfully," Beale recorded, "Indian signs having been observed." The next day they traveled only four miles because they found pools of water in the rocks at Aleman. They stopped for the day and watered the stock.

Little is known about the men from the Middle East who accompanied the caravan to care for the camels, except that they were in all likelihood the first Muslims to set foot on the Jornada. Beale treated his camels better than he treated these men. After a night in Albuquerque he wrote, "This morning I was obliged to administer a copious supply of the oil of boot" to some of the "Turks and Greeks," as he called them. One man in particular "had not found, even in the positive prohibitions of the prophet, a sufficient reason for temperance, but was as drunk as any Christian on the caravan." The man wanted to stay in town, and he would have done so "but for a style of reason much resorted to by the head of his church, as well as others, in making converts, i.e. a broken head." Beale then writes about the weapon he used to subdue the man. "To move a stubborn, half-drunken Turk, give me a good tough piece of wagon spoke, aimed tolerably *high*."

The camel caravan eventually made it to the eastern slope of the Sierra Mountains of California. Although the voyage proved the efficiency of camels for warfare, the Civil War soon distracted the army. After the war, trains reduced the demand for efficient beasts of burden in the West.

Having served their purpose, the camels were abandoned in California. Some were sold, while others were left on the desert. Camels were reported still living in the remote American deserts in the early 1900s.

I descend into the dry wash and climb up the other side.

As soon as I reach the top I hear a vehicle. I stop dead in my tracks. It has been days since I've seen another human, much less heard an automobile, and the sound is so foreign that for a moment I'm frightened. I search the horizon and see the cloud of dust it has raised on the road into the ranch. I reach the back gate of the main ranch yard just as a pickup truck enters it from the opposite side. I unlatch the rear gate and swing it open.

The truck slows, and I lean over to introduce myself. Inside is a man and a squirming load of youngsters. "Some my kids, some my grandkids," the man explains. His name is George, and he is Ben Cain's hired man. George lives six miles southeast of the ranch headquarters, at the end of a dirt path. He's a big man: a big, warm hand, a big face, a walrus mustache, and a big cowboy hat. The kids are patient while George and I talk. He tells me the children travel each day to schools in Truth or Consequences, fifty miles away.

Education has always been a hardship for people on the Jornada. At the time the camel caravan stopped at Aleman in 1857, the Territory of New Mexico had only four schools and enrolled a total of six students. Some scholars maintain that because of racial stereotyping, the earliest white Americans believed the local Hispanic people were incapable of being educated. This in turn led to a campaign by the Spanish-language press for the creation of local schools. After the ranching and homesteading boom at the turn of the twentieth century, Anglo families on the Jornada created several small, local schools where children from neighboring ranches would gather to learn their three R's. Those schools are long gone, so now George's children face the daily hundred-mile round trip.

I stand aside and let George and his family head home. I swing the gate closed and watch the truck disappear in a swirl of dust.

I cross through the yard to where my tent is pitched just beyond. Although the sun is low in the sky, it still broils the tent. I gather up my cooking utensils and head for the shade of the Cains' front porch. As I'm boiling water for my freeze-dried lasagna, I sit on one of the porch's two swings and gently rock back and forth. A nighthawk flashes in the sky. I hear a strange squawk as it swoops to catch an insect, the sweep of air on its feathers creating a metallic buzz.

Next to me on the porch is an old-time workbox, built to withstand rugged use. The heavy-duty handles on either side of the large box were used to lift it onto the back of a wagon. The front side opens to form a sturdy workbench. The surface of the box is covered with a hundred different cattle brands. They are burnt onto the surface of the wood. They look like the hieroglyphics of another civilization.

In the last years of the nineteenth century many cowboys rode the ranchlands of the Jornada. One of them, Gene Rhodes, worked for the Bar Cross at Aleman. Later in life Rhodes gained considerable fame as a writer. By the 1930s his realistic short stories and novels of life in the West often outsold those of the era's most popular writer, Zane Grey.

I stand on the porch. The blood-red sunset pours down the distant tip of Victorio Peak. What is it about the Jornada that caused Rhodes to devote a lifetime to trying to capture it in words? Was it this old porch and its view? Or was it the quiet? Was it the smell of mesquite on the breeze? Or was it the men and women who meet here by chance?

I shut off my stove and leave my dinner to simmer on the porch. I walk out onto the cooling desert. The sun paints the air in limitless color. Off toward Victorio Peak up by Hembrillo Basin, low storm clouds are slashed with brilliant flame. In the west the setting sun burns the rocky slopes of Apache Pass to flakes of gold. In the shadows: purple darkness, deep blue, and black.

"Every sunset which I witness inspires me with the desire to go to a West as distant and as fair as that into which the sun goes down." Henry David Thoreau wrote that in Massachusetts in 1862, the year he died. He never saw the American West, but he, more than anyone else, understood the importance of such wildness. During the final decades of his life Thoreau turned away from philosophy and began to study nature more as a scientist would. Everywhere he went in those days he tried to identify plants. He loved to – as he called it – "go a-botanizing."

El segundo Alemán, the second German to visit Aleman, also loved to go a-botanizing.

In 1835, at the age of twenty-five, Dr. Frederick Adolph Wislizenus emigrated from Germany to southern Illinois, where he practiced medicine for a few years. Just before the outbreak of the Mexican-American War he set out on a long-planned scientific expedition to the Rio Grande. Wislizenus naively believed that if a war came it would be short-lived.

Everywhere he went, Wislizenus studied the plants. Each night at camp he would carefully flatten specimens in cumbersome, bulky presses. He meticulously gathered seeds, leaves, needles, and the spikes of his favorite species, the yucca. He kept a daily journal and filled it with descriptions of the new world opening before him. Wislizenus was the first to describe the majestic Ponderosa pine of the western mountains and the gnarled, half-dead piñon pines that dot the dry, grass hills of the desert Southwest. He wrote about Gambel's quail, roadrunners, and a tiny, marbled wonder: the beautiful Inca dove. Like Thoreau, Wislizenus sometimes recorded his data with the precise exactitude of science, while at other times his prose burns with awe and wonder.

As he approached the Jornada, he saw his first cholla cactus (*Opuntia arborescens*). He described the spiked, porous stems of the four-foot-tall cactus tree common to many parts of the Southwest. He recorded that when the green branches of the cholla die, they shed their spikes and flesh and dry into lacy wooden sticks. These unusual dried branches, Wislizenus noted, make excellent torches.

He reached Aleman on August 3, 1846. He didn't know the name of the place, only that here was a spot "where sometimes a water-pool is found, but which is now perfectly dry." El segundo Alemán, the second German, camped here near an old grave, "distinguished by a cross." He never knew that the grave held the bones of the primero Alemán.

Discovery is not so much a process, or a progression that sheds light onto the unknown, but simply a name we give for those rarest of moments – those nearly ignored needle-pricks of time – when now becomes eternity. A few days later, at the southern end of the Jornada, Wislizenus caught a fleeting glimpse of the unspoken before it was made into words. "I met on the road with the largest cactus of its kind that I have ever seen," he wrote. "Enormous fish hook–like prickles" lined the ridges of the massive, upright barrel cactus. It stood four feet high and was six feet, eight inches in circumference. He correctly identified the plant as a member of the genus *Enchino*, but beyond that the plant was unknown. Later another botanist honored Wislizenus by attaching his unusual name to the "fish-hook cactus," *Enchiocactus Wislizenii.* "I really felt sorry that its size and weight prevented me from carrying the whole of this exquisite specimen with me," he wrote.

After he crossed the Jornada, Wislizenus reached Chihuahua City. By then the deathly war had begun. The Mexicans arrested him and held him captive. Six months later Colonel Doniphan's troops arrived and freed him. Wislizenus then joined Doniphan's men as a part of the army's medical department. After the war he eventually returned east.

I wander about the ranch yard. Mountain ranges grow dark in the twilight. Heat lightning flashes from silver clouds on the far horizon.

I stand amid a clutter of ruins a short distance from the ranch house. An arched stone fireplace marks the remains of a Civilian Conservation Corps camp that existed at Aleman in the 1930s. At places all over the ranch country of the American West, the "CCC boys," as they are still called by old-timers, shoveled rocks and gravel into circular berms called "tanks" that could hold water. They built the tank Ben Cain still uses to hold water from his well. The young men slept where my own tiny tent now flaps in the sudden breeze.

The setting sun is a holy golden host, held in a chalice of clouds.

I return to the porch and eat dinner. Afterward I unzip my tent in the dusky darkness and climb inside, dodging the first of the evening's mosquitoes. Stretched on top of my sleeping bag, I listen to their faint hum as they bump against the window of my tent. I think of the bones scattered at Aleman, and the march of camels and cactus and oryx, and the humanity passed by here and gone. Just before falling asleep I hear the hoo of an owl. Then I sleep.

Hours later I awake to the dogs' frantic barking. Then, less than a hundred yards away, a pack of coyotes begin to yodel. The dogs stop barking as if to listen, then answer with a chorus of their own. One of the great chroniclers of southwestern history, Fray Angelico Chavez, traced the name "coyote." Today nearly everyone pronounces the word ki-yo-*teee*, but pronounce it as if it were written in Spanish, with the last syllable rhyming with "day," and you'll be speaking Nahuatl, the proper name for the Aztec language. I listen to coyote and hear the voice of the Aztec speaking to me across the centuries. The animals are so close I can hear the faint yipping of the pups as they pass by my tent.

I wake before dawn to a sound like someone softly shuffling cards. The faint tap-tap-tap of the windmill blades marks the early hour. Behind that sound a few birds call in the cool air.

I get up and walk to the porch. I make coffee and sit with a hot black cup of the stuff, sweetened by a dollop of honey. The iron springs on the sliding couch squeal softly as I rock back and forth. The ranch dogs try to scratch, yawn, and sleep all at the same time.

First knowledge, they say, is best knowledge. When we first encounter something we see it as an innocent might: shape without meaning, structure without form. On first sight the world is neither evil nor divine, neither black nor white. On first sight, for the briefest of moments, the world simply is; only with time is it misshapen into words and given meaning by memory.

There is a fiery fringe along the tips of the San Andres Mountains.

Then, like a torch, the sun comes vanquishing the cool breeze.

12. Valverde

On a snowy mid-February morning in 1862 a man stood on a roof at Fort Craig. Using a pair of binoculars he looked south over the fort's imposing wall in order to get a glimpse of the large Confederate army amassing to the south. He saw "parks of artillery, towns of shelter tents, grazing horses, lounging men, curling smoke, all framed within the disc of field glasses."

Four miles south, thousands of Confederate soldiers readied themselves for battle. These soldiers, under the command of the often-besotted Brigadier General Henry Hopkins Sibley, were part of a far-fetched Confederate plan to seize several western territories.

Nearly four thousand Union soldiers, under the command of Colonel Edward Canby, waited for them at one of the largest forts ever constructed in the American West. The sprawling, adobe-walled fortress included a hospital, three barracks, officers' quarters, a bakery, a store, and a library.

The Union forces at Fort Craig included hundreds of local Hispanic men who had volunteered to defend their homeland. One such native New Mexican was Rafael Chacón. He had been born in Santa Fe when the territory still belonged to Mexico. At age thirteen he had been a military cadet with the Mexican forces who had first encountered General Kearny and his invading U.S. Army. Chacón fought in the Ute Indians Wars during the 1850s and later traded goods east onto the Great Plains. Since Colonel Canby spoke no Spanish and Chacón spoke no English, they communicated through an interpreter. Chacón was twenty-eight.

Other soldiers at the fort came from more distant lands. When the Civil War began, twenty-five-year-old Alonzo Ickes of Ohio had been prospecting in the Rocky Mountains. He joined a company of Union volunteers in Colorado, believing it was "the duty of every single man to enlist and do all in his power to end this war."

In the Confederate camp, well-educated Alfred Peticolas passed the tedium of the march west by reading everything he could get his hands on, from the trashy *Reveries of a Bachelor* to an eighteen-hundred-page history of the French Revolution. A native of slave-holding Virginia, Peticolas now hailed from Victoria, Texas. Despite his mere twenty-two years, he had already been a schoolteacher and a lawyer. He had enlisted having recently suffered a broken heart.

FEBRUARY 19, 1862

Well before dawn, the long roll of drums cracked the dark silence of the fort, calling all soldiers to the ready. At 4 a.m. the well-known scout and Indian fighter Christopher "Kit" Carson and his company of New Mexican volunteers were ordered to cross the river and occupy the high shoulder south of Black Mesa.

At almost exactly the same moment, Peticolas and the bulk of the Confederate army were fording the bone-numbing Rio Grande. The Confederate plan to lure the Union troops out of the fort and into an open battle had failed, and Sibley's men were on the move. Over the course of the next few days, Peticolas and the rest of the Confederate soldiers advanced up the Rio Grande on the edge of a wasteland they called "the Horn," a mispronunciation of the Spanish *jornada*.

Once across the river, the massive Confederate army set up a new camp near the small village of Fra Cristobel. An adobe village of about two hundred existed for a few decades during the mid-1800s near the old Fra Cristobel campsite on the Camino Real. Despite the difficulty of the location, the village prospered for a short while by virtue of being located at the last access to the river. Most of the inhabitants – farmers, housekeepers, and laborers – had fled in advance of the gathering armies and were not witnesses to the thousands of men, wagons, long supply train, and massive beef herd that constituted the large, mobile force.

The Union commander ordered Chacón and his New Mexican volunteers out to investigate the recently abandoned Confederate camp. Chacón and his men reached the area and found two fresh graves – soldiers who had died of dysentery.

Back at the fort by nightfall, Chacón joined the other soldiers in anticipation of war. Within a space of about four miles, thousands of men from both sides bedded down and tried to sleep. A cold, wintry sky brought an early and dark night to the Jornada.

FEBRUARY 20, 1862 – DAY

In the cold predawn darkness, Texan Alfred Peticolas moved north from the Confederate camp at Fra Cristobel near the front of a long line of soldiers, artillery, and horses. The Confederates had decided to avoid the fort completely by traveling around the far side of the imposing bulk of Black Mesa. They started up a wide arroyo that led to the desert plain high above, but soon the thin-wheeled wagons sank to their hubs in the loose sand. The men double- and triple-teamed the wagons, and when that wasn't enough they got behind and pushed the wagons up the arroyo.

At that same time, Rafael Chacón led about six hundred New Mexican volunteers out of the Union stronghold. They were ordered to occupy a rimrock shelf opposite the fort. They too struggled up through sandy soil, and by early afternoon they held a position amid lava rocks near a sandy arroyo that provided them with a clear view to the south. Chacón and his men could see thousands of Southern troops snaking their way toward the high, bleak plain above. Directly above them a number of Confederate soldiers formed a battle line. Chacón watched as the Confederates aimed their large cannons down at him. From their brass band, strains of "Dixie" drifted out over the Jornada like ghost music. When the first cannon's blast exploded, the Confederate soldiers clapped and cheered.

The incoming balls shattered the lava ledges into slivers of flying rock and shrapnel. The arroyo where the men hid served as a barricade so Chacón's position was safe, but the debris wounded two men.

Colonel Canby immediately sent additional men to Chacón's right. Among them was Colorodoan Alonzo Ickes. "The enemy has a position where their guns can throw round shot among us," he wrote that night in his diary. "And we cannot return the fire as we are far below them." A boy, "the youngest and smallest boy in our company was seriously wounded with a round of shot." A few days later the boy died.

By 4 p.m. the firing ceased and both Chacón and Ickes returned to the fort.

FEBRUARY 20, 1862 — NIGHT

By nightfall the Confederate camp was less than two miles from Fort Craig. Only a steep slope separated the two sides. Men from one side could see the other's fires; they shouted to one another and listened to the other's laughter and taunts. On both sides men prepared for the battle that everyone knew would come the next day. They repaired equipment, shoed horses and mules, or sat cleaning their weapons and casting lead bullets over campfires.

A thin snow floated down on the dark land. At dusk a Union spy came up with a plan he thought could disrupt the entire Confederate force and isolate them on the barren Jornada. James Graydon, a thirty-year-old ball of fire, was ten years away from his home in Northern Ireland. The Union army used certain men like Graydon as spies. Ickes called Graydon "a daredevil and as reckless as can be," while Chacón, perhaps aware of Graydon's reputation for mistreating Hispanics (he usually threatened the life of any local man who resisted "induction" into his troops), called him "a braggart and arrogant."

Graydon's idea was a nineteenth-century version of stealth tactics. He loaded two mules with boxes of twenty-four-pound howitzer shells. The plan was to lead the mules close to the Confederate camp, light the explosives, and then head the mules into the heart of the enemy's herd. The explosion would cause a stampede, Graydon thought, and without horses and mules the enemy would be immobilized.

Under cover of darkness, Graydon and three other men left the fort on foot, leading two old mules loaded with explosives. They waded the cold river and climbed to within 150 yards of the Confederates' mule herd.

Graydon lit the fuses, but instead of joining the enemy's animals, the two mules turned and followed Graydon and his men as they scrambled back down the steep slope. The bright fuses sparkled like stars in the snowy air.

The explosion lit up the night; the deep, hollow thumps of the two bombs echoed off the black-rimmed mesa. Graydon and his men were not injured, but the mules were killed in the blast. Both camps were fully awake.

FEBRUARY 21, 1862 – MORNING

There were enough patches of clear sky in the cold and cloudy dawn that some soldiers on both sides caught a glimpse of red Mars rising in the east.

Drunk (as he was to remain for the better part of this battle day), Confederate commander Sibley ordered his entire army to move around Black Mesa and regain the river at Valverde.

Alfred Peticolas ate a quick, waterless breakfast of dried beef and then helped to burn some of the wagons that could no longer move in order to prevent their cargo from falling into enemy hands. Along with the first line of Confederate soldiers, Peticolas then rode north across the relatively flat shoulder of the desert behind Black Mesa.

Before first light, Union commander Canby sent Rafael Chacón, the spy James Graydon, and about one hundred other men up the Rio Grande to intercept any Confederates who reached Valverde at the far end of the mesa. Chacón reached the lower ford at Valverde and crossed the river "just as we were able to see the sun behind the hills."

An advanced guard of 180 Confederates opened fire on them from amid the cottonwood bosque. It was a "substantial discharge of their carbines," Chacón later recalled.

Meanwhile, Peticolas had "struck a brisk trot and rode rapidly over the high table land and down a long slant to the river bottom." They had reached old Pedro Armendaris's beautiful Valverde. "When we had gotten nearly to the bottom," Peticolas wrote that night in his journal, "we heard the discharge of a cannon." Peticolas, "in high spirits and singing songs," dismounted among the cottonwoods and advanced rapidly on foot.

Just then he looked up "and saw a man climbing the high table land to our left."

It was Graydon. While Chacón fought off the initial skirmish in the bosque, Graydon and a few of his men had scrambled to the top of Black Mesa in order to assess the situation. When he reached the top he saw that the entire Confederate army had abandoned the southern end of the mesa and were now moving northward toward Valverde en masse. Using the sequence of flags known as semaphore, Graydon signaled distant Fort Craig of the enemy's movements. At Fort Craig, Colonel Canby then ordered all but a few of his Union command to rush to Valverde. By midmorning the ever-increasing number of soldiers arriving from both sides began to fan out all across the cup of the three-mile-wide green valley.

Peticolas hid behind a small, sandy hill. A snow squall began. "After we had been lying [under cover] some ten minutes listening to the balls whistling over our heads," he wrote that night, five artillery guns "came thundering down and in a moment had taken position directly in front of us, and commenced firing directly at the infantry and artillery."

It was Colorodoan Alonzo Ickes and a number of other soldiers who had just crossed the river. "Our battery of eight guns opened upon them sending forth a volley of grape and canister," he later wrote to his brother. Then "the ball began in earnest."

"Shell and round shot and bullets came whistling in showers over our heads," Peticolas wrote. "Bombs burst just behind and before us. Trees were shattered and limbs began to fall. A horse or two was shot, and presently they brought back a man severely wounded."

Valverde

The snow flurries hadn't let up. By midmorning more than six hundred Union soldiers had joined Chacón's position. A little after noon, these men were ordered to fix their bayonets and draw their sabers.

At the same time, Confederates noticed a number of Union soldiers crossing the river just to the north. In order to meet this new challenge, Peticolas and other men galloped about 250 yards and then "dismounted in a perfect hail of bullets." Within moments many horses were killed and several men wounded. One soldier was hit in the mouth and his tongue was nearly shot away. Peticolas watched as "he pulled out a part of it which was hanging ragged to the edge of his tongue and cut it off with his knife." For the remainder of the long day Peticolas would see all of his action from the tentative protection of a few sandy embankments at this position not far from the river.

Chacón, who was within a few hundred yards of Peticolas, wrote that the fighting was so violent that "in a quarter of an hour that renowned enemy cavalry was left stretched out on the ground, completely destroyed, their horses and men dead and dying on the field."

The men with Peticolas fought back. "They began paying dearly for getting so close to us," he wrote. "Not a man shot without taking sight, for Texas boys are accustomed to the use of arms and never shoot away their ammunition for nothing. Although our balls were not as numerous as theirs, they went with more deadly intent, and our fire soon became extremely galling."

One of Peticolas's companions wounded a Union soldier, but the man still shot at them. "Captain," the Confederate soldier asked, "out yonder is a dammed son of a bitch that I have shot who is lying behind a tree shooting at us. May I go out and kill him?"

The fierce fight had been going on for more than six hours when finally the desert grew silent. An uneasy quiet fell over the battlefield.

Valverde

Virginian-turned-Texan Alfred Peticolas sat in the sand of the old riverbed. "I ate a little piece of dried beef and suffered for water," he wrote in his journal. At first the sudden quiet on the field of battle shocked him. "During this lull in the fight the suspense began to be very painful, and I heartily wished the battle was over."

On the eastern ridge, General Sibley was so drunk that he was incapable of making any decisions. At about 1:30 he acknowledged his incapacity to lead and sent his staff to report to Colonel Thomas Green; then he retired to his ambulance at the Confederate rear for the remainder of the battle.

Colonel Canby arrived about this time with the remaining soldiers from Fort Craig. He immediately faced the problem of getting his troops across the river. He ordered Kit Carson and his company of New Mexican volunteers to hold a defensive position in the cotton-woods near the middle ford.

Graydon and his company doubled back to the south, where they found thirty Confederate wagons abandoned in the deep sand. They set them on fire and then whirled their ponies around to return to Valverde.

Chacón and his men had been in the heart of the battle all morning and were now tucked up under rocks at the base of Black Mesa. Chacón saw an unmanned Confederate cannon standing alone in the cottonwoods. He ordered his men to advance. He rode down from the stronghold playing out his lariat. As he reached the cannon he flung open a wide loop in the rope, and after a couple of deft swings he lassoed the cannon. His horse jolted to a stop as if bringing down a heifer. Cowboy style, Chacón and his horse pulled the cannon through the trees and back to the Union lines.

Then Union artillery opened fire, and just as suddenly as it had stopped, the fighting began again.

FEBRUARY 21, 1862 – 2:00 P.M.

Ickes and about seventy other Union soldiers didn't know it, but the slaughter they were about to impose would signal the end of a weapon

134

of war that dated to medieval times. From an arroyo at the north end of Valverde came a strange sight: "Three companies of Rangers, each armed with a long lance, made a charge on our company," he wrote to his brother.

As historian John Taylor explains, "the troopers were armed with nine-foot lances, each tipped with twelve-inch blades and sporting red guidon banners, emblazoned with a single white star." Lances were an anachronism by the outbreak of the Civil War, "though one still favored by many senior officers on both sides."

Ickes sat in the arroyo and watched as the strange formation "turned smartly" toward him. They were three hundred yards away.

"We all were anxious for the deadly conflict," Ickes wrote. The captain of the Union men steadied the soldiers and commanded them to wait until he told them to fire. The soldiers' guns were loaded with a potent cartridge known as "buck and ball." It contained both buckshot and a bullet.

"The boys waited until they got within 40 yards of us when they took deliberate aim," Ickes wrote. The Union soldiers fired, and the brief, bloody slaughter began. The first volley "sent many brave Texans to bite the dust," Ickes wrote. "They wavered for a few moments then on they came . . . fierce looking fellows they were with their long lances raised." Ickes reloaded and waited. "When they got to us we gave them the second volley." As more lancers fell, the survivors stood by bewildered and uncertain what to do.

"It was fun to see the Texans fall," Ickes wrote.

Fun.

"After the second volley there were but a few of them left."

In all more than twenty Confederate lancers lay dead or dying. A few made it back to Confederate lines. "The others were shot and bayoneted," Ickes wrote. "Simpson ran his bayonet through one of them and shot the top of his head off."

That night after the battle, the surviving Confederate lancers piled their "hog pokers" and set them ablaze. When Ickes learned of this he wrote, "I guess they found they were not the things to fight Colorado Volunteers with."

One surviving lancer's arm was so badly mutilated that it had to be amputated. He died within days. Nine days later, another who had been grievously wounded in the battle asked his slave to bring him a gun and then killed himself.

FEBRUARY 21, 1862 — 3 P.M.

By midafternoon the 2,750 Union soldiers were in a nearly continuous line, concentrated at each of three fords across the Rio Grande. The Confederate line, numbering about 2,300, faced them in an arc that stretched one and a half miles in and along an old riverbed.

Chacón was with hundreds of other Union soldiers as a part of a thick wall of troops pivoting toward the southern flank of the enemy, much like a door about to slam shut. Additional troops, sent from the center of the Union forces, were streaming in. Graydon's spy company was a part of this force, as were Kit Carson and his men.

The Confederates at the south end of Valverde charged. When the Texans were within 150 yards, Chacón and the other soldiers opened fire. The soft pop of canister shot hitting flesh filled the air. A few men fell; many of the other shots hit the horses. Peticolas was not witness to this particular battle, but he described a similar one: "Men rallied around their captains about the ground where the horses were shot. Wounded and dead horses were hastily stripped, and those that were able to move were turned loose to feed around or to shiver and die." The Southern troops fell back under heavy fire, while the Northern cannons were ordered to advance.

Colonel Canby heard the intensified fighting to his south. He was "unaware of the true strength of his opponent," wrote John Taylor, "and concerned that the loss of the last Union cannon would make the lower ford vulnerable, Canby made a fateful decision." He withdrew most of his troops from the center of his line and ordered them to move south. This decision created a defensive gap and isolated Ickes and other Union soldiers to the north. They now faced Peticolas and the other Confederates without support.

THE BLOODY BATTLE

At first Ickes was confident of the Union's superiority. A cottonwood bosque sheltered him and several hundred other soldiers. "A battery had been throwing shot among us with but little effect," he wrote. "Our sections were brought to bear upon the enemy as well as the ground would permit." They positioned their cannons as best they could and turned them on the Confederates.

Confederate colonel Green now rode in place of the drunken Sibley. Unaware of the Union's weakened position, he remained with the troops at the north end.

Then the Union's gunners set fire to their fuses.

Peticolas was on the receiving end of this initial volley. "Six pieces of artillery ran out and pointed point-blank range of us," he wrote. The Confederates set up their own big guns "within ten yards of where I was lying and opened fire upon the enemy. . . . When the fire was hottest our horses were being killed . . . I saw several horses horribly wounded. A cannon ball shot off the right forefoot of one within ten yards of me. Another had both forelegs shot off, and the last I saw of him he was trying to use and stand on the shattered stumps."

Lying amid the carnage, Peticolas reeled from thirst. He and the other Confederate soldiers had not had any water for over twelve hours. Men's tongues were swelled, and the horses' and mules' eyes bulged. The heavy bombardment from the close cannon fire "meant that our men could not long hold out against the galling fire." He thought that within two minutes they would all be dead. "The bombs were bursting and flying all around us and sweeping the trees far behind us."

According to John Taylor, this Confederate battle line was about seven hundred yards from the Union cannons. There were about 750 Confederate soldiers here, not including the decimated lancers who were being held in reserve.

Ickes and the 630 other Union troops were driving these Confederates into a box. Green knew he had to act. He shouted to Peticolas and the others that they must make a charge straight at the Union cannons. Immediately, several men turned and fled. Green rushed at them and drove them back to the line. "Would you disgrace yourself and your country here?" he yelled. "Don't forget that you are Texans!"

Green quickly implemented a plan of attack. To prevent a retreat, he ordered that the assault be made on foot. There would be three waves: the last would be the strongest, with 300 men; 250 men were to make a second charge; the first group – which included Peticolas – was the smallest.

"Boys, I want Colonel Canby's guns," the commander shouted. "When I yell, you raise a Rebel yell and follow me!" He thrust his arm in the air. "Charge boys, charge!"

"And at that command," Peticolas wrote, "two hundred men – a mere handful – started up and with a wild yell and dashed forward through the shower of Minnie balls and grape shot towards the belching cannon and the solid lines of infantry supporting them." They scrambled down the hill in a semicircle formation, shooting as they ran.

Although such frontal attacks accompanied by the wild Rebel yell would become common before the end of the Civil War, most soldiers fighting on the Jornada that day had never seen such a thing before. Ickes was among the Union soldiers who received the thrust of that first charge. "Our battery boys played the canister into the enemy," he wrote. "At every shot you could see their ranks open and pieces of men fly in the air."

Peticolas reeled from the carnage. A captain rode past him, his saber in the air. "Come on, my boys," the captain shouted. "Don't stop here." Despite the heavy pounding from the Union guns, the Confederates continued their charge.

Because they had been isolated from the rest of the Union troops, Ickes and the Union soldiers could not defend the cannons. Retreat meant surrendering the cannons. Ickes and the others fired at the advancing Confederates. "But on and on they came," Ickes wrote.

The Union forces wavered. Cautiously, a small band of Confederate sharpshooters advanced on the Union cannons, moving from one great gray cottonwood to another in the snowy and faltering light. "As we neared the lines," Peticolas wrote, "our short range guns began to play with telling effect on their lines." One by one the sharpshooters killed the soldiers protecting the cannons.

When Peticolas and the other Texans reached Ickes and the Coloradans, they fought hand to hand.

One of the Union commanders ran wildly about. "For God's sake," he shouted, "help me save the guns." His right arm hung limp and bloody, the bones shattered by a jagged wound.

Peticolas ran up an exposed arroyo and toward the cannons. Just as he reached the big guns he saw two of his fellow soldiers killed. The second, a close friend, had just reached a cannon. "This one is mine," he shouted, and at that instant he was shot dead. Peticolas then saw a Union gunner get hit just as he was about to touch off a cannon.

The second wave of Confederates now poured toward the cannons. Vainly the Union tried to hold their position. "But, there were too many of them," Ickes wrote. "It was no go."

Both men recorded the climax of the battle.

Ickes wrote: "One of the battery boys sprang on a powder magazine which was near and cried, 'Victory or death.' "

Peticolas wrote: "One of our men who had just killed a gunner" climbed up on the same ammunition cart. "He leveled his pistol at the gunner."

But the gunner, said Ickes, "then coolly fired his [own] pistol into the ammunition." Since the men were fighting "as thick as they could stand," the "dreadful explosion" killed several men on both sides.

The Union retreated to the river, leaving many cannons behind. The Confederates rushed after them and "poured a deadly fire upon them."

Ickes ran past a man who was writhing on the ground; one of his legs had been blown off.

The Confederates continued to shoot at the retreating soldiers, but they did not cross the river in pursuit.

Later that night, Peticolas reflected on the victory. "I thought that I had experienced a good many moments of exquisite pleasure, but never before have I felt such perfect happiness as I did when we took the battery from our enemy. Then I knew the tide of battle had changed, and my feelings with it. We raised a loud shout of gladness and I did not forget to feel thankful to the great King of Kings, who is the God of Battles."

Who is this Kings of Kings, god of such bloody battles?

FEBRUARY 21, 1862 – DUSK

Just as the sun was setting on that cold and unforgiving February day, Rafael Chacón, Kit Carson, and the spy company of James Graydon were ordered to retreat from their successful fight under towering Black Mesa. Chacón was confused at first. "I, who had already found myself very deep into the enemy zone because of the violence of our attack, did not understand the order, for we considered that our charge had won the battle." He was so hesitant to leave that he and the other native New Mexicans of his company were the last Union soldiers to retreat from Valverde. After they forded the river they learned of the Union defeat to the north. The entire Union army then withdrew while a rear guard held off sporadic Confederate gunfire. When they reached Fort Craig the numbers of wounded men simply overwhelmed the fort's surgeons.

FEBRUARY 21, 1862 – NIGHT

Scattered Confederate campfires cast a feeble and gloomy light across the dark battlefield. Men combed the area. The wounded were taken to the nearest campfire and made as comfortable as possible.

After dark, Alfred Peticolas wandered the battleground looking for the bodies of his friends.

FEBRUARY 22, 1862 – DAWN

In the early hours of the next day, George Washington's birthday, Chacón and a burial detail from Fort Craig returned to Valverde. "The field was covered with blood," he later wrote, "horses torn and dismembered limbs, and heads separated from their bodies – a spectacle that was horrible." Chacón's New Mexicans worked alongside Confederate soldiers. He added: "It was a great pleasure for us to see the chivalry and courtesy with which we treated one another, forgetting the anger and antagonism of yesterday in the solemn presence of the dead."

But the evil of human prejudice runs deep.

Both sides of the conflict incorrectly blamed Hispanic men like Chacón for the Union's loss at Valverde. Ickes – who had just fought to put an end to slavery, called the native New Mexicans "cowards" and hung the nasty epitaph "greasers" onto their name.

Confederate soldiers like Peticolas boasted that the "Mexicans" were so cowardly they simply fled in fright.

Despite the fact that Kit Carson's success at Valverde was *because* he led a company of New Mexican volunteers, a soldier later falsely wrote that the all of the New Mexican soldiers deserted Carson. The soldier falsely claimed that "Kit went in single-handed and fought the fight out."

Men of all colors suffered at Valverde, but of the 111 Union soldiers killed at Valverde, 29 were New Mexicans.

The Confederates buried most of their 230 casualties in mass graves gouged into the Jornada's bleak sand. "We dug a ditch four feet deep," one soldier reported, "wrapped 40 of our boys in their blankets, and placed them in the earth without so much as marking the spot."

In the 1970s an elderly resident of the Jornada named Vigil reported that farmers at Valverde occasionally "would plow up skulls and other human bones when they prepared their fields for spring planting."

Eight miles south at Fort Craig, Ickes used the quiet time to catch up with his journal: "In America this is a great day of rejoicing – all join in celebrating the anniversary of the birth of the immortal George Washington. Alas! How different with us – the shrieks of the wounded and dying together with the ghastly appearance of the dead form an impression upon our minds that time will never erase.

"Many of the boys with whom I was acquainted are dead. I visited the dead room to search for one of my friends who was missing. I went to the room where they were piled one upon another. I climbed over the bodies turning some over. Men were mutilated in every conceivable manner. I was seeking for a friend and all of this without a shudder. *Who will say war is not degrading?*"

CODA

"I feel extremely sad today," Alfred Peticolas wrote the day after the battle. "My feelings have undergone another change, and another wave has come over me." He scratched a simple prayer into his journal: "May a Good God soon deliver us from this unnatural war that has been forced upon us."

Although victorious at Valverde, the Confederates would be soundly defeated several weeks later at Glorieta Pass in northern New Mexico.

13. The Life and Death of Victorio (On Seeing Apache Plume)

Victorio sat on his pony and studied his Apache warriors securing the stronghold below him. He wore a bandanna around his head. A weatherbeaten leather vest covered his tattered, checkered shirt.

Directly below on a low ridge, three men lifted stones to form breastworks from which to kill soldiers. The army was near. More trouble lay ahead.

Across the way a half dozen warriors, including his sister Lozen, rode northward along the rocky slopes of the high San Andres range. They followed an ancient trail that overlooked the Jornada; in a little while they dismounted and waited.

The holy mountain rose beside him, the cool, wet springs at its base. He turned to look back at the *wickiups* the others had built of yucca stalks and grass. In the camp people busied about, readying for whatever might come next. Some cooked, while others gathered water and prepared for a quick flight. His old warrior friend Nana was there, guarding the people. Although both of his wives were now dead, somewhere down there a woman carried his youngest son strapped to a wooden *tsach* on a her back.

Victorio raised his binoculars. His right hand shook slightly from palsy. He scanned to the east, down the narrow canyon that led to the white sand desert and Tularosa.

A flash: the sentry's mirror: once, twice.

He raised his gun in the air. The shot reverberated across the basin. In his high-pitched warrior's cry he shouted, "Soldiers are coming up the canyon!"

In the spring of 1880, Victorio – whose name might have been a corruption of his Apache name, Bi-duye' – was about fifty-five years old. Six months after this battle on the Jornada, he would be dead, killed – the Apache say by his own hand – in order to fulfill a vow to not be taken by the enemy.

No account of Victorio's death can ignore the mystery of his birth. Victorio's origins are largely unknown. He was probably born around 1825. One legend has it that he was a young Apache boy who had been captured and raised by Mexicans. Another has it the other way around: Victorio was Mexican and was then stolen by the Apaches. According to historian Dan Thrapp, no contemporary ever said anything about his origins and "no white man knew him well. He was an *Apache*, a man apart."

When Victorio was about twelve a band of scalp hunters (most likely James Kirker and his Indians) attacked his village. The young boy and his sister Lozen escaped, but the men slaughtered the rest of their family and many of their friends. The bloody horror of that day set the path for both lives. Lozen would never marry; instead she picked up a rifle. Perhaps the greatest female Indian fighter in American history, she would become legendary for her bravery in battle and for her holy powers.

As a result of that day, Victorio dedicated his life to protecting his people. Honest to a fault, he was known far and wide as a man of his word. If treated fairly, Victorio would have been a man of peace.

I grab the edge of my seat as Jim Eckles turns west up a jagged stone road into Hembrillo Canyon. He steers the truck around a couple of rocks in the middle of the road.

Jim is the director of public affairs at White Sands Missile Range. Because of the missile range, most of the Jornada's eastern flank is off limits to the public, so I jumped at his gracious offer to take me to the site of Victorio's battle. He warned me it would be a very long day.

We left his office at range headquarters at dawn. That was two hours ago.

Jim drops the truck into a lower gear.

I stammer, "You just let me know if you want me to get out and move any of these rocks. I'd be happy to if they're in our way."

Jim smiles. A fit, bearded man in his early fifties, he wears wide, dark sunglasses and an outrageously colorful Hawaiian-style shirt. "Nah," he drawls, "this is a *good* road for around here."

The ruts climb higher into the rugged San Andres Mountains. We bounce around a mesquite tree and pass a low, symmetrical berm of rocks and earth. "That's a multi-launch system for rockets," Jim explains with nod. "They put equipment on the back side of the berm for protection and they put the launcher on this side."

We rattle higher until we reach a barred gate. Two large, official-looking signs, one in English and the other in Spanish, warn the trespasser of the dire consequences of going beyond. Jim flips me the key. I hop out to open the gate. The canyon has narrowed considerably, and now craggy rock walls close in on either side.

Jim pulls through, and I get back into the rig. "This is a pretty good place for an ambush," I say.

Jim doesn't answer, but a moment later he pulls to a stop. Ahead of us the canyon passes through a tiny slit in the towering walls of light-colored stone. Then he says, "This is probably where Victorio's warriors first shot at the soldiers."

On the afternoon of April 5, 1880, Lieutenant John Conline and about thirty-five black soldiers approached this spot at the mouth of Hembrillo Canyon. These were Buffalo Soldiers, former slaves and sons of slaves who had enlisted in the U.S. Army after President Lincoln allowed for regiments of black soldiers. Between 1866 and 1900 close to four thousand blacks served in New Mexico. White officers like Conline led all such regiments.

Conline wrote: "At 4:20 I struck a fresh trail of about 50 horses and 10 or more head of cattle headed up the canyon a short distance from its mouth. I followed the trail about 1 1/2 miles to a point where the canyon became much narrower, or boxed up."

He and his men dismounted and, "owing to the strong impression that Indians were not far away," left a few men to guard the horses and proceeded on foot. Near here, Conline placed several of his men in the rocks and sent a few further ahead.

"I made a careful examination of the canyon in every direction through a powerful pair of field glasses," he wrote. High on the rocks he spied two Apaches, then others. "I discovered about 35 to 50 more Indians coming down the hillside into the canyon on a run."

Shots ricocheted off the rocks. Soon they were under heavy fire. When the Indians drew close, Conline heard an Apache shouting orders. The enemy built one large fire to block the way and another on top of a hill about two miles further up. Rifle fire continued until after dark. Realizing he could not go up the canyon, and having no water, Conline retreated back down the canyon. The casualties were two men slightly wounded and "one public and one private horse killed, and one public horse wounded."

Jim pulls the truck through the tight cleft in the canyon. "Conline's Buffalo Soldiers were one of four such companies looking for Victorio," he says. "A guy named Captain Henry Carroll was in charge of all four companies. Carroll now knew Victorio was in this canyon, but he also realized that Victorio was now aware of *their* presence." He pauses. Jim has given this a lot of thought and wants to be sure I understand. "I think Carroll knew he had lost the element of surprise, and that's why he decided to circle to the north and attack Victorio up in the basin itself."

Most of the Buffalo Soldiers under Carroll were seasoned soldiers who were stationed at places like Fort Craig in segregated bunkhouses. The real work of most soldiers in the American West more often involved building roads and guarding traffic on stage routes than fighting Indians. These men had protected railroad construction crews, escorted stagecoaches, and defended water holes. And, like all soldiers, they also tended to the more tedious tasks of survival: they cut and gathered firewood, repaired the fort, served as bakers, assistant quartermasters, clerks, and cooks, and – when the supply of locally contracted beef ran low – hunted for fresh game. As was also the case for fellow white soldiers, the boredom of life in such a desolate land sometimes led to gambling and fighting and drinking.

Now these men of the Ninth Cavalry were about to come face-to-face with the legendary Victorio.

A quarter mile up the bumpy canyon, Jim stops alongside a nondescript patch of catclaw bushes. "See that little mound and that cracked limestone?" he asks, pointing. "See how it's kind of out of place? That's the site of an agave roasting pit. The agave was an important food source to Native people like the Apache."

The word *Apache* probably came from the Zuni word for enemy, *apachu*. The Apaches speak the Athapascan language and simply call themselves people. Several distinct tribes, including Navajos, Mescaleros, and Chiricahuas, share the Athapascan language. Despite the common background of language and similarities in culture, some of these groups did not get along. Sometimes a local incident caused the bad blood – men arguing over a woman or a horse – and at other times the reasons for such animosities were more complex.

Each of these groups was further divided into nomadic bands. Known historically as the Warm Springs Apaches by the English-speaking community, and as Ojo Caliente by the Spanish, Victorio's band called themselves Tchene, or Red Paint People, after the red paint they used for decoration. At the time of Victorio's death the Red Paint People had lived in the Jornada region for more than six hundred years.

Except for a few years in the 1700s when the Spanish established a successful reservation system, the Apaches were at a nearly constant state of war from the moment Europeans first arrived. The Spanish conquistadores used captured Apaches as slaves. Then came the scalp hunters' wars when men like James Kirker roamed the land looking for human bounty. After that, when the United States took possession of New Mexico, the Apaches faced new intruders.

The history of U.S. relations with the Apaches is shameful. Treaties were ignored. Political infighting, greed, broken treaties, lies, and incompetence brought continuous sorrow for the Apaches.

One of the earliest records of Victorio's band of Red Paint People is from 1846, when William Emory, a botanist who accompanied General Kearny's invasion, came upon Victorio's village near Warm Springs just a few miles west of the Jornada. Ever the scientist, Emory carefully noted that he saw "several Indians [who] wore beautiful helmets, decked with black feathers, which – with the short skirt, waist belt, bare legs and buckskins gave them the look of antique Greek warriors." Victorio, then twenty-one years old, was among the men

Emory saw. "Most of the men were well armed, and wore cartridge boxes on thick leather belts around their waists." Emory noted that they were excellent horsemen and that they always mounted and dismounted their horses on the right side.

Victorio next entered the historical record in 1852 when he agreed to keep peace in exchange for a reservation. The official U.S. plan was that Apaches would be trained to become farmers. Victorio's people were placed on a reservation, but no tools, not even a hoe, were ever provided. Starvation soon beset them. They were promised food rations to offset this tragedy, but shipments came months late or not at all. Despite these deplorable conditions, Victorio kept his side of the bargain, but the treaty he had agreed to uphold languished in Congress for fifteen years before it was finally rejected.

According to Dan Thrapp, "Had the Americans been as diligent and trustworthy as the Indians in keeping the bargain . . . the Apache-white hostility might never have resumed . . . but greed and ignorance and callous disregard for the rights of others entered in, and interminable misunderstanding and bloodshed resulted."

On December 4, 1860, Victorio's camp was surprised by gunfire. A group of twenty-eight miners made an unprovoked attack on the Red Paint People in the Black Mountains west of the Jornada. Thinking there must be some kind of mistake, one of the few warriors who was in camp that day tried to parley with the miners. He was "lifted out of the saddle" by a miner's rifle shot. Enraged, Victorio fled into the hills and began a series of raids over northern Chihuahua and southwestern New Mexico.

The Civil War gave the Apaches a short respite from all this weary warfare, and for a short while they were able to roam their traditional lands. They found, however, that life had grown much harder. Game that had once been plentiful had been nearly hunted to extinction. In addition, the few meager rations they received were now being diverted to feed the soldiers in the Civil War.

The official Confederate policy was to capture and then exterminate all Apaches. Lieutenant Colonel John R. Baylor spelled it out in an order to his troops: "You will use all means to persuade the Apache to come in for the purpose of making peace. Buy whiskey and such other goods as may be necessary . . . and have a sufficient number of men around to allow no Indian to escape, and when you get them together kill all the grown Indians and take the children prisoners and sell them to defray the expense of killing the others."

The Union command was hardly more humane. Colonel James Henry Carleton, who replaced Valverde's Colonel Canby in 1863, ordered that all Indian men were to be killed.

At the end of the Civil War there was a moment of brief hope. Victorio said he wanted to make a chain between the Red Paint People and the whites that would never be broken. He said, "I and my people want peace – we are tired of war – we are poor and we have little for ourselves and our families to eat or wear – it is very cold – we want to make peace, a lasting peace." For unknown reasons, however, Victorio hesitated when asked to inspect a place for a potential reservation and disappeared into the mountains.

Then, in 1869, as one of his last acts as governor of the Territory of New Mexico, despotic Robert B. Mitchell declared war on a *different* band of Apaches, but he made it legal for citizens to shoot *any* Apache at will. The bloody ten years that resulted reinvigorated the grim ritual of war.

A government agent named Charles Drew recorded one contact with Victorio's people during this period. Drew had been sent to Warm Springs with several others to try to negotiate with the nervous and distrustful Apaches. He had been traveling up the stunningly beautiful canyon that leads to the Warm Springs Reservation when Victorio and forty other warriors appeared among the rocks. The Apache leader Loco did most of the talking. He said they were willing to stop fighting in exchange for food and clothing. "They were very suspicious and all came well armed, a great many with guns, the rest with lances and bows," Drew later recorded. He told them they would get their provisions but that it would take time. The Red Paint People agreed to stay at Warm Springs. Before Drew left he noted Victorio's military strategy: "The Indians took every precaution. It is impossible to get near them with soldiers."

But then Washington decided to remove Victorio's people from their home at Warm Springs and concentrate them at the San Carlos

Reservation in Arizona. They couldn't have picked a worse place, as there was bad blood between Victorio's people and the people at San Carlos. Apaches from there had recently murdered Red Paint People. The people there stole from them. The water in Arizona made them sick. The crowded conditions meant there would be even less food for them to eat. Victorio said they were willing to do as the government asked and move, but he pleaded that it be somewhere other than Arizona. It didn't matter. The government once again was deaf. In 1875, and despite the fact that many of his people were too sick with smallpox to travel, Victorio was forced to leave Warm Springs and move to San Carlos.

After enduring the sorrows at San Carlos for two years, Victorio had had enough. On September 2, 1878, he and his band fled the Arizona reservation. After he had secured himself in the mountains, he sent word that he would surrender and accept "anything but concentration" in Arizona.

Colonel Edward Hatch, who was in command of the Ninth Cavalry in the Southwest, reported that Victorio's people were well armed with Springfield, Winchester, and Sharps carbines as well as a variety of revolvers. The women and boys had muzzle-loaders, and the entire band had plenty of ammunition. Victorio told Hatch that his people were starving. He said that while he wanted peace, he could not control the actions of the young men who were then raiding neighboring ranches for food. He said that the government had broken too many promises. He did not want war, but if it came, he said, "I will not surrender the hair of a horse's tail."

The army negotiated a peace but did not know where to take the Indians. Having promised not to take him them back to Arizona, they decided to hold them temporarily at Warm Springs. For Victorio, this settled the matter. They had been placed at their familiar reservation at Warm Springs because it was to be their home. He could not have known about the existing political squabbling between the army, which had jurisdiction over Indians who were not on reservations, and the Department of the Interior, which had jurisdiction over Indians on reservations. Technically, Warm Springs was no longer recognized as a reservation, and that meant the army had control of the Indians' fate. Winter came on. Just as Victorio's people settled down to life in Warm Springs the army told Victorio that he would have to leave Warm Springs again.

In January 1879 Victorio met with soldiers and apparently agreed to be taken to the recently established Mescalero Apache reservation, seventy miles east of the Jornada. Since there were many family and cultural ties with the Mescaleros, he said the Red Paint People could live at such a place.

Then: a simple twist of fate.

On the evening of February 7, 1879, the army camp at Warm Springs was alarmed by shouts. Distrustful and apparently thinking the army had reneged and was planning to take them back to Arizona, Victorio shouted, "I will die first!" and fled.

They hid out in the mountains and survived that spring by raiding ranches and villages in the border country. Although their raids were limited, every crime in the country was soon placed on the head of the "outlaw" Victorio.

That summer Victorio sent word that he would go to the Mescalero reservation. In the meantime, however, a county judge had put three indictments out on him. One was for murder. They were trumped-up charges. From the time he first started to live at Warm Springs, Victorio never killed an American.

Still, local hysteria reached a fever pitch. Sensing that it would be impossible for him to be treated fairly at a trial, and probably fearing prolonged confinement (which to an Apache was worse than a sentence of death), Victorio made his final flight for freedom. Over the next several months – from the autumn of 1879 until he was killed the following May – his stealth kept his people free.

"Astute and tireless, cunning and sleeplessly vigilant – this man has made his very name a proverb of terror," proclaimed the March 21, 1880, issue of the Silver City *Daily Southwest.* "When he has retreated it has been as though he fled through the air; and when he has stricken a blow, it has been as a bolt of death descending from a cloudless sky." The terror was overstated, but Victorio's cunning was not. Other contemporary accounts called him "the greatest commander white or red who ever roamed these plains."

But by April 1880 the noose was tightening around Victorio's neck.

The truck jolts down into a deep rut and then bounces up the other side. Jim fights the steering wheel as if steadying a bronco.

"How many spare tires do you carry?" I ask.

"Just one," Jim says, and then sees my face. "Hey, don't worry, man!" The truck swerves around a mud hole and rattles across a stony arroyo. "Must have gotten a little rain in here," he says.

We stop and get out. The rock walls of the deep canyon tower above us. A half dozen cottonwoods cluster around a cool springs. On the ground are an empty tuna can and a steel fork. I turn and follow Jim through the cottonwoods and up a steep slope.

He stops and then points to a ledge just above us. Red figures dance across the rock. They have odd-shaped, nearly triangular bodies and round, space-alien heads. "Over in Rhodes Canyon we'll see much older Paleo-Indian petroglyphs, but these are Apache pictographs," Jim says. "It's a pretty rare thing to find Apache drawings, since they didn't stay in any one place for very long."

It's easy to make out the drawings. A small trickster figure with a horned headdress follows a parade of dancers. A figure mounted on horseback watches from the left. The pictograph depicts Apache mountain spirits known as Gans. "The dance of Gans is done to drive evil spirits away," Jim tells me.

We return to the truck and drive on. In a few miles the narrow canyon begins to broaden. The road climbs up a steep incline, and then the land opens to expose a series of hills surrounding a wide, rugged valley.

"This is the Hembrillo Basin," Jim says. The odd name probably came from the Spanish word for female, the opposite of *macho*: *hembrilla*.

On a high slope Jim stops and shuts off the truck. Below us, the canyon we drove up looks like a deep knife slash in the dark earth. He grabs his hat and a bottle of water and hops out of the truck. I scramble after him, and we climb to the top of a rugged hillside. We stand in the center of an irregularly shaped basin. "Carroll's men came in through that place over there," he says, pointing to a distant gap between two hills.

On the late afternoon of April 6, 1880, Lozen's holy powers told her that soldiers were approaching from the north. She fired a single shot as a signal to the others. A little while later Captain Carroll and seventy-two Buffalo Soldiers under his command cautiously entered Hembrillo Basin from the northeast.

Then: gunfire.

A horse fell screaming. Then other horses were hit. Soldiers scrambled for cover near the crest of a rocky hill. Carroll ordered every fourth soldier to hold onto the horses and pack animals. The remaining fifty soldiers set up defensive positions amid the rocks.

Apache gunfire rained down on them from the steep slope to the west and from a more distant hill to the east. One military historian has called Victorio's opening strategy "a classic V-shaped defensive trap."

The Buffalo Soldiers were outnumbered two to one. "I am sure that I did not kill any Indians," one soldier later said, "because I did not see a single thing to shoot at – in fact I saw nothing except a long ridge from which came smoke and bullets."

I follow Jim as he walks along the top of the hill. He stops and nods at something near his feet. "This is an Apache breastwork," he says. Amid the sharp blades of a catclaw bush is a wall of oblong stones. It could have been built yesterday. Flat rocks form a tight, two-foot-high bunker. One space in the top tier of stones has been left open in order for the shooter to take aim on the hill below.

We talk awhile about the various details of the battle. Unable to move against the Apache sharpshooters hidden behind the breastworks on this ridge, Carroll focused on the Apache warriors to his east. Victorio predicted Carroll would do exactly that, and as a consequence he had concentrated his forces on the more distant, eastern ridge.

I mention one long-standing piece of misinformation about the battle. "I've heard there never was any poisoned water," I say.

"I think Karl's research totally killed that legend," Jim says. "When I first started my job the story I heard was that Carroll's Buffalo Soldiers were almost annihilated because they stumbled into Victorio's camp sick and half dead from drinking bad water. Karl determined that Carroll and his men weren't sick at all but had purposefully engaged Victorio in order to hold him there until reinforcements arrived."

Karl is Karl Laumbach, an associate director for research and education for a company called Human Systems Research, which has provided much of the historical and archaeological knowledge of the extensive White Sands Missile Range. Karl and a man named Harold Mounce discovered the location of Victorio's battle site in the Hembrillo Basin, and Karl led the extensive archaeological survey that revealed intricate details of the battle.

Jim waves his hand along the ground behind the Apache breastworks. "Karl's team found a lot of cartridges all over this area here," he says.

Carroll was in a tight spot, but at least a limestone ridge provided his men with their own natural breastworks.

As always, the Apache warriors fought in small groups; each member of a group used the same kind of repeating rifle and hence could share ammunition. Victorio kept his short-range rifles in his strongest positions and placed his long-range weapons on the most distant hills.

Carroll and the Buffalo Soldiers were a good distance from the Apache positions to the east, so – initially at least – there wasn't as much danger of getting hit from these. Carroll hoped that when darkness came and the Apache guns grew silent, he could buy some time. But the Apaches did not relent. Half a dozen warriors attacked the arroyo where the horses were being held, and others crawled across the desert to take up positions closer to the soldiers.

Jim points down to the rocky place below us. "As night fell Carroll's ridge was a field of fire," he says. "Karl's team found more spent lead down there than anywhere else in the basin."

As night came on, about five Apaches moved in close and fired at the soldiers. As darkness fell they shot several more horses and mules.

With the darkness Carroll bunched his men into two groups so that lone soldiers would not become easy targets. During the night several of the soldiers' horses were stampeded. Three Apaches got to within yards of Carroll's position and fired into the black soldiers.

During the night Carroll faced another serious problem: thirst. Neither man nor beast had seen a trace of water since early morning. Despite the fact the springs at the base of the mountain would be heavily guarded by Victorio's men, Carroll determined that he had to reach it before the moon rose. Karl said the water was "tantalizingly close." Carroll himself led a small group of men. They crawled toward the spring. The Apaches never let them get near. Two Buffalo Soldiers, Isaac James and William Saunders, were hit and killed, and Carroll himself took a shot in the chest. He struggled back to the hilltop. Carroll would survive, but it would take him a year to recover from the wound. "Given the number of Apache moving around in the dark," Karl said, "someone should have gotten a medal for the attempt."

The thirsty soldiers waited for dawn. In the bleak early hours they could hear Apache women singing. One soldier later wrote to his mother that he could hear Victorio's high-pitched tremolo singing and taunting them. Victorio was "shouting continually that he could whip the whole Ninth Cavalry."

At first light the full force of the battle resumed. Gunfire was everywhere. Several dozen warriors held positions within easy range of the soldiers. Other Apaches were above them on the ridges. The bulk of the Buffalo Soldiers were pinned down, firing, ejecting, and reloading. Twenty others fought with their pistols because the Apaches were so close.

Then, at about 7 a.m., the firing inexplicably stopped.

Lieutenant Conline's Buffalo Soldiers, who had seen action a few days earlier at the mouth of the canyon, had been kept in reserve. Now they arrived from the north. About that same time, additional soldiers who had been hunting Victorio arrived from the west.

The army suddenly numbered close to three hundred. Victorio probably had less than half that many warriors, as well as fifty noncombatants. Realizing that he was outnumbered and outgunned, he pulled his warriors to a position just below the sacred mountain. During the rest of the morning he used this strong rearguard position to hold off the strengthened army's attacks while the bulk of the Red

Paint People slipped away. By early afternoon Victorio and the last warriors had vanished.

Once out of Hembrillo Basin, the Apaches traveled in several smaller groups, making it necessary for them to be tracked almost individually. One such group narrowly escaped detection by a large number of additional soldiers under Colonel Hatch who were arriving from a camp at Aleman. A few days later Victorio's Apaches regrouped in the mountains west of the Jornada. For a short while they hid out there while Victorio and the other warriors raided sheep camps and mining operations west of the river.

In late May Victorio suffered his first real defeat of the war. A civilian scout working with a number of Apache scouts attacked the hidden encampment and killed thirty people. Victorio himself was wounded in the leg. During the melee the enemy Apache scouts called to the Red Paint People, urging them to surrender. The women shouted back, "We will not come out, and if Victorio dies we will eat him so that no white man should ever see his body."

That was Victorio's last escape. For a few months during the summer of 1880 he and about three hundred Red Paint People traced a zigzag pattern along the border country of New Mexico, Texas, and Mexico. When Victorio's bloody end came, many said it happened because his sister Lozen, the woman with the holy sight, had not been with him that day.

On the afternoon of October 14, 1880, low on ammunition and strung out in a long line so that they could travel, the group of Indians was surprised by a large number of Mexican soldiers at a place called Tres Castillos. "By all accounts," Karl Laumbach told me, "Victorio's final battle was a massacre." Caught in the open desert of Chihuahua, the Apaches dove for the scant cover and soon exhausted their ammunition. At the end, those still living fought with knives and with their bare hands, until, one by one, they too were killed.

Once the fighting ended, any remaining men were taken to an arroyo and shot. The surviving women and children were kept as slaves. About forty Red Paint People escaped. Mexican authorities paid two thousand dollars for Victorio's scalp.

Years later, one of the survivors of the massacre said that Victorio died "with his own knife in his heart."

Victorio's battle in the Jornada's Hembrillo Basin was the second-largest military engagement of the Apache Wars. At the height of the battle close to five hundred people were in the basin. People who, in Karl Laumbach's words, "would have preferred to have been elsewhere."

Victorio's only wish was to be given a home. But "few ever seriously considered acceding to their [the Apaches'] simple request to remain where they were, in their traditional homeland where they had been raised and whose mountains, valleys, deserts and canyons they knew and loved," Dan Thrapp wrote. "They must be moved. Why? Search the records from end to end, the thousands upon thousands of documents, and you discover no valid reason. There was no reason. It was simply that, since they desired to remain, they must be moved."

The truck bounces back down the steep canyon road out of Hembrillo Basin. I look out to a hillside ringed with green. I see a metallic flash of light. "What the dickens was that?" I ask.

"Oh, that," Jim says. He pulls to a quick stop; a cloud of white dust as thick as smoke blows up around the truck. As the dust settles I see blades of yucca and ocotillo amid a scattering of juniper trees on a grassy hillside. Jim leaves the truck running and says, "Karl thinks that the vegetation here is coming back to more what it was like before ranching." Since 1945, when the White Sands Missile Range took control of this large region, the entire area has remained a kind of nuclear-age nature preserve. Just in front of us is an Apache plume, the Jornada's most beautiful plant. A member of the rose family, the *Fallugia paradoxa* produces exquisite solitary star-shaped flowers the size of apple blossoms, but the feathery, downlike plumes of the plant's fruit are its true beauty. The shoulder-high bush is covered with hundreds of delicate plumes of the softest down; each white, feathery plume sways in the slightest breeze.

For a long moment, Jim and I are silent.

The Red Paint People seldom spoke their heroes' names. The Apaches believed that you must not use the names of the dead; otherwise their spirits will haunt you.

Then I see it again on the far hillside. A metallic silver arrow the size of small truck punctures the earth near the top of the hill. "What is that thing?" I ask.

"They call those tow-dart targets," he explains. "They are made from cardboard and wooden frames and then covered with an aluminum skin. They used to tow them behind planes using a long towline. Then the planes would drop it and they would shoot at those big darts for practice."

Arrows from other wars, yet to come.

14. Two Writers of the Purple Sage

CAPTAIN JACK CRAWFORD

Just a few weeks after Victorio's battle in the San Andres Mountains, thirty-three-year-old John W. Crawford, already well known by his stage name Captain Jack, rode east from Fort Craig onto the Jornada. The popular stage entertainer and scout had been hired by the U.S. Army to help search for the renegade. He rode all morning so that by midafternoon he had crossed the lava badland, the malpais, and had entered a particularly desolate part of the Jornada just under the Oscura Mountains. A little while later he saw a single horseman crossing the desert from the east.

Captain Jack rode toward the horseman at a steady pace, the clipped, hollow ring of hooves on the packed sandy desert the only sound. Too long ago to change the way things now stood, each man in his own way had forsaken a sweet mother's warnings and taken a path that eventually led him here, to a chance meeting on the desert.

There had been no mistaking the lone rider. Only a strong and brave man, or a desperate man with nothing to lose, faced the parched basin alone. When Captain Jack met Billy the Kid on the Jornada del Muerto, the boy was already the most notorious outlaw in the West. Dime novels had already emblazoned *his* legend onto the hearts of millions who hungered for romance and adventure while trapped in the smoke-chocked cities of the East.

When Captain Jack met him, Billy the Kid – *alias* the Kid, *alias* the Billy Kid, *alias* Billy Bonney, *alias* Billy Antrin, *alias* Henry McCarty, *alias* Henry Antrim – had already killed twelve men.

He was just a kid, Jack saw right away, not much older than his own son – it was just that *this* boy was on the other side of hope.

The boy slouched in his saddle and grinned. He chewed on a twig fifty miles from the nearest tree. Captain Jack too knew the Apache method of slacking a thirst, but he still had plenty of water in his canteens. The Kid took the offered water, then reached into a saddlebag and pulled out some jerked deer meat. The men sat on their horses, shared what they had, and talked.

Billy loved fiddle music, he told Jack. The worst thing about running, he said, was that he hated to miss a single *baile* on the Ruidoso River. He sure did like the way them cousins, the Coe boys, fiddled. They'd saw out "Arkansas Traveler," "The Irish Washerwoman," or "Fisher's Hornpipe" on their fiddles and stomp the wooden floor with their heavy boots in time to the music. "I'm a mighty fine dancer," Billy said. "I like that tune 'Turkey in the Straw.' I always yell to ole Frank Coe 'Don't forget the *gaillina*.' "

This was no legendary romantic but simply a young man who liked to twirl the young ladies on a sawdust-covered dance floor. This was no dastardly dime-novel outlaw waging a private war for freedom, with double-barrels blazing fire and a sleek pony to carry him like the wind, but just a kid who'd let his own reckless desires drive him so far away that he could never find his way back home.

"Whiskey done it," the Kid said. "That and the boys I joined up with." He stuck the twig back between his buck teeth and turned in the saddle to look behind him. "Seems I been at war ever since." The boy seemed about to say something else, but he drew back and said simply that no one would ever believe the real truth of matters.

Captain Jack nodded and offered the canteen again. The Kid refused it.

It was said of Billy the Kid that he was unscrupulous, that he would sacrifice the lives of a hundred men who stood between himself and freedom. You can say of Billy the Kid that he was a cunning, self-righteous, daring, desperate, smooth-talking, cold-blooded killer.

The earth tipped slowly away from the blistering sun. On the desert plain, their shadows grew longer. Purple mountains lined the far horizon.

The Kid cocked his head a notch and smiled. "Obliged," he said. He prodded his horse awake and moved aside, waiting.

Captain Jack touched his heels to his horse and moved past the Kid. "Adiós," he said.

"Hasta la vista," said the Kid.

A mile later, Captain Jack turned to look back. The sun was low in the sky. A small, dark, and distant figure moved toward it, a black shape on the featureless plains on the Jornada.

When Captain Jack met Billy the Kid, no blazing rifles lit up the western sky, and no desperadoes spurred lathering ponies across a fenceless frontier. When Captain Jack met Billy the Kid there were just two men: one a killer, one a dreamer. They had shared a meal, circled one another, and moved on.

Five years earlier, John W. Crawford had left his wife, Maria, and his two small children in Pennsylvania and headed west. The Civil War captain had first spent a few years roaming the Black Hills and earning his living as a correspondent for the *Omaha Bee*. When the Sioux and Cheyenne rose up in a losing battle to keep their sacred Black Hills, Crawford served the army as a scout.

Shortly thereafter he joined up with his friend Bill Cody and formed the *Buffalo Bill Combination*, a traveling entertainment destined to popularize the realities and the myths of the American West.

On stage Captain Jack wore buckskins; his long, wild hair billowed from beneath a wide sombrero. He often wore pistols, and carried a knife jammed into his belt. Audiences loved him. Instead of reading from a prepared script, Captain Jack captivated audiences with his spine-tingling tales of life in the West. Despite the flair of his outrageous appearance, a contemporary said "there was nothing of brag or bluster about Crawford in either speech or manner." He spoke with the voice of a worker speaking to other workers just like him. He railed against the popular dime-novel accounts of the "Wild West," while he himself blended fanciful fiction with his firsthand knowledge in wry moral tales of a mystical land.

Shortly after Victorio's War, Maria and the children finally came west and joined Jack on the Jornada. Jack tried to settle down and cobble together an income for his family. He ran a store at the now-abandoned Fort Craig and started a small herd of horses and dairy

cows. He speculated on the mineral wealth of the Jornada and published books of poetry. Then, in 1885, Doc "Evil Eye" Carter offered
Crawford a place in his traveling show *The Great Wild West Combination*. In the blink of an eye, Jack left Maria in charge of things at Fort
Craig and lit out for the territory ahead.

From that point until his death in 1917, the "Poet Scout" remained
one of the country's most popular writers and platform entertainers.
For the remainder of his life Jack split his time between the stage and
life with Maria and the children on the Jornada.

In 1894 the owners of Pedro Armendaris's land, then known as the
Valverde Land and Irrigation Company, sued Jack in order to eject
him from his ranch at the abandoned Fort Craig. Begrudgingly, Jack
relinquished his claim there. "I regret that I could not have made a
permanent home for my old age under the old cottonwoods at Fort
Craig," he wrote. Instead he built a spacious home for Maria and the
children at San Marcial, another short-lived community not far from
the fort.

Although he wrote Maria frequently during his long periods away,
his attempts to secure a living meant more long absences, and this
strained the already unusual relationship. They argued over a divorce
but finally agreed to simply go on as they always had – she remained
on the Jornada with the children while Jack traveled the world. He sent
most of the money he earned to her.

Maria was a jovial woman with a good sense of humor. She was a
strong pioneer woman her husband once described as "equal to any
emergency." Although they spent precious little time together, when
they were together the time always seemed rich and full. At dawn the
morning after a loving Thanksgiving at home, he wrote in his diary
that their life together was "as quiet and still as a summer's dream."

And yet he never returned to the Jornada after 1912.

By the time he died in 1917 hundreds of his short stories had appeared in popular magazines. He had published seven books and
four plays.

In the words of his biographer, Darlis A. Miller, Captain Jack
"taught Americans what they knew about the Western experience."
During the final years of his life he was driven by what Miller calls a

"frenetic drive for fame," but his once-gigantic audiences were growing smaller and smaller. He even took a bit part in an early silent movie, but he had less and less money to send back to Maria.

In January 1917, while attending a performance by baseball player-turned-evangelist Billy "Pop" Sunday, Jack caught a cold. Two weeks later he died of pneumonia at the home of his female secretary in Long Island. The *New York Evening Sun* reported that on his deathbed Jack said, "They'll be sounding taps over me pretty soon. Well, when Bill Cody and I meet Tall Bull and that tough old codger named Sitting Bull on the other side and say 'How! Kola!' there will be a lot to talk about."

Maria died in 1925 at San Marcial.

EUGENE MANLOVE RHODES

Eugene Rhodes's life story reads like one that he himself might have written: in the same year Pat Garrett killed Billy the Kid, a devil-may-care nine-year-old and his homesteading family arrived on the Jornada. Born with a cleft palate that made it impossible for him to correctly pronounce his own name, Gene early on learned how to fight. Ready for a brawl at the drop of a hat, he always defended the downtrodden.

Although the young man cowboyed for a while at the Bar Cross Ranch, his true talent was breaking horses. Like some real-life John Grady Cole, no one on the entire Jornada could saddle-break a horse better than Gene Rhodes. He loved to gamble, to tell tales around a campfire or poker table, and to ride out into the Jornada on a good horse, his head deep in a book. Like most boys in those days, Gene became addicted to tobacco early on. One company provided coupons with its tobacco tins. His mother had taught him how to read, so he used the coupons to send away for small, cheaply made books of classic literature. (The only reason they were the classics, he later realized, was because the "soulless tobacco corporation" could reprint them copyright free.)

Tales of Rhodes's escapades still swirl across the Jornada like dust devils on the alkali flats. There was the time he won a bet that he could read the first chapter of a brand-new book while riding a wild horse, and then repeat the plot verbatim. There were stories of gambling and bloody, bare-fisted fights, stories of his horsemanship and his gallantry. "No man could be more loyal to a friend than Gene," one man recalled, "and that loyalty was without reservation."

His wife would describe him as a small, wiry man, "permanently sunburned, with a heavy mustache, strong toil-scarred hands, and a pair of blue eyes that seemed to look right through you. His face was battered."

He first worked for the Bar Cross Ranch when he was thirteen. His job was to dig out the old Martin ranch well at Aleman.

The ranch manager asked Rhodes to teach his children to read. Gene obliged. He worked intermittently on the Bar Cross chasing thousands of cattle strung out from Engle to Point of Rocks and beyond.

When the drought of 1890–93 shriveled up the Bar Cross and most of the other ranches on the Jornada, Rhodes built a small cabin in a canyon northeast of Engle and holed up there. He lived free, working horses when he felt like it. Visions of this mystical place from his youth forever haunted the dreams and stories of his adult life.

It was while living in Rhodes Canyon that Gene fell in love with a pretty girl he had met in Engle. She was the one true romance of his life, but nothing came of it: the mothers did not like one another, and that ended that.

A short time later his parents moved to California, where his mother soon found a suitable match for her son. She knew of a woman with the poetic name of May Purple who had recently been widowed. May lived with her two young sons far from the Jornada on a farm near Binghamton, New York. His mother told Gene about May, and soon the two were exchanging letters. He sent her his poetry, which she thought the grandest she had ever seen. After two years of nearly nonstop correspondences, he decided to pay her a visit.

When the twenty-eight-year-old hopped onto a cattle train at Engle on that blistering July day in 1899, he didn't know he would spend the remainder of his life in a fruitless attempt to return to the Jornada.

He worked his way east as a "shipper" for the railroad, using a sharp-pointed cattle prod to load and unload stock. Not long after he arrived in New York, Eugene Manlove Rhodes married May Purple. Gene first tried to move his new family to Tularosa, New Mexico, a town not on the Jornada but within thirty-five miles of his beloved cabin in Rhodes Canyon. Frustrated, worn by the harsh desert life, and probably homesick, May didn't wait long to move their now three children back to New York. Gene said he would follow her soon. "Soon" turned out to take four years. Part of the problem was that he was perpetually broke. A flood destroyed his old cabin in the San Andres, and he had to sell his herd of horses. He worked whatever odd jobs he could find and sent money back east for May and the children. He washed dishes, dug wells, mopped up saloons, hauled bags of flour in a local mill, and helped build a pipeline across the Tularosa basin. During this time the famed musicologist John Lomax visited the area, and Rhodes loaded him up with dozens of cowboy songs he knew by heart.

About this time Rhodes also tried his hand at writing fiction. Soon he began getting occasional checks by selling stories to magazines like *McClure's* and the *Saturday Evening Post*.

According to one biographer, Gene gambled away any extra money he made. "Eventually Gene was forced to the realization that he was not living up to his own strict code. That code demanded that a man accept and face up to his responsibilities." In 1906 he left his beloved land for a second time; twenty years later, when May and he were finally able to return to the general area, they would stay only a handful of months.

Rhodes moved to his wife's farming community in New York. For most of his previous thirty years he had lived with not much more than a bedroll and a wide-brimmed hat for a home. He took to farming like a barn cat takes to the family dog.

He also detested the East. Part of his hatred came from the fact that his youngest daughter died shortly after he moved to the New York farm. May claimed her husband never overcame his grief. Despite this great sorrow, and his longing for the Jornada, he became a much more productive writer while farming. Still, as would always be the case, he had trouble making ends meet.

His finely crafted stories of life in the desert West gained him loyal readers. He was a perfectionist who insisted on rewriting and polishing his work. He seldom sent a story out to be published until he was absolutely destitute, and claimed if he could make as much money any other way he'd give up writing in an instant. Perhaps his greatest flaw as a writer was that he was easily distracted from the task.

With the skill of our best writers, he captured the moment the American West turned from horses and open range to cars and trucks and missile ranges. You can see Gene in his best-known novel, *Paso por Aqui*, or in stories like "Good Men and True" where a law-clerk reads Carlyle's *French Revolution* and then tells a cowboy about that book's influence on Dickens. The tobacco-smoking cowboy himself can quote Shakespeare, classical poetry, and cowboy doggerel. The plot of the story involves murder and conspiracy and is as well written and complex as any by Arthur Conan Doyle.

In 1925 May's mother died, leaving the couple free to abandon the New York farm. The following year they drove a broken-down Huppmobile to New Mexico and soon moved to Alamogordo, about a hundred miles southeast of the Jornada but close enough to make him temporarily giddy with joy. "May and I are flourishing like two bay horses," he wrote a friend. They had just moved into a rent-free rock house in an isolated canyon. Gene had spent several months making the big house comfortable; it had running water and a modern toilet, but it was twelve miles to the nearest neighbor. Both of them soon found the dusty, hard life at the isolated house too much. After a lifetime of trying to find a way to return to the land he loved, Rhodes left the desert for the last time.

He spent his final years in California. The couple bought a small house overlooking the sea. They lived there with their cats and their memories.

Champion of the underdog until he died, Rhodes bemoaned poverty, senseless war, and the plight of workers. He believed that all races should be treated equally. He knew that there were both saints and sinners everywhere in humanity.

Late in life he started writing "The Desert Road," a long-planned history of the Jornada. It remained unfinished at the time of his death.

Rhodes didn't care much for what he called a "blue tin" heaven or a "comic-supplement" hell. "I'm interested in the here and now," he wrote. "I like to help out at whatever comes my way."

In 1933, with only a half dollar to his name, he sold his final story to the *Saturday Evening Post*.

He died on June 27, 1934.

"We're in eternity now," he once wrote of life, "every minute of it – as much as we ever shall be."

"His creed was kindness, decency, and simple stout heartedness," read Rhodes's obituary in the Santa Fe *New Mexican*. "To these things he gave new vitality for millions of readers. In his own soul he found the value of life on mountaintops amid great distances and among the simple people herding cattle. His tales were imbued with the true genius of the Southwest. He was loved here because of the magic words in which he could say what so many of us feel about the country."

Up near the crest of Rhodes Pass, tall soapweed yuccas grow in profusion; the trunks are as thick and as tall as men. From the cluster of dagger-like leaves at the top of each yucca rise stalks covered with thousands of brilliant flowers the shape of bells.

Rhodes chose to be buried at this isolated spot.

The faint path to his grave passes through the yucca and into a thick stand of one-seed juniper and single-leaf piñon. There is no sound here but the constant ringing of insects.

A large boulder marks his isolated grave.

"I would not push my littleness upon this so large a world," he once wrote. "One of my earliest ambitions was to have graven upon my tombstone this epitaph 'Pass, traveler, nor ask who lies beneath the grass.'"

On a brass plaque bolted to the granite boulder are the words: Eugene Manlove Rhodes – *Paso por aqui*.

15. Virtual Fences and Real Neighbors

Jane Cain sets the glass of iced tea on the table and sits back down. "You go on and use one of those napkins," she says and smiles.

I reach for a napkin from the holder on the table.

"Tell him, Ben," she says to her husband.

Ben Cain sits across from me. He chuckles. "I will," he says, and then begins yet another tale. "We've lived here at the Bar Cross Ranch since '54," he says, pronouncing it "fifty-*four-your*." "I was born in '28 and lived over to what we call the Buckhorn Ranch up towards Rhodes Pass." Ben was born on the Jornada and, except for two years when he moved to Missouri because of his skin cancer, has lived all of his seventy-three years here.

"Go on and take a look at that napkin holder," he says. Both he and Jane watch me. "Did you know Eugene Rhodes' first job was here at the Bar Cross . . . ?"

I remove a handful of paper napkins and take the heavy holder in my hands. It is an odd-shaped ring of metal about the size of a child's face. The flattened edge of the metal oval shows signs of wear.

Ben continues. "Well, here about thirty years ago I found a saddle out on the range. It was falling apart: all the leather was gone; there was just the tree and the horn. Then I found that old stirrup nearby."

Jane leans forward. "I cleaned it up and we use it for a napkin holder."

Ben continues, "Well, then several years later I remembered that Eugene Rhodes once worked for an outfit called the Circle Cross and I thought, 'Well, I've seen that circle cross brand somewhere before . . .'"

Jane says, "Turn it over." Her smile might be the sweetest thing this side of Tularosa.

I turn it over. Scratched onto the bottom of the old stirrup is a circle with a cross inside of it. Next to the brand are the initials E.R.

"Eugene Rhodes," I say automatically.

Jane laughs. "Isn't that something?" she says.

Jane has not lived on the Jornada for quite as long as her husband, having moved here when she was six. She and Ben met during her senior year at Hot Springs High School. She pronounces her husband's name as if it had two syllables. "I chased Be-yen for two years, and boy – I caught him."

We laugh.

For the first few years of their marriage they lived pressed up against the San Andres Mountains at the Buckhorn Ranch, but shortly thereafter Ben and his brother Lewis bought the Bar Cross Ranch at Aleman and split it into two ranches of about thirty-six thousand acres each. Ben still runs about four hundred head of cattle on his part.

"My brother Lewis died here, oh, nineteenth of February this year," he says. He pauses, and then goes on. "There's been five or six different owners of the Bar Cross between Rhodes' day and mine," he says.

He talks about his childhood home. "We had to leave the Buckhorn," he says. "The army kept squeezing us out." During World War II the U.S. military picked the remote Jornada to test a top-secret weapon they had developed. They began evicting residents like Ben Cain from their ranches. The fifty-year-long battle that ensued between those residents and the U.S. government is often called the White Sands War.

"And now they want to take this place too," Jane says. She explains how the Bar Cross is smack dab in the center of a possible site for the world's first "Space Port." "They want 450 sections for a place to shoot a rocket straight up," she explains, "but it'll be a rocket that can land like an airplane. You would be able to get to Tokyo in forty-five minutes, or get here in an hour from any place on earth."

"But you'd still be a four-hour drive from here to anywhere else," I say.

Ben laughs. "It's really the Lockheed defense plant who is behind it. They don't own the military reservation, and the regulations there are too stiff, so they want private land."

169

Most ranchers on the Jornada and elsewhere in the Southwest range their cattle over large tracts of public land. Scattered over those sections, men and women like the Cains own small patches of private land around water sources or other improvements. That patchwork represents a rancher's investment in his entire cattle business, but, because of their isolation, the separate pieces of land have very little value when sold as real estate. When the government took land to create the White Sands Missile Range, many ranchers were paid only for the market value of their isolated "deeded" land rather than the worth of their livelihood that the land represented.

I ask, "If whoever had control of the public land came in here and said, 'We'll give you only 75 cents an acre for your deeded land,' that'd be all you could get?"

Ben and Jane speak at the same time. "Yes," they answer.

"There's a lot of state land over here, and the state is very involved in this Space Port idea," Ben says. "They want to co-use the land. They said they won't bother our cattle and our cattle won't bother them. We told them, yeah, we know all about trusting the government. They don't want another White Sands War on their hands."

The afternoon goes by in the slow, easy way that time passes on the Jornada. They unfold their lives for me: tales of childhood pony rides to school, of the bad, dry years and of good, happy ones. Eventually the conversation comes back around to the government. In a few days the Jornada will be evacuated. They explain how the government has a co-use agreement with them and some other ranchers on the Jornada. Once or twice a month they are paid to vacate their home for six to twelve hours so that White Sands can use the Jornada for a test. "They never really do tell you why," Jane says. "But we go to town and make it our monthly shopping trip."

The sun has dropped behind the Lombardy poplars outside the kitchen window. I make motions to leave, but Jane's words stop me.

"You know the train used to stop right there, just outside there by the windmill and the old Aleman well." She turns to her husband. "Oh Ben, tell those stories."

Her husband of a half century picks up his cue without missing a beat.

"We used to ride the train a lot. We'd take the train to El Paso, even Albuquerque. It was pretty handy. The train'd come by here at nine in the morning. We could get all the way to Albuquerque, shop and be back here at 9:30 at night. They stopped carrying passengers in 1963 or '64, the same time they stopped shipping cattle.

"When you carry cattle on a train you have to unload them and let them rest. So my brother and I spent a lot of time loading and unloading cattle right out there. And it seems we never did load a train with cattle but at two in the morning. If you carried bulls" – he pronounces it *bools* – "in the same car with cows you'd have to tie them up so they wouldn't hurt the cows. The way you'd do that is you'd load up the railcar and then crawl across the backs of the cows so you could tie the bulls up to the sides of the cars."

"Doing that at 2 a.m., now that's trouble, isn't it?" Jane says to me.

Ben continues.

"We had this old depot agent in Engle – he was a real nice old man, and he'd always help us load cattle. He'd shine a lantern in there to try to show us where the bulls were. Well, one night the engineer took it as a signal and away we went!" He bursts into laughter. "We went only a quarter mile, but we thought – Socorro, here we come!"

We stand. Jane takes our glasses and dishes to the sink. I feel I have overextended my welcome, but they insist that I see the rest of their home.

Until they moved here in 1954, the Cains had never lived with electricity or indoor plumbing. "But this place had four baths with a commode in every one of them," Ben recalls, "and our kids went around flushing each one – they thought that was the darnedest thing!"

The sprawling fourteen-room adobe house dates to 1865, when the first room was built to serve as a stagecoach station along the Camino Real. Over the last 140 years rooms have been added one at a time.

We move from room to room and finally come to the long, cool living room. It is tastefully decorated with old ranch items and family artifacts.

Jane takes up the tour. "We were Cattlemen of the Year in '94. There's our trophy from the Cattleman Association," she says. "We're quite proud of that." She points to a painting. "Our oldest daughter did that," she says. "She's real good with horses. We pretty much ran this ranch as a family. Our other daughter lives a few miles up the Jornada from here."

We walk to a shelf that holds two framed photographs. "Here's what I really wanted to show you." She takes one of the photographs into her hands and holds it gently. "This is our family in 1975," she says. "This is our son and his wife . . ." She stops. "We lost Steve in 1976. He and our little grandson Cody Cain were killed in a car accident in Oklahoma," she says. "For the next twenty years our therapy was hard work." She replaces the photograph to its place on the shelf and then points to a second, much more recent photograph. Jane and Ben stand amid their middle-age daughters and a scattering of grandchildren. "I told Ben I would never have a picture as great as that one from 1975, but then this last fall we took this picture and it is *just* as good as the one from long ago."

We walk onto the porch. "We've had a good life here," Jane says. She stays on the porch as Ben and I walk away. She waves. "You say hi to Flo Martin next time you see her," she shouts. "She was our neighbor when we lived over on the Buckhorn."

I follow Ben across the yard. He stoops when he walks, and walks with a little shuffle, but his lean, strong frame seems more suited to a man of thirty. We enter an old adobe room. Heavy cottonwood *vigas* support a ceiling of willow *latias*. A few wasps float back and forth in front of a paper nest in a corner of the ceiling. "There was more to this building," he says, "but in 1960 we had a freak snow – three feet or more – and the roof collapsed." Ben hauled away the old roof. "Under the dirt roof was this grass," he says, "old, old grass over 150 years old. Well, you never would have thought it, but I took that old grass and my damn horses ate it right up."

We step back outside. We walk along a long, narrow wall. The old adobe building forms a barrier between the blistering Jornada and us. A space about ten feet wide breaks the long facade of the low building. Ben tells me that at one time the ranch was a stage station. Because of Apache raiders, the walled ranch served as a small fortress. Stagecoaches pulled into the protection of the yard through that narrow space.

In a guarded moment I stare at Ben's right ear. The flesh is virtually gone. All that remains is a gnarled stub of a skin-colored bump. He notices me. "Skin cancer," he explains. "That was a bad thing – they pulled all the muscles out of my ear – they had to rebuild my face. Every skin doctor I'd go to they'd say, 'Man, you'd better get out – you'd be best living at the bottom of a coal mine.' So we tried living in Missouri, but it wasn't any better there so we said to hell with that and came back here."

As if shrugging off skin cancer like a pesky horsefly, Ben continues his tour. We stand in the yard of the ranch. The afternoon's heat has raised darkening clouds in the July sky. "One foreman killed another foreman right here." He says with a hearty laugh. "Shot him down right here."

"How do you think Eugene Rhodes' saddle ended up out there in the middle of nowhere?"

"Oh, the horse broke lose, or it died, there's no telling," Ben says. "They talk about him being so wild as a cowboy. They still tell stories about him." After a moment he adds: "You can't be bored out here, because there's something new every day: a different problem or a different blessing."

We reach my van. I tell him I'm headed north to his neighbor Ted Turner's ranch.

"Back when the Armendaris was for sale a number of us ranchers got together enough for the down payment on the spread," he says. "We had it all figured out: we'd each get ninety sections and put heifers up there. Ted Turner bought it instead."

He smiles. "Then it didn't rain for two years and the price of cattle went way down. We would have been flat broke! Every morning we thank the Lord," he laughs, and then adds, "we thank the Lord and Ted Turner."

I drive north from the Bar Cross. Despite a changing climate, the Jornada supports a wide diversity of plants and animals. There are more than five hundred species of plants, while animals like the black-tailed deer, pronghorn antelope, and the African gemsbok, the oryx, all range free on the Jornada del Muerto. Periodically, black bears show up along the river. Lately elk have been coming down out of the high ranges to the northwest to wander up onto the edges of the Jornada plain. The Jornada is home to mountain lions, desert bighorns, Barbary sheep, prairie dogs, lizards, four species of rattlesnakes, and Ted Turner's bison.

A cowboy who worked this area in the late 1800s said there were "worlds of cattle" here. The Bar Cross alone ran twenty thousand head. Meanwhile, homesteaders like Eugene Rhodes's parents, who were lured to the area by a short-lived mining boom, raised domestic sheep and goats. Along with climate and other factors, early grazing practices contributed to the rapid invasion of shrubs like mesquite, creosote bush, and tarbush. Scientific records from the Jornada Experimental Range show the speed of the invasion. In 1858 good grass covered 90 percent of the Experimental Range, but by 1963 it had virtually disappeared from one 144,000-acre parcel. Grazing practices and climate changes have contributed to the disappearance of grasslands, as have the suppression of fires. That transformation continues today, threatening perhaps the largest remaining stand of black grama in the world.

For several miles north of the Cains', shrubs dominate the Jornada's desolate landscape. I cross a cattle guard. A few miles later I pass a dark, sloping hill. A small sign on the railroad tracks announces Cutter. In 1900 Cutter had a massive two-story hotel and was home to more than three thousand people. The place had drinking water from dug wells, but when drought after drought ruined cattle ranching and the railroad abandoned it, the town shriveled up and died. Today even Cutter's cemetery has all but disappeared under the blowing sand.

Three cows stand near a tall yucca. I watch as they push their heads through the spearlike leaves, knock over the central stalk, and begin to munch on the plant's ripening fruits.

In two miles I pass a large, dry playa. The water that briefly collects here after summer storms provides enough moisture for a scattering of grass. In the distance a few cattle wander the lake bed.

I hold my map with one hand as I drive. The road swings slightly eastward and climbs up Jornada Draw on a gentle hill. On the slopes beside the road, creosote and mesquite shrubs give way to more stands of black grama grass scattered amid the daggerlike leaves of yuccas.

In a moment I stop and get out.

I know from exploring this area on foot that traces of the old Camino Real come down off that nearby ridge, cross the modern road and the railroad tracks, and head toward the saucer-shaped valley of yellow grass that glimmers in the heat waves to the northwest.

Just beyond where I stand, a wire fence cuts the horizon like a knife. On the fence in formal, red print is a sign:

> Private property. No trespassing.
> Hunting, fishing, trapping, camping,
> digging or woodcutting is prohibited
> without written permission of the owner:
> NM Ranch Properties Incorporated
> Violators will be prosecuted

I've reached Ted Turner's Armendaris Ranch.

Most of the scientists who study such things agree that preserving the diversity of plants and animals is crucial to the well-being of places like the Jornada. Aside from climate – which may affect the desertification of the Jornada despite (or because of) humanity's efforts – proper management of natural resources is critical. But what is happening is that modern economic pressures are in the driver's seat. Our fast-food lifestyle demands that hamburgers all taste pretty much the same and that steaks be a certain size for easy packaging. Currently almost all the beef grown in the United States is sold to one of only four different companies, which then slaughter and distribute it. Those companies insist on a uniform product, and that demand for conformity has strained the natural resources of places like the Jornada.

Current research to solve the problems of range management on the Jornada has an odd, twenty-first-century ring to it. Some scientists are trying to create a variety of desert-tolerant cattle by cross-breeding an ancient, desert-wandering species with beef cattle. Others discern long-range weather trends in the dance of isotopes.

And then there are virtual fences.

Virtual fences are located on the cow, not on the ground. Each animal wears a collar that contains an electronic "map" of a virtual fence line. A beeping satellite sends GPS signals to each computer-chip-carrying cow. When a cow approaches a predetermined location, the collar activates sound or electronic cues to the animal. Software in the device determines the cow's angle of approach and then cues the animal to turn either right or left.

"The proper distribution of plants and animals is a challenge that has been around since the beginning of civilization," said scientist Dean Anderson, who invented the device. Dean has been an animal scientist at the USDA Jornada Experimental Range since 1977. He says that one problem with traditional fences is that they are limited by topography. Wire fences also require a lot of hard work to build and maintain. They are expensive. In the areas of the world where proper animal control is most needed, fencing is least affordable, so virtual fences could help properly manage rangeland.

Dean has always had a knack for creative thinking. When he first came to the Jornada, he heard about the Beales' 1857 camel caravan on the Jornada. Since camels eat prickly, spiny, sharp things that cattle won't touch, Dean thought they might be useful to control the shrub invasion, and he thought camels might have economic promise as a specialty food. Before long he had imported eight feral camels from Australia's Ayres Rock region. Then he made a mistake. He turned them out on a strange land filled with unfamiliar plants. "I don't think they reacted much differently than you or I would if we were suddenly turned out in Islamabad, Pakistan," he said. The camels might have taken to tarbush if they had been trained to eat it. Instead they began eating a gnarly, pungent bush known as Mormon tea. "The concentrated smell of the urine of eight camels eating Mormon tea is an unique olfactory experience," Dean said of the failed experiment.

Later, at Los Alamos National Laboratory, he created electronic identification devices that allowed him to monitor the internal temperature and weight of cows as they approached remote watering tanks.

Enter flerds surrounded by virtual fences.

A flerd is a blend of a *herd* of cattle and a *flock* of sheep. Sheep social behavior is modified so that they learn to mingle *within* a herd of cattle rather than to flock alongside them. Among other advantages, flerds have reduced the number of sheep killed by coyotes. When coyotes are near, cattle defend themselves by facing them in a circle. The sheep, now integrated as a flerd, shield themselves behind the cows like wagons circled against Indians.

Using the virtual fence, Dean can program an entire flerd to stay within a certain area. He can also create individualized programs in order to control the location of each animal. And, unlike traditional fencing, the virtual fence can march itself across the landscape. By programming additional map coordinates, animals can be moved from place to place at a moment's notice: virtual roundups by wired-in cowboys.

Chances are the virtual fence could work just as well on mountain lions, desert bighorns, and bison.

I am nearing Turner's ranch headquarters at Engle, a small collection of low buildings alongside the railroad track. Because of its location at the intersection of the north-south Jornada road and a road that once led from the Rio Grande east to Tularosa, Engle thrived as the hub of the Jornada for the first half of the twentieth century. It was home to the Eugene Rhodes family and the Blue Goose Boarding House, and it was here that cowboy Joe Turner started his store and gas station and raised his five children after his wife took sick. Since White Sands Missile Range closed the road east of town in the late 1940s, Engle has all but disappeared.

There has been no traffic since I left the Cains' place twenty-five minutes ago, but I stop at the empty intersection anyway and look. The jagged teeth of the rugged Fra Cristobel range fill the near horizon, and to their right lies the open plain of the Jornada. Far beyond, a wall of dark mountains encloses the land. Everything I can see – near mountains, distant mountains, plain and basin and buildings – belongs to Turner. Fifty miles long and twenty miles at its widest, the 360,000-acre Armendaris Ranch is one of three large ranches Turner owns in New Mexico.

Other wealthy visionaries owned the Armendaris before Ted Turner.

In 1873 Wilson Waddingham's U.S. Land Improvement Company owned the Armendaris and controlled more than 1.25 million acres of land in New Mexico. Waddingham sank his money into the cattle industry and speculated on a plan to irrigate the river sections of the Armendaris and then sell that land at a great profit.

By 1890, when the cattle industry hit the skids, Waddingham was in deep trouble. He had robbed the Peter of his cattle business to pay for the Paul of his irrigation scheme. For the remaining nine years of his life he grew ever more desperate trying to keep the shell game going.

Waddingham was not alone in his dreams. Since ancient times people have known the value of the Rio Grande's water. In the late nineteenth century the U.S. government blocked private attempts to dam the river while it worked out its own plan. In 1902 Congress passed the Reclamation Act, and groundwork for the "Engle Dam" project began. Engineers soon selected a site seventeen miles due east of Engle for the project that they claimed "will do much for Mexico and a great deal for the U.S." As a part of the legal maneuvering, the United States negotiated to send sixty thousand acre-feet of water to Mexico.

Elephant Butte Dam was completed in 1915. The high, V-shaped wall of concrete plugs a narrow gorge on the western edge of the Armendaris. The river at that place must have been spectacular.

Waddingham's main headquarters were at San Marcial. The town, located on the distant northern side of the Armendaris property, lasted only a few years longer than Waddingham's dreams. Its citizens suffered terribly as a result of the Spanish flu epidemic of 1918. Then, in 1929, after Elephant Butte Dam had been built below the town, a flood destroyed San Marcial. Today Waddingham's village of San Marcial is no more than a salt-cedar, mosquito-choked flat along the river.

After Waddingham died the Armendaris came under the control of various companies and corporations. Kern Cattle Company, Victorio Land and Cattle Company, the Diamond A Ranch, Strand and Perkins, Lawrence and Stengal, and Oppenheimer Industries Incorporated all held the land before Turner's 1994 purchase.

I turn right on what was once a street and park the van next to a white pickup truck just across the street from an old, comfortable hacienda. In front of me is the plain, single-story building that serves as Turner's ranch headquarters. A house trailer sits just behind the building, and beyond it is a lone pink-colored shack.

A young woman at the front desk smiles as I walk in. "You're here to see Tom, aren't you," she says, laughing. "He's temporarily engaged in an important job."

A round, stocky man appears in a hallway just beyond the front room. He wears a western dress shirt and a pair of jeans held up with a square, silver buckle the size of a cereal box. The toilet plunger he holds in his left hand is dripping wet. "Yes, sir," he says, "one of my most important responsibilities around here is fixing the jammed commode."

Ranch Manager Tom Waddell has gray, short-cropped hair and deep-set, steel eyes. Despite a slight middle-age paunch, his strong, stout frame shows years of hard work. He sets the tool down and offers me his big hand. I follow him down a hall to his office. He has a slow, easy, nearly shuffling way of walking. When he speaks it is with a faint southwestern accent.

"Fixing the commode!" he repeats. He waits until I sit down before he takes a seat behind his desk. "The problems on this ranch haven't ever changed," he says. "I've got a letter from a manager on the Armendaris that's a hundred years old. He's writing about his problems collecting from debtors, about horses getting out, and about trespassers . . ." He chuckles. "Nothing's changed in a hundred years."

Tom was born and raised in Arizona and had spent most of his life there. He had just retired from the Game and Fish Department there when he was asked if he was willing to manage the Armendaris Ranch.

"I wasn't sure," he says, "but once you've worked for Ted you realize there's no better place to work. There's 150 percent support for everything you do. The managers make the decisions they feel comfortable with, and if they don't feel comfortable, they call and Ted . . ." he pauses. "Any decision in this company takes probably less than a minute." He laughs heartily. "There are no long meetings in this company: when there are too many meetings that means there's a lack of leadership."

Turner owns two million acres of land in the western United States, making him the country's largest private landowner. From mountain lions to prairie dogs, he is trying to reintroduce native species on his land while still keeping the properties economically viable by raising bison for commercial sale, by promoting eco-tourism, and by attracting big-game hunters who pay high rates to experience the wilderness of the American West firsthand. In addition, Turner is willing to give up some potential profits in order to promote biodiversity. Local opinion on such an endeavor is mixed. "Ted Turner's got more dollars than he has sense!" eighty-eight-year-old Flo Martin told me.

Tom says Turner's purchases of western properties are not reckless. He explains how the Turner ranches are managed through a system of administrative divisions. Tom is the manager of one of fourteen Turner ranches. Each ranch is further divided into divisions. "There's a livestock division, a wildlife division, a biodiversity division, and an endangered species division," he says. Each division's goal is to determine the endangered, native, and non-native species and then determine how to get the area back to its best possible condition. "So every time we buy a ranch we have to address all those things," Tom says. "It's not so simple. The livestock division has to build fences and to make planning for grazing, the wildlife division handles the commercially hunted game species, and the biodiversity division handles all the inventories of species that aren't covered by one of the others." Tom's job is to coordinate the various divisions on the Armendaris and to offer support for whatever they might need.

Tom says that Turner is intimately involved with the ranch. "He knows how deep every well is; he knows how big every pasture is," he says.

Tom himself knows a fair bit about the Armendaris. He tells me of Pablo de Aballos's 1620 mine up in the Fra Cristobels; he can talk for an hour on the history of the ranch's Tucson Springs, which has long been the most reliable source of water in the area. He tells me of the caves in the malpais to the northeast that shelter one of the largest concentrations of Mexican big-eared bats in North America. "In the late 1800s over three thousand tons of bat guano was mined from the cave," he says. The caves contain one of the largest and purest forms of nitrate. The Spanish conquistadores walked right past it, Tom says. He thinks that if they had they discovered such a rich source of gunpowder, the history of North America might have been different.

Above: Gene Rhodes around 1898. New Mexico State University Library, Archives and Special Collections.

Below: Captain Jack Crawford. Courtesy Palace of the Governors, Negative # 15747.

Flo Martin around the time she married Frank.
Courtesy Flo Martin.

Ben Cain in 2001 near old Martin's Well on the Bar Cross Ranch.
Author photo.

Georgia Green in 1942. Courtesy of Bill O'Connell.

Georgia Green and her brother Bill. Courtesy of Bill O'Connell.

The author on the Jornada in 2001. Photo by Dan Perry.

Ruts on the Jornada found during the author's final walk. Author photo.

Above: Joe Turner in the 1930s. Courtesy
Ronnie Turner.

Below: Joe Turner in 2001. Author photo.

"You ever see a Folsom point?" he suddenly asks, and then slides open a drawer on his desk. He removes something from an envelope and then hands me a thick, nearly oval spear point. "You see that fluting right there with the fine edge to it? That's maybe ten thousand years or better. It's from the ranch."

The woman from the front room comes in to discuss a problem with a contractor. When she leaves, he turns back to me. "This is one of the oldest places in North American history," he says of the Jornada. "And it's being lost. It's a very old, old culture, and this new age of communication is jerking it up pretty fast."

He pulls out a large book of pressed plants. He flips through the pages. Each page holds a different, beautifully preserved plant. Each plant is labeled. "One of the botanists did this," he says. "It's all the flowers on the range."

Turner allows his ranch to be used as a no-frills laboratory for scientists, including botanists, prairie-dog specialists, and people like Myles Traphagen, who is studying the effect of fire on black grama grass. The ranch contracts with the scientists and also has permanent full-time employees for other projects like the reintroduction of Alplomado falcons, mountain lions, and desert bighorn sheep.

The most obvious additions to the wild landscape on the Turner ranches are buffalo.

"We run seventeen hundred bison on the Armendaris," Tom says. He notes my amazement. "Shoot, the company owns about thirty thousand bison, and it'll be bigger, see, because Ted's never going to sell a bison heifer. That's why we're buying so many ranches. He's not just buying land for the sake of land. The heifers come first, then the land comes. The heifer production is driving the land purchases. We have to buy out in front of our projected heifer production. And there's no ceiling. The bison market is excellent – the commercial value is about three or four times what it is for cattle. Of course the value may drop as we get more bison, but you can raise bison as economically as you can raise cattle." Tom explains that the bison serve another purpose as well. "We're essentially using bison to bring back all the native species that were extricated out of here for one reason or another," he says.

He knows that bison and cattle are both bad for the land if they aren't managed properly. At the same time, he admits that there is precious little information about how to manage bison. "There's been people who have raised bison commercially, but they've been backyard, small-acreage operations. We're the first to raise such large herds, so we're kind of on the cutting edge of management. There's very little known about bison. People for years compared them to cattle. They compared blood chemistry or they compared grazing; they compared everything to cattle. But they're nothing like cattle. So the whole industry is in the process of learning about bison."

Tom tells me that bison are also easier to raise than cattle, but quickly adds that he gets along fine with his cattle-ranching neighbors. "Whenever you move in," he says, "the wild range of Ted Turner rumors run amok, but the fact of it is we're very good neighbors. We've had no problems with our neighbors, and they've had no problems with us."

When I finally stand to leave, Tom walks me back to the reception area. The young woman is making small talk with a man seated in a chair. He wears a tan cowboy hat and types onto a laptop computer.

Tom shakes my hand. "You know, this old culture right here has remained intact for a long time," he says. "It's finally catching up with modern technology, but the Jornada is still the last place ever settled in the West." He pauses. Then, as if describing Ted Turner himself, he adds, "it's the last place you'll ever find frontiersmen."

I walk outside into the early evening and stand at the van. Jornada scientist Ed Fredrickson told me that things are changing for the ranching industry. "To survive we have to diversify," he said. Turner hopes his bison will make a difference in the world. Down the road a bit there's old Ben Cain – still kickin', ear-chewed by cancer, still punching cattle and living out life the only way he knows how.

Standing at my van, I think of the Jornada's fragile human diversity: of Eugene Rhodes, riding with his head buried in a book; of conquistadores resting at the Cross of the German, Aleman; and of Victorio, come down from the battle at Hembrillo Basin and dashing westward to his coming death. Life stories fading into the sands of the Journey of the Dead, vanishing but for tiny fragments of flint, pottery, and stirrup.

I gaze to the east. I take a deep breath. Find the center: look up, look now, look there.

From a silvery distant cloud, a dark plume of smoke snakes its way to the ground. They are testing another weapon out on White Sands Missile Range. The old, old question rises up from the Jornada: Can nature survive amid the power of human technology and might?

16. Flo Martin Puts Down Her Monkey Wrench

Eighty-eight-year-old Florence Martin remembers the last roundup of wild horses on the Jornada as if it happened yesterday. She and her husband were living at their ranch on the western flank of San Andres at the time.

"Frank and I never fooled with wild horses," Flo says, "but we stood in on this last deal."

Periodically, area ranchers rounded up the wild horses that still roamed the Jornada and sold them to the Mexican army. It was in the spring of 1945, just a few months before the atomic blast at Trinity.

"They started gathering wild horses from a great distance," Flo says, "and as they moved on, different ranchers would throw in. They'd take them to local corrals, and then they'd move them on to the next ranch."

Flo was at the house the day the last herd of wild horses rode past. She was staying close to home, keeping an eye on her firstborn, who was then a toddler. About midday she saw a cloud of pale yellow dust to the northeast. She knew instantly she would have to deal with their troublesome stallion, Tom. "That horse was the meanest old son of a gun you'd ever seen." Because the wild horses would be coming right past the ranch house, she would have to tie him up. She had to act fast. He was already snorting at the air. "I threw a rope around old Tom and lashed him to a post just inside the corral's gate."

She quickly herded five or six other horses inside the corral and then grabbed her child and threw the gate closed. They watched as the wild horses thundered past. "I'd guess they had maybe five hundred horses. And those horses were wild! It took a real cowboy to handle them, and all of those ranchers, well . . ." she smiles. "They were real cowboys."

She waited four hours until the herd was long gone before she turned the stallion loose. "Ol' Tom he just went haywire," she laughs. "He'd get out and he'd snort, and he'd rare, and he'd charge, but all of them horses was gone!"

Her husband, Frank, died a few years back, and Flo now lives alone in their modest house in Socorro. Out back is a large aluminum ranch shed that looks out of place. The big shed is as gray as gunflint in a neighborhood of bright gardens, kids' bikes, and trampolines.

In her living room is an oil painting of their home on the range. "This was the ranch headquarters," she says. "The poison weed was so bad down on the flat that we'd have to throw our cattle up there in the high country." She pauses. "It was a beautiful country, a lovely country. And it was a good life. We were always busy; we had something to do all the time."

Almost every Sunday there was a potluck where area families gathered to socialize, play games, and catch up on news. When Flo hosted, no one ever minded the flour-sack curtains she had made for the windows.

Flo loved the ranching life. "Truth is, I learned to ride a horse before I learned to walk." She laughs. Despite her years, her skin is as taut and deeply tanned as a woman of twenty's. "My brother put an extra set of stirrups where the back cinch goes; and I sat on a cushion behind him. Then off we'd go to cover the hills!" She laughs. "I learned ranching on a cushion behind my brother's saddle."

During the early years of World War II, before she married Frank, Flo taught school. She taught all over the state – at sawmills, at mining camps, and on the famous Bell Ranch – before she landed a job in Tularosa. When she was single, Flo loved to kick up her heels. Despite the fact that the citizens of Tularosa didn't approve, she started going to local dances. "My superintendent took me aside one day and told me that if I was going to go dancing, for goodness sakes get out of Tularosa to do it."

That's how she met Frank Martin, a local rancher she fell in love with the moment he twirled her about the open-air dance floor. Although folks frowned on that kind of thing back then, Flo and Frank went together a long time before they got married. Only single women were allowed to teach in New Mexico, so that allowed Flo to keep her job. When they eventually married, she was fired.

Willard Frank Martin grew up on a ranch in the low hills west of Mockingbird Gap. When he was eleven his father died and his mother took over the ranch. After Frank married Flo they took to improving the old ranch and starting a family. "We had a fifty-section ranch," Flo says. "You think of it: seven square miles – and that was just a small ranch. Of course the army came in and took it all away from us. . . .

"Our horse pasture fence was on the boundary line of where the bomb went off," she says and pauses. "My husband loved horses. He loved to rodeo."

In 1941 the federal government had told the Martins and about ninety other families it needed the use of their ranches for a bombing range but that they could get their homes back at the end of the war. The government offered to lease the grazing rights, but said that if the ranchers could not negotiate a fair price, their property would be condemned. "With the war going on," Flo says, "the ranchers did the patriotic thing." They abandoned their homes and their land and turned their leases over to the government.

The ill feelings began immediately. Most families were given only two weeks to evacuate and were not given funds to resettle. Cattle had to be rounded up and shipped to whatever grazing could be found. The economic and social impact of the move was devastating. Many families were forced to sell their livestock on a depressed market and find some other way to make a living. Flo and her husband at first thought they were lucky. They found pasture for their three hundred head of cattle. "But then the army didn't pay us for our lease," she says. "They didn't even pay us."

Thus began the long-simmering White Sands War.

In the government's view, ranchers had no right to argue about how much they got paid in compensation, since each owned so little property. As was common in the West, ranchers usually owned a few acres around their house and a few acres near water sources, and they ranged their cattle on large tracts of leased public land surrounding these improvements.

From the rancher's point of view they were not compensated fairly, since they had given up not only their homes but their livelihoods as well.

Luckily, Flo got a job at a local school. Because of the shortage of teachers during the war, married women were being allowed to teach.

Even though she and Frank were not allowed to use their property, they still had to pay taxes on their deeded land. Then, when the government finally offered them a lease, it was very small.

"Frank said, the hell with it," Flo says. "He went back home. He went back to the ranch."

The search for a place to test a strange, secret weapon that scientists had nicknamed "the gadget" began in 1944. Search teams scoured the West looking for just the right location. The requirements were strict: the site had to be isolated and yet close to Los Alamos, New Mexico, where the device was being created. It had to be flat, have predictably good weather, and – as a last-minute addition by the Department of the Interior – be in a location where no Indians would have to be displaced. By early 1945 they had narrowed the search to a spot on New Mexico's Jornada del Muerto.

Anyone on the Jornada during the summer of 1945 could tell that something was happening. Bulldozers and road scrapers driven by young, hardworking soldiers scoured the land. Youthful, pipe-smoking scientists were holed up at the McDonald's ranch house eight miles north of the Martin ranch.

"Those scientist boys down at the McDonald place would slip away and come up to our ranch," she says. "They liked coming there. At the time we had this one man who worked for us, old man Jim Milton." Milton knew more about horses and cattle than any other man Flo ever met. "They loved hearing how Old Man Milton could pick the winner of a horse race by studying the space between the animal's shoulder blades."

On the day the sun rose twice, Flo was in Tularosa and didn't witness the detonation, but Old Man Milton and Frank were at the ranch. "Frank told me he was asleep in a room on the south side of the house. He said it felt like his bed flew up and hit the ceiling," Flo says.

"Frank looked out. There was a bunch of horses in a pen away from the house, and those horses were running and running." The family pet, an ancient horse named Old Lum, reared up on her hind legs and threw herself wildly against the poles.

Three weeks later, on August 5, 1945, the world's second man-made nuclear explosion devastated Hiroshima. On August 9 a third bomb leveled Nagasaki.

Almost immediately following the detonation at Trinity, captured German v-2 rocket parts began arriving in New Mexico. As the war in Europe ended, Germany had developed rockets they could fire from great distances and had used them to destroy large areas of London. The United States wanted to use the captured materials in order to unlock the secret of German rocket technology. The wide-open spaces of the area were an ideal place to test-fire the new devices. The Jornada's railroad was soon crowded with hundreds of boxcars all carrying captured parts headed for the desert bombing range known as White Sands Proving Ground. In 1946 a reconstructed German v-2 fired from the range became the first rocket launched from U.S. soil.

At the same time – at the dawn of the arms race and the Cold War with the Soviet Union – the original leases the government held with the ranchers expired. Congress failed to provide any additional money, so many more ranchers simply moved back to the Jornada. What they found only infuriated them more. Many homes were in ruins. Any cattle they'd left behind had been slaughtered, and now the land was being overgrazed by army cattle.

In 1950 the Army Corps of Engineers produced ten- and twenty-year leases and told the ranchers they had to sign.

"We were getting a small payment," Flo says, "but they called all of the ranchers in and the Corps" – she pronounces the *s* – "said, 'We'll give you ten thousand dollars for your ranch.' Frank told 'em go to hell. We'd been standing-in with the army by then, but now we just went in and took our place back." So did many others.

Over the next few years, however, the other ranchers sold out, took the offered lease price, or were evicted. By now the Martins had a second child. By a combination of luck and stealth, the family continued to avoid eviction and live on the missile range. "We were able to last longer than the rest of them because we always hid out when we needed to," Flo says. Eventually the Martins, an old rancher named John Prather off over by Alamogordo, and a few others were the only holdouts. Years later Edward Abbey would base his heroic novel *Fire on the Mountain* on Prather's story.

Meanwhile, the weapons race with the USSR had reached break-neck speed. By 1952 German and American technicians had built and test-fired nearly one hundred v-2 rockets from the missile range. Scientists were testing larger and larger nuclear bombs in Nevada and on islands in the Pacific Ocean. The combination of larger nuclear weapons and rockets with long-range delivery drove the government's need for more land. The Department of the Army now demanded a large, single, integrated missile range. This range would combine the rocket-testing area with the area around the Trinity site. The missile range soon grew to be more than one hundred miles in length and included both an air base and a small city.

"When Holloman Air Force Base started we would sometimes entertain the officers," Flo says. The officers didn't mind that the Martins still occupied the land. "Frank and I knew where to trail the deer up." They knew where all the big bucks were, and Frank always made sure that each of the officers got a trophy to take back. "We were living out there and pasturing out there. But the top brass at Holloman said they didn't care."

Then, in 1954, the army expanded its New Mexico claim by having hundreds of thousands of additional acres permanently withdrawn from public and private ownership.

"I remember the day they came in," Flo says, her voice even and measured. "They came in and ordered us off. They ordered all of the cattle off. I had a military escort out of there." A day or two later she returned to pick up a few belongings. What she found embittered her. Soldiers had taken over her house. They had butchered her beef and killed her banded chickens. They had gone through all of her things. They had stolen her radio and shot her cat.

"It was at a time of drouth," she says, pronouncing it that way. "Our cattle were in terrible shape, and there wasn't any pasture anywhere that we could go to." They looked for a ranch to move to. "We didn't own anything – we had to save the cattle," she says. There was a place up near Crownpoint they could get – Flo knew the owner. "We went to the federal land bank to see if we could borrow money to buy this ranch," she says, "and they turned us down." She repeats each word, slowly, "they . . . turned . . . us . . . down! 'You have no collateral,' they told us! We *had* a ranch, but it was in the missile range and it was worthless."

They used what little money they got when they sold their cattle for the down payment on a house in Socorro. Frank started a car parts business, and Flo taught in the Socorro schools. Eventually she went back to school to earn a master's degree in education and then became principal of a Socorro elementary school.

In 1959 the military decided to extend the missile range. Ranchers living in this new area did not have to vacate; instead, the government said they could "co-use" the land. Ranchers could continue to stay on the range, but they would have to evacuate for short periods of time during testing. Unlike earlier, when it had taken exclusive use of the land, the government would now pay ranchers for the inconvenience of vacating during testing. The Martins never got this compensation because their home (as well as homes of people like Ben Cain and the McDonald brothers) was in an area the government claimed for its exclusive use.

In 1970 the government announced it would no longer pay leases to ranchers whose land was a part of the "exclusive use" area. Commissions were formed, contentious public meetings were held, and complex legal issues worked their way through the courts. The Martins and two other families were selected to represent the ranchers.

Flo and the others' claim that leasing their grazing rights was not the same thing as selling their entire livelihoods was defeated at the U.S. Court of Appeals. Assistant U.S. District Attorney James Grant, who represented the government, said, "I hope they understand it's one of the necessary functions of government to condemn the land."

"We were in court for days and days and days, and we had to hire more lawyers and blah, blah, blah, blah," Flo says, "but the truth of it is they stole our cattle, they vandalized our homes, they capped our wells, and never did pay us the value of our land."

Then, in the early hours of Wednesday, October 13, 1982, the White Sands War flared into the nation's headlines. Armed with two rifles and a pistol and driving a pickup truck loaded with water and supplies, Flo's former neighbor, eighty-one-year-old Dave McDonald, snuck back out to his old ranch house on the missile range. He and his niece Mary erected a barbed-wire fence around his house and then posted some handwritten signs: "Closed to U.S. Army. Deeded Land. No Trespassing."

The story hit the front page from coast to coast.

"A month earlier his niece and I had gone out to look the place over," Flo says. "We got permission to go in and all that kinds of stuff."

As they approached the old familiar land, they stopped to watch the Jornada's beauty. "I saw the clouds start to build over Salinas and Silver Top Mountains, and I watched them grow dark as the rain came through Mockingbird Gap. I knew the browse would freshen with that rain." What she found on her old place made all the old injuries seem fresh. Although she and Frank could no longer ranch, another rancher had been given permission and his cattle now grazed their land.

"When Dave McDonald heard that, he decided he was going back. He was just going back to his ranch.

"I was the one who . . . I contacted a reporter from the *Albuquerque Journal* I knew from a long time ago. We got Dave all geared up and ready to go, and all the statements were in the hopper all ready to hit the papers." She pauses. "You know, Dave hadn't *ever* accepted any money for his place. He just wanted his ranch back. He had always just wanted to go back home, just to go back home."

Dave McDonald had just wanted to go back to a familiar place, to a dream place, to a place that existed before the world grew dangerous. Just like Eugene Rhodes in his writing, or Captain Jack on his stage, just like Victorio armed and bloodied, or Ted Turner dreaming of the wide open range, Dave McDonald just wanted to go back, to go back home.

Once fortified at his old house he immediately began to clean the place up and tinker around fixing this and that, but of course the government couldn't let him stay, and probably he wouldn't have survived had they let him – an old man, with no cattle, no range to run them on.

Flo had arranged to have an interview with Congressman Joe Skeen on the morning Dave snuck back onto his ranch. Just as Skeen stood to signal the end of their meeting, Flo told him that an old rancher had eluded security and had returned to his ranch on the White Sands Missile Range. The congressman's jaw fell open. "What?" he stammered. Flo knew that by then it had already hit the papers.

Skeen and New Mexico's Republican senator Harrison Schmitt were up for reelection that fall. Within hours bigwigs and top brass showed up to talk to old Dave McDonald holed up at his old ranch. It was agreed that a congressional-level hearing would be held concerning the ranchers' compensation and other issues surrounding the long-standing feud. The commander of the military range promised that a committee of ranchers would be formed to give advice on measures regarding how best to protect the resources of the range. After three days of negotiations, Dave and his niece left the ranch peacefully.

During the 1983 congressional hearings that followed, Flo and other Jornada ranchers argued to no avail that they should have a co-use agreement just like the one granted to ranchers in 1959, that they should be allowed to graze their cattle on their old land, and that they should be paid to vacate during missile tests.

As a part of their winning argument, the Army Corps of Engineers claimed it had taken the Martins' land the way it did in order to save taxpayer dollars.

After Frank died in the late 1980s, Flo took over the auto parts store in Socorro. She and her daughter ran the store for several years until she finally retired.

In the 1980s and early 1990s, Flo and other area ranchers were interviewed for an oral history project conducted by the Department of Defense. The interviewers were told not to let the ranchers talk about the White Sands War.

In 1995 the missile range built a new launch complex in the forty-mile expansion north of U.S. Highway 380. "It is not our policy now to condemn land for use by the military," said an official of the Ballistic Missile Defense Organization. Ranchers at the time were skeptical. They'd heard such talk before.

Flo shakes her head. "The government figured it would simply wait until we were all dead," she says. "This is what is so tragic: so many families had such a large ranch interest, and they are now all gone . . . and all the relatives get to feudin' and fightin' and the big ranches all gone to seed."

Today, officials on the missile range are trying to preserve Dave McDonald's ranch house. They have installed a new roof and sealed the windows in order to keep the elements out.

Trinity National Historical Landmark is closed except for two days each year when public tours are given to the remote site. Coming south from the gate on U.S. 380, visitors pass the "Large Blast/Thermal Simulator," where the shock and the thermal effect of a nuclear weapon are simulated using the world's largest shock-tube. Twenty miles later the road reaches a bleak, featureless area where the Defense Nuclear Agency currently conducts tests of large above-ground explosions. Near a place called the "Permanent High Explosive Test Site" is a high, nondescript chain-link fence. The fence surrounds a low, oval-shaped area the size of two baseball fields.

No one knows how Trinity got its blasphemous name. None of the stories – that it was named after a local mine, that scientist J. Robert Oppenheimer chose the name from a John Donne poem or from lines in the *Bhagavad-Gita*, or that it was named by a Catholic soldier in order to match the religiously flavored name of a nearby railroad siding named Pope – have proven reliable. The least-romantic story seems the most likely: the name simply denoted the fact that the test bomb was to be the first of the three such nuclear devices being built.

The ground here is pale yellow: nearly white. Very little grows. Dead center inside the enclosure, a lava rock monument with a bronze plaque marks ground zero.

"My daughter Wanda and I drove out to the gate just two or three days ago," Flo says. "There's not much to see on that missile range. There's no feed on the land. It's bad out there, it's bad. Ranchers used to have soapweed for feed. We had an old chopper and you'd take your soapweed and chop it up and it's the best cow feed there is. Now there's no feed for anything but oryx."

Scholars have written of the government's role in the White Sands War: "In failing to allow the ranchers to return to their lands, in the destruction of their homes, improvements and equipment, and by constantly holding out the hope that one day, the ranchers could return to their homes, the federal government laid waste to the hopes livelihoods and dreams of almost a hundred families."

Lately some ranchers have stopped talking to Flo because they're worried she will cause problems when their co-use legislation comes up again.

"If you had ten thousand dollars extra a year coming in: gravy!" she says. "Those ranchers think I'll throw a monkey wrench in it, but I'm past doing anything like that. I mean, what's the use?" she says and then repeats it. "What's the use of fighting anymore? There's nothing left. There's nothing left. All the old-time ranchers are gone."

17. The Georgia Green Story

Out on the windswept flats of the Jornada they still tell the tale of how the God of Death once danced with the virgin bride.

It happened at Fort Craig during the bloody Victorio's War.

In one of the fort's large rooms a wedding party was in full swing. People were crowded everywhere, laughing and talking. A few children ran about. Men stood around smoking, while the women stole glances at the pretty bride dressed all in white.

The musicians had just finished a song and were tuning their violins and guitars when the door swung open.

From out of the burning desert there entered a ghastly figure dressed in black. The room fell deathly quiet. No one moved. The phantom swept across the room to the bride. He bowed ever so faintly, then took her hand. Later the members of the band said they did not know what possessed them, but they began to play.

The dark specter took the young bride in his arms and stepped to the center of the room. The crowd stood transfixed as they began a slow waltz. He twirled her gracefully, but she fell limp in his bony arms. He held her a moment and gently let her body slide slowly to the floor. He stood at the lifeless form, then stepped back to the door and disappeared into the Jornada.

Georgia Green never had a beau; she never married, but she too waltzed with the God of Death made manifest on the Jornada.

This is no folktale, but the true story of a brave and unusual woman.

When Georgia was born in 1925, one of her eyes was deformed. The pupil was much larger than normal. Nobody knew what to do. The hideous eye continued to swell. When Georgia was three years old doctors had no choice but to remove it.

She soon lost the use of her other eye as well. Some say the cancer spread, others recall an accident or a childhood illness, but by age seven Georgia was virtually sightless. For the rest of her life she could only distinguish vague patterns of darkness and light.

That same year, her family left Fort Sill, Oklahoma, for a homestead in the magnificent Magdalena Mountains at the edge of the Jornada. For the rest of her brief thirty-four years, Georgia lived without seeing the expansive desert landscape of her new home. Instead, she came to know the Jornada through the shape of sounds and the color of touch.

She spent her girlhood on a 640-acre homestead at the mouth of Water Canyon. She helped with the cooking and, because she was so mindfully aware of everything around her, kept the house immaculately clean and tidy.

On hot days she went outside and climbed down into the root cellar. There she sat in the fragrant, dark cool air peeling potatoes for the evening meal. Sometimes after supper her mother taught her Braille or her brother Bill read to her, but the best nights were when the family had a sing-along. They would sit on the porch in the deep, cool evening singing song after song while her mother played the accordion. Georgia's mother, Abbie Lucina, was her eyes, her teacher, and her strength. Guided by Abbie's strong and devoted hand, Georgia learned to face the world with confidence and skill.

One day her mother handed the accordion to Georgia. "I'll teach you," she said. Georgia took to music with a passion. Before she started school that fall at the small, rural school in Magdalena, her nimble hands could fly faster than her mother's. Soon she had memorized hundreds of songs. By the age of eleven, just before they left the homestead and moved into Socorro, she was playing at every dance in the area. She played the piano or accordion while brother Bill strummed the guitar. There wasn't a song she didn't know. Her favorite was "Home on the Range," and her sweet, powerful voice caressed the lyrics like a cool breeze from those very skies that were not cloudy all day.

The young girl – with one glass eye, the other eye always unfocused and drifting – stood out in Socorro like a sore thumb. Everyone knew her, although few knew her name. She was "the blind girl." Instead of growing timid as a result of her new status, Georgia just became more confident and self-assured.

When she was a young teenager her father drove her across the Jornada to Alamogordo, where she took classes at the New Mexico School for the Blind. When she eventually started high school back in Socorro, she excelled at her studies. Her classmates still remember her outstanding talent. She was smart. She could play the piano like a master and could sing almost as well as she could play. In high school she began teaching piano to students from around the area. On weekends she played at dances. Sunday morning found her at the church organ. She began touring the state, giving concerts at town halls and school auditoriums.

Shortly after she graduated from high school in 1942, Georgia made her most extensive concert tour. She and her mother traveled all over New Mexico in order to raise money for the new Methodist church in Socorro. Her solo concerts of popular ballads and classical music were so successful that it didn't take long before she was playing organ in a brand-new church building.

In the days before anyone every heard of gender discrimination and accessibility, the young, severely visually impaired woman enrolled at Socorro's largely male School of Mines. She studied geography, geology, English, Spanish, and economics.

A year later she enrolled at the University of New Mexico in Albuquerque. By 1945 she was working toward her degree in education, taking summer classes in Albuquerque. Georgia came home from school almost every weekend that summer. One weekend in July she was home to the Jornada for a visit. Very early on Monday morning, July 16, Georgia was awake in the dead of the night dancing her fingers over the pages of a Braille book, reading there the words that she touched. She felt the first rumble of distant thunder before anyone else awoke. One of the desert's massive monsoon storms was building above the town. Then the violent storm roared over School of Mines Mountain and crashed full force upon the town. For ten minutes the ground shook and white bolts of lightning blasted the earth. Then the universe calmed and a gentle rain fell.

Hours later, Georgia's sister Elizabeth began stirring. Then her brother-in-law Joe got up. They were going to drive her back to classes in Albuquerque. Georgia packed up her things and ate breakfast. Before dawn the three of them were in the car driving north out of town.

She had traveled the route so many times she knew each bump, every curve, and each swale by heart. She felt the cool night's air as it blew in through the partially opened window, and she smelled the sweet cottonwoods along the river.

In the next instant the world changed forever. A flash later estimated to be a thousand times brighter than the sun burned the calm desert darkness in a white, blinding light.

"What was that?" Georgia Green said.

The car swerved. Joe pulled off onto the shoulder.

When the world's first nuclear device exploded, Georgia Green was thirty-five miles northwest near the volcanic buttes at Lemitar that mark passage out of the Journey of the Dead. At that same instant, Rowena Baca's grandfather was standing outside the Owl Bar, twenty miles from the blast. Several nearby ranchers had just started their morning chores out on highlands of the northern Jornada. Rancher Frank Martin was fifteen miles south of the explosion at his old homestead. Scientists, military personnel, and other guests were watching from shelters on Compania Hill in the Stallion Range. Only a handful of people were any closer, and they were in heavily fortified observation bunkers 6.7 miles from ground zero.

Sitting in the south bunker, scientist Enrico Fermi was calm enough to conduct a simple experiment. Just before the final countdown he had ripped a sheet of paper to shreds. The instant his bunker flooded with light, he released the paper and watched the pieces float toward the ground. When the violent blast of the nuclear thunder shoved the shreds aside, he watched the displacement and then calculated that the explosion was three thousand times greater than anything previously known.

It blew out most of the windows and crumpled the barn roof at the unoccupied George McDonald ranch house two miles away. The blast and firestorm scorched everything any closer than that.

Absolutely nothing at all remained at ground zero. The detonation had vaporized the massive steel tower that had been built to hold the device. For hundreds of yards in every direction the pale yellow sand had melted to a sickly green glass.

The God of Death had been set loose to roam the Jornada del Muerto.

A red fireball filled the sky. Some scientists had feared the fireball would expand until it engulfed the entire world. Georgia got out of the car. She stood at the side of the road. A faint shock wave came first, and then she felt a force so powerful it shook the ground like an earthquake.

The worst radiation fell in an area twenty miles north where the heaviest particles from the blast came to the earth. This was world's first nuclear fallout. Several ranchers and homesteaders who were in that area that morning later died of cancer.

We still do not know the extent of Trinity's legacy.

A recent government study estimated that fallout from the first several years of nuclear weapons testing has probably caused fifteen thousand cancer-related deaths and twenty thousand nonfatal cancer cases.

A recent study by the National Academy of Sciences concluded that nuclear test sites could remain a permanent threat to life on earth. Since we do not know the ultimate effects of such contamination, the report states, and since we do not know how to prevent that contamination from spreading, the danger will remain "for tens of thousands of years."

In her time on this dangerous earth, Georgia Green led a brief but triumphant life. When people tried to be kind by telling her that it was her blindness that made her so talented, Georgia shook her head. All her blindness did, she said, was make her more sensitive to people.

Georgia Green died of liver cancer in 1960.

18. The Final Walk

I parked the van and got out. I stood before a tiny cemetery enclosed by a single strand of barbed wire. The old boneyard consisted of a dozen stone tombstones worn down to stony stubs by the wind. Secured by a rock beneath one such remnant was a single, and very faded, plastic flower.

This was to be my last hike onto the Jornada for a while, and I wanted to find the most remote area possible to explore. By the looks of things I had found it.

I hoisted the big backpack onto my shoulders. The sun was less than four hand's widths above the horizon. That meant I had two hours until sunset. My plan was to hike as far as I could during the next several hours, then set up a base camp. Tomorrow I planned to explore the Jornada beyond camp, then return to camp before I hiked back to the van the following day.

Although I kept my supplies to a minimum, my backpack was weighed down by the amount of water I carried – enough, I figured, to last the forty-eight hours I planned to be away from the van. Properly equipped I should be safe, but the water situation was critical. The problem was that to go as far as I wanted I had to carry a lot of water, and carrying the heavy water meant I would get thirstier faster.

I stood at the van, stalling. Nothing about this spot was inviting except, perhaps, its remoteness. From the forlorn little cemetery, a sparse, flat landscape of low scrub spread out in every direction. The attraction, if it can be called that, was the desolation itself. I had a naive notion that the solitude might provide me with inspiration. I wanted to think about the nature of time and history, and I hoped the remoteness would aid my contemplation.

I lingered, checking my thermometer. It was still ninety-six degrees. I shook my head and then pushed away from the van and began following a faint trace just beyond the cemetery. After a moment, I stopped to look back. The Jornada had swallowed the graveyard. With some relief, I saw a shimmer of light and located my van, minuscule against the enormity of sky and sand.

After a while I passed an old, empty house in a bare yard consisting of an even older wooden shed, the skeleton of a large truck, and sand.

I trudged slowly along. I sucked down water from a tube connected to a bottle in the big backpack. Small drops fell from the tube onto my shirt pocket where I carried my map, compass, and notebook.

Just before sunset I picked my base camp simply by unbuckling my pack and letting it slide to the sand. I could hear birds in the low shrubs as I cooked a meal and ate. The day's hot winds had finally quieted. Just after sunset, I set up my sleep netting. Then the mosquitoes came. I quickly crawled into the netting and zipped it closed. When I held my hand against the fabric, over a hundred mosquitoes swarmed in a whining cloud trying to alight on my hand.

I lay on my back and stared through the netting. At first I thought the dark band in the eastern sky was a cloud, but as the shadow moved westward I realized it was true night – a line of stark darkness sweeping its way across the Jornada sky.

Shortly after that I fell asleep. I was startled awake by the sudden, sharp crack of a nearby branch. I ignored it and fell back to sleep. A little later a sound like a vehicle woke me again. I listened until I realized it was a train, many miles away. I slept soundly then until just before dawn. When I awoke the bright pinpoint of Venus hung in the black sky.

The Mayans believed that if Venus rose as a morning star it meant that a time of death and war was coming. Venus spared no one: not the old, not the young, not the crops, not the king. Because Mayan astronomers could predict the arrival of the morning star, they were believed to possess mysterious powers, including the ability to foretell death's arrival.

For a few moments I just lay absorbed in the light of the star-filled sky. The coolness of the night had quieted the mosquitoes. Infinite silence – like time itself – engulfed the expansive Jornada, broken only by the faint, momentary call of a bird.

I got up, put on some coffee, and packed my day bag with four quarts of water, the garbage from last night's meal, a first aid kit, a map, a compass, and a pair of binoculars. I left my last three quarts of water near my tent under the backpack. Before the sun rose, I started walking.

When the sun was one hand high I heard coyotes calling from somewhere back near my base camp. It was unusual enough to hear them in daylight, and this howling was unlike any I had ever heard: a single, modulating, and clear voice ran up and down almost like speech; a few other soft whines encircled it. I was glad I had decided to carry my garbage in the day pack, but I worried that the scent on my small stove would attract them and they would tear the big pack to shreds.

I walked on, moving carefully, watching for snakes. Four different kinds of rattlesnakes inhabit the Jornada. Like a blind man tapping his cane in order to find the way, I beat the sides of the path with my walking stick. I heard something scurrying into scrub, and once I panicked at a sudden buzz until I realized it was only an insect.

Later I passed some beehives stacked near the faint trace I was following. The pleasant but incongruous hum and swirl of bees was still in my ears when the path crossed a shallow, rocky draw and then dropped down into a nearly impenetrable mass of salt cedars.

The mosquitoes found me instantly. Thick clouds of them surrounded me. Hundreds bit my face, my neck, and my arms while thousands more swarmed around my head.

Luckily, I remained calm enough to realize the danger. Rattlesnakes love such shady, bug-infested places. I knew that if I gave in and began swatting wildly at the swarms of mosquitoes, their biting and whining could easily make me panic just when I needed to be most alert for snakes. It took great concentration for me to focus on simply getting out of the thick vegetation. The deep sand made running nearly impossible. I walked forward as quickly and as carefully as I could, still slapping the brush with my stick. Mosquitoes covered every inch of my exposed skin: my arms were black with sheets of them.

I never thought I'd love the white heat of the Jornada, but stepping out of the salt cedars into that furnace was a relief. Still, several hundred mosquitoes followed me out of the bosque. A slight wind thinned their numbers, but others remained with me for a long while.

I followed a sandy path for several miles until it disappeared. I searched the area until I found a faint cattle path. Creosote bushes blocked the way, but I followed that path, plowing my way through the scrub. A quarter mile later that trace disappeared at an ancient gate through a run-down wire fence. I stopped, took a long draft of water, and looked out on the pathless and empty Jornada beyond.

In the fourth century, a handful of monks willingly sought out such solitude in the forlorn deserts of the Middle East. According to Thomas Merton, in order to survive both the physical and spiritual trials a hermit "could not dare risk attachment to his own ego, or the dangers of the ecstasy of self-will." The hermits believed there could never be a "religious state," a political state where those of a "true religion" gathered, because true union with God was something of the spirit, far beyond the mundane workings of human society. "Society was regarded by them as a shipwreck from which each single individual man had to swim for his life. . . . Obviously such a path could only be traveled by one who was very alert and sensitive to the landmarks of a trackless wilderness."

I stepped through the gate.

I set a vague course toward a distant hill and began to walk. Most of the time I slogged through sand dunes where the sensation was of walking on a slippery mud – but mud so fiery hot that it burned right through the thick soles of my hiking boots. At other times the surface became more firmly packed, but then I had to tiptoe in order to avoid walking on the delicate, living soils that stabilize the desert and eventually allow other plants to take hold of the ground and grow.

I stopped often for water.

When he heard what I was planning to do, an old-timer warned me that when you're out on the Jornada and getting dehydrated, the world gets smaller and smaller and smaller. "And then it's easy to get turned around and lost," he had said.

The sun climbed higher into the empty sky. It seemed now as if the heat was a great weight that bore down on me. I tried not to think about my thirst. I remembered that Apache children were taught to walk with their mouths closed in order to conserve moisture. I tried to keep mine shut as I trudged along.

The slope of a lifeless ridge in front of me limited the view. I moved onward, but with each step under that blazing sun I slowed down.

I stood a moment, removed the day pack, and took a long, slow drink. I swirled each sublime mouthful, savoring the feel of it. Water.

I walked on. My mind drifted from notions of the future to a litany of ghosts from my past.

By noon I had used only a fourth of my water, but the hottest part of the day was still ahead of me. I was going to need every bit of my remaining water to get back to base camp.

I stood numbly for several minutes idly toying with my compass and map before I put them away and simply looked around. Each tiny dry *thing* grew in its own isolation, surrounded by a half acre of sun-baked sand. Yellow rock stood against a turquoise sky. Sun and mountain and plain and sky spread spectacular and huge in every direction. Everywhere were multitudes of shapes, emotions, light, and shadow.

To be alive. To stand in mute witness to an instant of time in a universe that was as indifferent to my hopes as it was to my sorrows and my crimes.

I turned my attention back to my map, compass, and water. I looked at the high angle of the sun and calculated the afternoon's walk. I imagined how good it would feel to be sitting in the shade of my tent back at base camp.

I took one last swallow, replaced the bottle in my day pack, shouldered the pack, and began the long walk back.

The heat drilled through the bones of my skull. I tried to conserve water by taking only a mouthful at a time and then swishing it around a long while before swallowing it.

My legs moved slowly and methodically, as if on a forced march. My mind dulled. I watched the sharp outline of my own shadow as it walked beside me. A large horned lizard suddenly appeared in front of me, but it barely registered on my consciousness. I was no different from sand and rock. I had become a part of the Jornada itself.

I trudged through the afternoon, footstep following footstep. To break the tedium and exhaustion, I began playing a mental game counting the number of steps I took for each breath. Six. Then five. Three.

"This is where I had some water on the way in," I said.

I stopped. Had I spoken the words out loud? I didn't know. I tried to clear my head. A dull and deep pain gripped my back. The thought idly occurred to me that death was no big deal. If I stopped fearing my own death, then I no longer needed the courage to face it.

Then I saw the trace. A fragment of an ancient road, no more than a pair of alkali-washed ruts, appeared at my side, ran for twenty yards, and then vanished in the sand. I stood and stared blankly at the fragment. Then, like other human beings throughout time who had stood here weary from their journey, I thought simply: "There. Go that way."

I walked on, disheartened now even by thoughts of reaching base camp. There would be no shade at camp, and I still faced the bosque and its mosquitoes. The pain in my back was much worse and had spread to my left leg. My tongue ached for water. Everything had turned to suffering.

As if they were tiny grains of rice, my past and my future were gobbled up.

I reached the fence at midafternoon and followed it to the ancient gate. Zombie-like I stepped through and began following the faint trail back toward my base camp.

I plunged into the salt cedars. The sudden, saw-blade whine of thousands of mosquitoes rang in my ears, and just beyond them, the sound of thousands more and millions more beyond, yet fainter and fainter: the world was nothing but the blackness of their wailing.

I ran wildly, fighting my way through the thick broom-bristled curtain of salt cedar. I ran blindly, insanely, desperately, until finally I broke out of the choking swarm and struggled onto the burning sand.

Although I saw the older-model white pickup truck, it took me a long moment to understand that it was real. I watched it slowly pull away from a beehive and roll to a stop not far from me.

A round-faced, deeply tanned man leaned out the window. These are the words he spoke: "You must have been putting one foot right in front of the other to have reached here today. You want a ride somewhere?"

I stumbled forward and fell into the front seat. I fumbled for the last of my water and drank the final hot splash.

He hadn't started to drive yet, but was looking at me carefully. From the expression on his face, I must have looked pretty bad.

I was thankful when he offered me his water and started to talk.

He was a beekeeper. These hives were his. "It's all I've ever done," he said. He wore a long-sleeved pale blue dress shirt, worn jeans, and a black felt cowboy hat. The hat was stained with reddish yellow dust that looked more like pollen than desert dirt. "See those hives over there?" he nodded to a large scattering of white hive boxes on the edge of a sandy place, "I'd say there's only about 10 percent of them still have bees." His voice was soft, with an accent I couldn't quite recall. "Bee mites. They've nearly wiped me out. I'm forty-four, and now I have to find other work. There's chemicals you can use to ease the problem, but I don't like using chemicals." I sat next to him in a heap as he talked. "A professor up in Michigan thinks the mites have a reaction to mesquite, so I've been burning a lot of mesquite in my smokers, but I don't know – it's gotten pretty bad," he said.

A half mile before we reached my base camp he stopped the truck in order to point out a large pile of droppings. "Oryx," he said. "They're everywhere on this part of the Jornada."

I mentioned the noise I heard the night before. He nodded once. "Mountain lions are nocturnal around here because of the heat," he said matter-of-factly. "They're dangerous, all right, but I think they should be allowed to roam free on the Jornada so people know what the West was really like . . ."

When we reached my base camp, he was reluctant to let me go. He kept asking if I wanted a ride back to my van. He jotted down his phone number and handed me the slip of paper. Twice he told me to call him if he could help me again.

I wanted to find the right words to thank him, but all I could do was shake his hand and croak out a good-bye.

He nodded his head and then slowly drove away, the truck stirring up small clouds of dust as it moved.

For the rest of the afternoon I just sat in the meager shade of my tent. I nibbled on some peanuts, and when I felt the heat begin to ease I cooked and ate a meal. Just before sundown, I felt the sting of the evening's first mosquito. I stumbled into my netting and collapsed onto my sleeping mat.

The blessed, cooling shade of dusk fell. Nothing moved – not the desert, not the air, nor, least of all, my body upon the earth.

Time is not an awareness of the future; nor is it a dream about the path we have taken in our lives. Time is always and simply this precise point on our voyage. It is the earth navel, the nan sipu from which, in the singularity of our birth, we rose, and to which, in the unity of our death, we all return. When, through the blindness of our pride or the mass hysteria of war, we fail to see the unity of our journey, we fight only ourselves to death.

Then came night. Stars filled the empty bowl of blackness, wheeling above me, rising and setting, intent on a stately mission not yet needful to declare.

19. Joe

All life trembles in the brief, brilliant light of existence. Whether in horror or in beauty, whether in tragedy or in triumph, each life story from the Journey of the Dead reminds us how very solitary is our own journey through time. Though their bones have long since turned to dust, and their stone markings have faded under the relentless sun, ancient people understood that time was but the instant we occupy between twin circles of eternity. So too are all the tales from the Jornada but scratched glyphs on the surface of human history.

I have come to a small, flat building on a dusty street in Truth or Consequences, hoping that one more story might provide a final lesson about the twin mysteries of time and timelessness. I have come to the apartment of ninety-three-year-old Joe Turner – no relation to Ted – who is the Jornada's oldest living cowboy. He was twenty-one when he rode horseback from Oklahoma to the Jornada in 1930. He lived out on the Jornada's open range from then until just a few months ago when his kids finally decided he had to move into town.

I knock on the screen door, wait, and knock again, harder.

A voice booms from inside, "Hello!" A moment later the screen door opens and a wiry, lean older man with glasses stands before me. He wears a western-style dress shirt and stovepipe-straight blue jeans. He is as tall and as skinny as a beanpole.

Joe invites me in. The apartment's living room is sparsely decorated. An ancient wooden trunk sits against a wall. Above it are three sketches of horses. Toward the kitchen is an ink portrait of a man in a cowboy hat sipping from a gourd-like cup. Near the trunk is a knick-knack stand, its shelves full of snapshots of kids, babies, loved ones, and horses.

Joe

Joe sits in a stuffed chair at the end of a worn couch. Next to his chair is a table with a lamp. The base of the lamp is a gaudy sculpture of a porcelain cowboy riding a bucking porcelain horse.

Although his hearing is poor, Joe is eager to answer my questions.

He came from a large family. He was born in 1908 and grew up across the Red River from Marietta, Oklahoma. "One of the first things I remember was one day when me and my dad went to town on business," he says. His father stopped to talk to a man outside the store. "The man had just set down a can of trash and a damn mouse jumped out of that can and went right up my leg! And I'm telling you, I never bucked so hard and high in all my life." He pauses and laughs. "Gul dang, I can *still* feel him scratching going up my leg! Gul-dang almighty!"

The father of six uses "gul dang" in most conversations, but anytime things get a bit exciting or rowdy it becomes "goddam." Born with cleft palate, he doesn't wear a mustache like Gene Rhodes did to cover the defect, and the scar where his upper lip had been crudely sewn together forms a jagged tear.

Joe Turner knew the Wild Man, and he's been around long enough to remember trading with the Mescalero Apaches. He played guitar at the dances up Rhodes Canyon where Flo met her husband-to-be Frank Martin, and he's known Ben Cain since Ben was "knee high to a puddle-duck." On the morning Trinity lit up the sky Joe was twenty miles away living at a cow camp on the Armendaris. Later he moved to Engle, where for years he ran a combination gas station, post office, store, and bar.

Joe nods to one of the horse portraits that hangs over the old, handcrafted trunk.

"I was a good rider, but anybody that rides a bronc gets bucked off once in a while. A man may say he didn't, but he's just full of bull. Ole Buck Smith was a good bronc rider, but by golly even he'd get bucked off once in a while."

After arriving in New Mexico in 1930, Joe and his brother prowled for cattle working for a rancher just west of the river. Joe then returned briefly to Texas to marry the love of his life, Grace Langford. He was twenty-three and she was seventeen.

Grace loved sports. The cowboys didn't like it much, but she could beat any one of them in a footrace. Her school record for making free throws stood for years. Joe was a lucky man to have found a woman like Grace. Everyone liked her; she never had an enemy her entire life.

They packed up a few things in a trunk and moved to New Mexico. He went back to cowboying on the west side of the river. Their first child, a girl, died in infancy, but by the time the first set of twins "were but little tid-bits of kids" Joe was working on the Armendaris for the Diamond A, the outfit that had leased Pedro's old grant from the Victorio Land and Cattle Company.

The first twins were only two when Grace had her *second* set of twins. A year later she had another girl. For a few years this family of seven moved from one isolated cow camp to another on the sprawling ranch, until Grace's illness made it necessary for them to quit the cowboying life.

Someone knocks at the screen door. Joe gets up out of his chair and moves slowly toward the door. He opens the screen, and an elderly man steps in.

"Hey, Joe, how you doing, you old bugger?" the man says.

"Oh my goddam!" Joe says. "Walter, I ought to kick your butt!"

"Well, you ain't big enough yet," Walter says.

"Gul dang, Walter Slayter," Joe says. "It's been a while."

"Twenty years or better," Walter says. He introduces himself to me and explains that he first met Joe in 1945. Walter had been a young kid and had hired on at the Diamond A. Joe was in his late thirties by then.

"You been out on that outfit lately?" Joe asks. "Ted Turner about shoot you if you get out there. He bought the whole damn country. He's shipped them old buffalo in; he's got some up near Deep Well, but there's none around Engle."

The two men talk, sharing stories of old times, friends, and families. Joe asks if Walter is still working for that ranch outfit in Hawaii. Walter tells Joe that he has finally retired.

Joe says, "Hell, Walter, you was retired all the time."

Walter laughs, "Well, I've been a-working like hell."

Joe pats his stomach. "I can tell," he says. "Plenty of work in bellying up to a table." Joe grins. "I remember the first time I ever saw you. We were down at Lava Camp: you rode an ole sorrel horse. We made a lot of drives together."

"You're damn right we made a lot of drives," Walter says. "You remember following ole Leland around? Damn he made you drive."

The fall cattle drive involved weeks and weeks of hard work. From every nook and cranny of the Jornada, cowboys gathered cattle and herded them toward the railroad at Engle.

Rounding up cattle worked something like casting a big net. Hours before daylight the cowboys spread out in order to cover a wide area. To avoid the heat, they'd start to gather cattle before they could see. Each day the herd grew larger as it slowly made its way toward Engle. The men wore no special gear – no chaps or gun belts. They had a cook wagon and often cooked sourdough biscuits in a Dutch oven over a campfire. Sometimes they just had canned goods for supper.

They would brand in the spring and ship in the fall. When winter came, Joe's job was to see that the cattle had plenty of cottonseed cake to eat. The cakes helped the cattle through the winter and were more economical than alfalfa.

Joe used an old team of mules and a wagon to deliver the feed. "We'd take about twenty sacks of cake and the cattle'd hear that wagon and you'd yell and they'd come," Joe says, "but you'd have to hurry and get around so you wouldn't be feeding some of them two or three times." In winter there would be a breed sale, where you could buy bulls and maybe some calves to raise with the bulls.

Walter says something about one memorable breed sale, but he has to repeat it several times before Joe can hear him.

Joe shakes his head. "I had two hearing aids and they both broke down at the same time. My son Ronnie is trying to get them fixed. In the meantime I can't hear myself fart."

Walter laughs, "Well, maybe that's a good thing . . ."

"Yeah, but the smeller's working just fine."

The conversation drifts to mutual friends and acquaintances who have passed away. After a while, Walter stands up. "Well, I got to see some more people," he says, "and I got to leave in the morning to get back to Hawaii."

"You gotta get back to work, huh?"

Walter roars. "Hell yeah – goddam," he says, "I gotta belly up to that table again. That's hard work." He steps to the door. "By god Joe, I'm glad to see you're in hell of good health."

"I'm doing all right."

"As long as you keep the old belly full," Walter says. "Goddam that's the main thing."

Joe says, "I get these Meals on Wheels."

"They feed you pretty good groceries?"

Joe says nothing.

Walter asks, "If they's a wagon cook, you'd fire them?"

"Damn right I would," Joe says.

Walter shakes the old cowboy's hand. "Joe, adiós!" he says. "I'll be back probably next year and have a little more time. I'd like to talk to you all day."

"We could tell some pretty big lies then," Joe says. He stands at the door and watches Walter get in his car and drive away. He turns back to the living room.

"Walter Slayter!" he says. "Walter worked with me at Deep Well Camp a while. He got married and had him some kids. It's been a long time. He's got white-headed since I saw him last. Gul-dang I didn't even ask him about his kids!"

In 1945, the year Walter started riding with him, Joe and Grace lived with their five children in a two-room adobe at Deep Well, not far from the lava malpais. At that place you can see from the towering San Andres to the dark Oscuras, everywhere the grandeur of range upon majestic range rising from the pale yellow plain.

"What did you do to survive the winter way out there?" I ask.

"You just buckled your coat up a little more and took it," Joe said. "We usually had kept three grain horses in the winter. We didn't keep any grass horses – we'd turn all of them out to pastures." He pauses. "We'd ride and ride and ride them grain horses."

When Joe was out on a drive, Grace had to handle things by herself. Despite her growing illness, she took care of the kids and tried not to worry about Joe. One summer, lightning killed two men. One of the men was a goat herder, but the other was a cowboy on horseback.

In one room of the adobe was a sink and a washbasin. Grace hauled water from the well and heated it up on the stove. She would bathe the kids, dry them with towels made from flour sacks, and then use the remaining hot water for washing clothes. The food they ate changed depending on the season. There was beef, of course, and deer meat, jerked or fresh. They bought potatoes at Engle, and Grace made pies from canned apples. Vinegar cobbler was everyone's favorite desert.

By 1945 the army was everywhere on the northern Jornada. Joe remembers the day an army plane crashed this side of the mountains. "It barely made it over the gap and then belly landed on the flats close to where we lived. These boys came and cleaned up the mess." Joe chuckles. "You know those army boys always gave our children Life Savers – that's the kind of thing you remember for a lifetime."

Joe says he was looking right at it when the bomb went off. "I was out at Deep Well. I was up early – and I happened to be looking right out the door. There was a flash. There was a big red ball. I hollered at Grace, I says: 'Get up! The sun's coming up before it should!' I had an idea it was something for the war."

By the summer of 1945 Grace's health had worsened. Her high blood pressure and kidney problems kept her sick most of the time. With five children under the age of seven, Joe knew he'd have to find a different way to provide for his family.

In 1946 they scraped together enough to buy a run-down, ramshackle place in Engle, where Joe started a store. Grace was bedridden by then and would live for seven more rough years. The rule of thumb on the Jornada was that you did your own doctoring and relied on your neighbors' help in the hardest of times. What little professional care she could find was expensive, and it was hard to get medical help living so far from anywhere. "They operated on her twice," Joe says of those difficult years. "Big operations." The second time they told her she had a fifty-fifty chance. "She took the chance but she didn't pull through," he says simply. She died in 1953. "The oldest kids were eleven," he says.

The Engle house had no electricity and no water, but since he'd worked so long for the Diamond A they let him tap into their water.

"It was a nice place to live, but I would never have started the store if my wife hadn't been sick. I couldn't take care of her and the kids and work on that ranch. But I could take care of her with the store.

"I made a living. I did everything. I had a bar and I sold liquor. I had a gas station and a little post office. They'd pay me forty bucks a month for that. I got a job taking care of the airport – there was an airport just east of Engle – I got a hundred dollars a month out of that. I worked like heck. It didn't bother me then to work that hard."

After Grace died the relatives wanted to split up the kids, but Joe wouldn't let it happen. "I raised them kids by myself," Joe says. "I just did it. We stayed together. It was all right raising them myself. I coulda used a bit more help, but it was all right – they got along real good, you know." He was a stern disciplinarian, and the kids didn't get away with much. If he told them to do something, he expected it to be done. But then his children had a lot of country to run around in, and Joe pretty much let them roam everywhere.

The gas station consisted of a single hand-operated pump. "You pumped the gas into a glass ball and then it gravity-fed the cars. I sold cheese, eggs, bread, and canned goods. The store was in a twelve-by-twelve-foot room, same size as the bar."

Some nights he kept the bar open until two or three in the morning. A lot of cattle were still being shipped out of Engle, and the kerosene-lit place attracted thirsty cowboys and other men. Joe never drank, and he never let the kids come in the bar. He ran the bar like he raised his children. When things got to the point of fisticuffs, he would order the men outside to fight.

Sunday mornings Joe had a preacher at the place. "People on the train always gave old Preacher Lewis a free ride. Every Sunday he came to Engle. He never charged for his preaching. He'd come and stay all night with us. I'd have my kids there and he'd preach right out on my porch. My oldest son, he'd take up a collection for him, you know: pass the plate. Old Preacher Lewis would get that money and he'd come into the store and use it to buy candy for the kids. He'd say, 'Take the money from me – I don't need any money.' " Joe pauses. "He was a real good guy."

Joe liked living on the high and dry Jornada. It was a healthy place for the kids. Despite the hardships, it was a good life. "If I die tomorrow, I will not have missed much," he says. That much is certain, Joe will not have missed much. He has spent a lifetime on an open wilderness, where from every direction the eternity of the desert beckons. His life on the Jornada has been full and rich. Living here meant he couldn't hide from the harshness of the world. He has faced many challenges, but whenever he needed to act, he did so without hesitation or doubt. He has taken whatever life has handed him, and he has triumphed.

Oh sure, he had to watch out for rattlesnakes, and then too he always had to worry about the kids and mountain lions. One day, for example, a cowboy and his dogs treed a big cat in the Fra Cristobels. "That old cowboy killed it with a single shot," Joe says. "The lion weighed 775 pounds and was seven feet, seven inches from tip to tip."

Joe thinks he might have a snapshot of that record lion. He stands up from the chair and walks to the old trunk. "This box right here a carpenter from Texas built in 1934," he says. "The whole thing cost me ten dollars. The man who built it was the best carpenter I'd ever seen. He told me to go down to this lumberyard and he told me what lumber to get. He sawed it and there wasn't a chip left over. He said, 'You should a seen my dad! He was a *real* carpenter. Everything he built was perfect.'"

"I don't want to take up too much of your time," I say.

"Hell, that's about all I got left is time," he says.

He lifts the top of the old trunk. Inside are a few boxes of photographs and a blanket. He takes out the top box and begins to shuffle through the images.

"Ole Joe Graham," he says, pausing at one. "He used to play the fiddle, he played the violin too – he drank a lot, but he was a good friend of mine."

He flips quickly past some of the images, and pauses at others. "That's my mother and my dad when they got married. Nineteen hundred I think it was. She was seventeen and he was thirty-four."

Other pictures are more recent. "I think those are great-grandkids," he says of one photo. "Hell, I've got twelve or thirteen. I got so many, I can't remember."

He falls silent. "Snapshots," he says.

He comes to an old black-and-white picture of several cowboys near a wooden wagon. "That's ole Skinny Davis," he says, pointing. "That's been a long time ago. I don't know who all these guys are, but that's the chuck wagon out at Deep Well. We were on to work." He stops, then speaks as if it were yesterday. "That's me on old Canary. Best horse I ever rode. He could do it all. When the horse got old, I gave him to my grandkids, but he took sand colic and he never could get over it." He pauses. "He was about fifteen years old then. Good horse, boy, that was a good horse . . ."

The next photograph stops him short. It is an old black-and-white photograph of little girls.

"Haa-ha damn!" he says, laughing.

"Who do you see?" I ask.

"A bunch of silly gals," he says with a soft laugh. He is still smiling when he adds, "Time sure does pass. Yes it does."

Acknowledgments

It would have been impossible to complete a project of this scope and duration without the assistance of many individuals, organizations, and foundations.

I wish to thank Centrum Arts for a residency that provided uninterrupted time to begin writing this book, and the Ragdale Foundation for a residency that allowed me the solitude to complete it. I am deeply grateful to both institutions for their support.

First and foremost among the individuals who have aided me are Virgil Lueth and Lisa Peters, whose generosity, optimistic outlook, and decades-long friendship far exceeds what I can ever offer in return. My New Mexico research assistant, Tony Freeman, spent countless hours in a number of libraries to locate several items that were otherwise unavailable to me. Without his intelligent assistance, tireless work, and uncomplaining help this book would not have been written.

I have been very fortunate to have several kind, generous, hardworking, helpful, and articulate people who provided me with much insight about life on the Jornada. Thomas Waddell patiently answered numerous questions, provided me with documents, books, contacts, and other sources for information, and was helpful and pleasant, despite my constant queries. In addition to providing me with critical information over the course of the creation of this book, Jim Eckles spent a day with me that began at 5 a.m. with a 250-mile circuit of White Sands Missile Range and ended with a delightful evening of pizza and conversation at his home with Jim and his wife, Debbie Edwards. Likewise, Flo Martin, Rowena Baca, Ben and Jane Cain, and Joe Turner opened their homes to me as if I had been kin. Without them there would have been no tales of the Jornada. I am grateful too for Mollie and Philip Freeman, who, as has been the case for over thirty years, accepted me into their New Mexico home as if I were their son.

Without the kindness of Butch Hammack, a fresh set of human bones might well have been added to the Jornada's artifacts. Bob Eveleth, senior mining engineer of the New Mexico Bureau of Mines, aided me on numerous occasions over the length of the project. Karl Laumbach spent the final hot hours of a Friday patiently answering my many questions about his remarkable research in the Southwest, while Florence Wesner Martin's cookies, iced tea, and long hours of interviews were invaluable. Dale and Alma Green of Socorro provided important background information on a variety of subjects. Thanks too to Richard Knezel, who stopped working on his tractor and instead spent the coolest working hours of the morning chatting with me about his modern-day homestead cabin on the Jornada; and to Hazel and Wayne Johnson, of Cutter, who served me the finest iced tea in the world while we talked about life on the Jornada. He may not know it, but Dane Liebel provided crucial inspiration for this project by his openheartedness as well as his enthusiasm for the Jornada. I am grateful as well for John Boye's companionship and enthusiasm while accompanying me to a number of remote sites in southern New Mexico.

My assistants Andrew Boye and Ben Boye were an important part of this project. Andrew's organizational assistance was an invaluable help for this complex and complicated project. More important was his never-faltering encouragement and good humor, which provided much inspiration. Likewise, Ben's technical help as well as his insightful questions and curiosity often stimulated my thinking and allowed me to see old issues in a new light. As always, without Linda Wacholder this project would never have been completed.

W. Clark Whitehorn first suggested this book one day over Mexican food in Lincoln, Nebraska. His initial encouragement and ongoing support for my work are deeply appreciated. I wish also to thank Gary Dunham for his patience and support, and Gretchen Albers for hers.

Poet Mike O'Connor and my friends Ted Senecal and Niels Holm provided the context of hope, the atmosphere of mindfulness, and the philosophical freedom I needed during the project's critical, earliest hours. Likewise, this book owes its existence to the insight and friendship of master photographer and bodhisattva Steven R. Johnson.

In addition to the friendship and help I got from naturalist Dan Perry at Bosque del Apache National Wildlife Refuge, Deputy Refuge Manager Gary Montoya, Mike Oldham, and Russ Scott were also invaluable.

I am particularly indebted to many people at the Rio Grande Historical Collection at New Mexico State University Library. These include Director Dr. Austin Hoover, Marah DeMeule, Linda Blazer, Bill Boehm, and Special Collections Librarian Cheryl Wilson. Likewise, I am grateful for the friendly staff at New Mexico Institute of Mining and Technology Library, who not only led me to many hidden archival materials but also tolerated several long-distance phone requests over the course of several years. Several people at the impressive and beautiful New Mexico Farm and Ranch Heritage Museum in Las Cruces provided me with research materials and valuable insights into ranch life on the Jornada. These included Director Mac R. Harris, Jane O'Cain, Robert L. Hart, Toni S. Laumbach.

A number of research specialists and scientists associated with the Jornada Experimental Range, the Long Term Ecological Research Program, and the U.S. Department of Agriculture took a great deal of their time over the course of several years to patiently walk this nonspecialist through the finer points of range management and other technical issues. Thanks especially to Eric Havstad, Ed Fredrickson, Al Rango, and Dean Anderson.

The staff at the Samuel Read Hall Library at Vermont's Lyndon State College was invaluable for all phases of my work, and I am especially thankful for the kindness shown me by Interlibrary Loan Specialist Phyllis Green. Thanks to Lisa VonKann and Lorna Higgs, co-directors of the beautiful St. Johnsbury Athenaeum, for use of the Writer's Room during the final editing of the manuscript. I owe a very special thanks to Yvonne Oakes at the Museum of New Mexico in Santa Fe, whose help opened many doors in the early phases of my research. In addition, I received generous help from Jeremy R. Kulisheck and Tim Seaman of Archaeological Records Management and from Tomás Jaehn, Hazel Romero, and Dedie Snow of the Palace of Governors.

Acknowledgments

A variety of people from all walks of life helped me by providing support, information, encouragement, or research assistance. These kind people include Ronnie Turner of Truth or Consequences, New Mexico; Mimi Wilson of Atlanta, Georgia; Joe Truett of Las Cruces; Rachael Armstrong and Steve Bobinski at the New Mexico Institute of Mining and Technology; Illene Renfro of the rare books archives at the University of New Mexico; John Williams, superintendent of the New Mexico School for the Visually Handicapped; Harry C. Richardson of Socorro; Gloria Richardson of Dallas; Emily Jojola and Jerry Howard at the Socorro County Sheriff's Office; Annette Boulden at the Socorro County Manager's Office; Jack Wilson of Las Cruces; Richard and Nancy Williams of Lampasas, Texas; Guy McDonald of Las Cruces; Jim McDonald of Carizozo, New Mexico; Ann Wellborn of Truth or Consequences; George Prisher of Aleman; Alan Ables, public affairs officer for the U.S. Department of Interior Bureau of Land Management in Las Cruces; Barb DuBois of the Socorro County Historical Society; Sherry Fletcher, assistant superintendent of Truth or Consequences Municipal Schools; Bill O'Connell of Norman, Oklahoma; and the Sitting Frog Zendo of Port Townsend, Washington.

I wish also to thank writers Daris Miller, Rolf Sinclair, and Thomas Steele, S.J., for their encouragement and advice. Finally, I wish to thank author Colin Fletcher, who encouraged me to pursue this project. I am grateful that his words have been a lifelong source of inspiration.

Notes

1. TRAVELING THE CAMINO U.S. 380

Much of the information about the climate of the Jornada and the Chihuahuan Desert is from "A Laboratory without Walls" and from Greenland and
Anderson, "Jornada Basin."

Information about Carthage can be found in Sherman and Sherman, *Ghost
Towns and Mining Camps of New Mexico*, 32.

Information about the area around Stallion Gate is from "The Road to
Stallion" and from my tour of the area with Jim Eckles.

2. THE WILD MAN

Eyewitness accounts of the Wild Man are from interviews I conducted in 2000
and 2001 and from Ackerley et al., *Ranching in the Tularosa Basin*.

Information about the posse and some of the descriptions of the Wild Man
are from Ernenwein, "Wild Man of the San Andres," 275–79.

The extended quote is from Underhill, *Mysticism*, 254.

Information about the Buddhist monks is from Bhikkhu, "Hunting and
Gathering the Dharma," 78.

3. ELEMENTS

Additional information about prairie dogs comes from my 2001 interview
with Ed Fredrickson, senior researcher, U.S. Department of Agriculture
Jornada Experimental Range. Fredrickson understands the desperation of
twentieth-century ranchers who worked to eliminate the prairie dogs: "World
War I is where the elimination of the prairie dog really started. We had
ranchers here who were fighting that war at home. We needed leather, we
needed meat, we needed fat, so ranchers were on the front line here. It was a
very noble effort."

Information about the depletion of the black grama grass is taken from my
interview with Al Rango, principal investigator with the U.S. Long Term

Ecological Research Network (LTER). LTER was formed in 1980 by the National Science Foundation in order to support research on ecological phenomena. Because of its isolation and unique features, the Jornada is one of several LTER research sites worldwide. Information on LTER can be found at http://lternet.edu/.

The factors contributing to changes in the grasslands of the Jornada were first outlined in Buffington and Herbel, "Vegetational Changes on a Semidesert Grassland Range."

"potentially represents a permanent loss in the productive capacity of the biosphere on which all life depends" is from Buffington and Herbel, "Biological Feedbacks in Global Desertification," 1047.

Additional information is from Fredrickson et al., "Perspectives on Desertification."

The information regarding mineral wealth on the malpais is from Stoeser, Senterfit, and Zelten, *Mineral Resources of the Little Black Peak and Carrizozo Lava Flow Wilderness Study Areas.*

That Oñate's colony named Muerto Arroyo is from Hammond and Rey, *Narratives of the Coronado Expedition,* 317.

5. GLYPH TIME

The quote from the Zuni man is from Young, "Images of Power," 187.

The ideas of John S. Dunne are from his *Time and Myth,* 39–41.

Augustine's views on time can be found in his *Confessions,* 11.13 and 11.16, and in *Expositions on the Book of Psalms,* 102.27.

Regarding the Hopis' symbol for the God of Death see Patterson, *Field Guide to Rock Art Symbols,* 105.

The quote regarding the significance of spirals is from Young, "Images of Power," 136.

"What occurred . . . prior to emergence is sacred" is from A. Ortiz, *The Tewa World,* 15.

"An earth navel is like an airport" is from A. Ortiz, *The Tewa World,* 24.

See Riley, *Rio del Norte,* 35–37, for information about the Orogrande cave.

For more on the Folsom shrine see Riley, *Rio Del Norte,* 44.

Sources on the earliest humans include Kirkpatrick and Duran, "Prehistoric Peoples"; Riley, *Rio del Norte*; Waldman, *Atlas of the North American Indian*; Marshall and Walt, *Rio Abajo*; Irwin-Williams, *The Oshara Tradition*; and Irwin-Williams, "Picosa."

For more on Mockingbird Gap see R. H. Weber and Agogino, "Mockingbird Gap Paleoindian Site."

For information about climate change, the sequence of human occupation, and mobility of the Jornada natives see Whalen, *Turquoise Ridge*.

Some material on Folsom is from Marshall and Walt, *Rio Abajo*.

Additional information about the places I visited with Dan is from Marshall and Walt, *Rio Abajo*.

Some of the information on corn is from "Native American History of Corn."

Ed Ladd and Leigh Jenkins are quoted in Widdison, *The Anasazi*, 35, 44.

6. ARTIFACTS

Some information about the Camino Real is from Welsh and Marshall, *El Camino Real de Tierra Adentro*.

Much of the information on de Vaca comes from Sauer, *Sixteenth Century North America*, 17–27.

The quotes of de Vaca and the other survivors are from Convey, *Cabeza de Vaca's Adventures*.

The information regarding Catholic missionaries reaping souls for religion, is from Simmons, *The Last Conquistador*, 61.

The Jornada proper is between 2,600 and 2,800 square miles. Connecticut is 4,845 square miles.

Most information regarding de Niza is from Hallenbeck, *The Journey of Fray Marcos de Niza*; the quote is from page xxvi.

Fredrerick Hodge's quote about Coronado's expedition is found in Castañeda, *The Journey of Coronado*, xix.

Additional information on Coronado is from Sauer, *Sixteenth Century North America*, 141–50.

"the captain . . . found four large villages . . ." is from Castañeda, *The Journey of Coronado*, 198.

"the Franciscans were elated by what they found" is from Simmons, *The Last Conquistador*, 24.

For the description of Coronado's caravan see Castañeda, *The Journey of Coronado*, xix.

The eyewitness quote about the defeated Coronado is from Castañeda, *The Journey of Coronado*, xxi.

Marshall's sentiments are from Welsh and Marshall, *El Camino Real de Tierra Adentro*.

For more information regarding the Franciscan missionaries' unnamed expedition to the gates of the Jornada, see Castañeda, *The Journey of Coronado*, 33, and *History of Sierra County*, 7.

The quotes about what the soldiers and missionaries saw are from Simmons, *The Last Conquistador*, 50–53.

What the soldiers saw is from Silverberg, *Pueblo Revolt*, 34.

The biographical sketch of Espejo is based on information from Hammond and Rey, *Narratives of the Coronado Expedition*, 17–19, and Simmons, *The Last Conquistador*, 55–56.

The quotes from Espejo are taken from Silverberg, *Pueblo Revolt*, 34-38.

The quote from the soldier regarding Espejo's killing of Indians is found in Silverberg, *Pueblo Revolt*, 36.

The quote about de Sosa is from Silverberg, *Pueblo Revolt*, 40.

The little-known expedition of Mexicans to follow de Sosa included Francisco Leyva de Bonilla and Antonio Gutierrez de Humana. Further information can be found in Moorhead, *New Mexico's Royal Road*, 7.

The quotes regarding the heritages of Oñate and his wife are from Silverberg, *Pueblo Revolt*, 42.

The official instructions to Oñate are taken from Simmons, *The Last Conquistador*, 61.

The quote about the benefits of becoming a don is from Simmons, *The Last Conquistador*, 65.

The Merton quote is from *The Wisdom of the Desert*, 7–8.

The quote describing the caravan is from Simmons, *The Last Conquistador*, 96–97.

That while north of Juarez Oñate used "a heavily used Indian trail" is from Simmons, *The Last Conquistador*, 101.

That they traveled five to ten miles day is from Silverberg, *Pueblo Revolt*, 45.

"We all fared badly from thirst" is from Simmons, *The Last Conquistador*, 103.

"On this day when a dog appeared . . ." is from Hammond and Rey, *Don Juan de Oñate: Colonizer of New Mexico*, 2:117.

"The clean, ozone-scented air . . ." is from Simmons, *The Last Conquistador*, 106.

The exact route Oñate took from Elephant Butte northward has been disputed. Most likely Oñate himself misidentified his location. Oñate says he arrived at Qualacu on May 28 but only *later* passed places such as Valverde, which are south of Qualacu. This sequence of landmarks suggests that the first inhabitants he met, on May 28, were from San Pascual or another nearby pueblo, not Qualacu. See Moorhead, *New Mexico's Royal Road*, 22–23, and Marshall and Walt, *Rio Abajo*, 250.

The quote on Oñate's disillusionment is from Silverberg, *Pueblo Revolt*, 65.

7. ROWENA

That women "have more love for the land" is from Hernandez, "The U.S. Southwest," 120.

Some of the general information about travel on the Camino was gathered from Moorhead, *New Mexico's Royal Road*; Espinosa and Bennett, "Don Diego de Vargas"; Hackett and Shelby, *Revolt of the Pueblo Indians*, 1:130-31, 212–13; and Bolton, *The Spanish Borderland*.

The "untold agony" that women faced is from Perez de Villagra's *New Mexico* and quoted in Hernandez, "The U.S. Southwest," 31.

For more information regarding food see Hernandez, "The U.S. Southwest," 166.

Information about women being charged with witchcraft can be found in Greenleaf, "The Inquisition in Eighteenth-Century New Mexico."

For information about the earlier Pueblo revolts see Silverberg, *Pueblo Revolt*, 87.

That the refugees were "without a crust of bread" and that the site was "incapable of supporting more than a few dozen souls" is from Silverberg, *Pueblo Revolt*, 127.

The information about Otermin's men saving the friar is from Morehead, *New Mexico's Royal Road*, 37.

"No heart . . . was not moved by compassion" is quoted in Hernandez, "The U.S. Southwest," 59.

"Because of the Revolt, we survived" is from "Rebellious Pueblos," 95.

That de Vargas found Jornada-area pueblos destroyed probably indicates troubles with Apaches.

That de Vargas ordered the sheep ahead to smooth the way is from Welsh and Marshall, *El Camino Real de Tierra Adentro*, 233.

That men and women pushed and pulled along with the animals is from Welsh and Marshall, *El Camino Real de Tierra Andento*, iv.

The screech of the cottonwood cartwheels is from information provided to me by the New Mexico Farm and Ranch Museum and from Simmons, *Coronado's Land*, 78–84.

The quote on eating "sweat soaked leather" is from Hernandez, "The U.S. Southwest," 90.

That Spain engaged in nearly continuous war with the Pueblo Indians is according to historians Espinosa and Bennett in "Don Diego de Vargas," 307.

Items carried on trade caravans are from Bolton, *The Spanish Borderlands*, 180–81; additional information on the caravans is from Welsh and Marshall, *El Camino Real de Tierra Adentro*, and Moorhead, *New Mexico's Royal Road*.

The first Frenchman on the Jornada is from Moorhead, *New Mexico's Royal Road*, 55–56, and the story of captured French trader is from 56 n. 1.

For the role of widowed women see Hernandez, "The U.S. Southwest," 37.

Information about the Inquisition and the Jornada is drawn from Greenlear, "The Inquisition in Eighteenth-Century New Mexico," 29.

That giving birth exemplified the courage of the male leaders was gleaned from Hernandez, "The U.S. Southwest," 159.

New Mexico experienced at least twenty smallpox epidemics between 1636 and 1816. Live smallpox vaccine was created in the area in August 1804 when a surgeon inoculated children with live cowpox. The fluid was then "transfused" into an uninfected person. The children were brought across the Jornada to Pedro Armendaris's ranch at Valverde. The vaccination was then administered widely throughout the province. See "What Is the Significance of a Road?" in Piper, *El Camino Real de Tierra Adentro*, 9.

8. THE COMING OF THE *INGLES*

Information on Malgares's route and quotes from Pike are from Coues, *The Expeditions of Zebulon Montgomery Pike*.

9. THE *VIEJO*

Much of the information about Pedro Armendaris can be found in Bowden, "Private Land Claims in the Southwest."

That Apache attacks had forced Pedro Armendaris to leave is from Cortes, *Views from the Apache Frontier*.

The 1821 canals and Mexico's claims regarding the loss of water based on prior rights is from Autobee, *Rio Grande Project*.

For a discussion of the differences in land-grant laws see Engstrand, "Land Grant Problems in the Southwest."

Some information on the post-Pedro ownership came also from Reb, "Armendaris Grant Is Local History."

For information on the Bell Ranch see Remley, *The Bell Ranch*.

Some information on black grama is from Hitchcock, *Manual of the Grasses of the United States*.

That the in-holdings were sold by the Oppenheimer Estate is from my interview with Tom Waddell, June 2000.

10. THE CAPTAINS OF DEATH AND THE YOUNG BRIDE

For information about Kirker I have consulted Ralph Adam Smith's masterful *Borderlander: The Life of James Kirker, 1793–1852*. Additional information is from his "The King of New Mexico and the Doniphan Expedition" and "The Scalp Hunters of Chihuahua 1849." Additional works include Dan L. Thrapp's *The Conquest of Apacheria* and *Victorio and the Mimbres Apaches.*

Comments about genocide having widespread roots can be found in Thrapp, *The Conquest of Apacheria*, 8.

"The bounty system had about it the smell of vengeance . . ." is from Thrapp, *The Conquest of Apacheria*, 10.

The date of Gregg's voyage is based on information found in Marshall and Walt, *Rio Abajo*, 286.

All other source material regarding Gregg is from Gregg's *Commerce of the Prairies.*

For Kendall's voyage I have used the 1929 Lakeside Classic reproduction of his *Narrative of the Texan Santa Fe Expedition*, especially pages 381–82, 444–48, and 548–63. I have taken the liberty of modernizing spellings and punctuation.

"They have done nothing to deserve death" is from Kendall, *Narrative*, 382.

Information regarding the jeering and the soldiers dragging the prisoners by ropes is from Combs, "Combs' Narrative, 1841," 307, 310.

". . . sought every occasion to insult" is from Kendall's *Narrative*, 563.

The Falconer information is from Falconer, *Letters and Notes*, 89–97.

"one of the best camping grounds" is from Kendall, *Narrative*, 548.

For Kendall's meeting of Samuel Magoffin see Kendall, *Narrative*, 444–45.

"It is a level, sterile and desolate plain" is from Kendall, *Narrative*, 548.

Kendall's recollection of the night is from Kendall, *Narrative*, 553-54.

For ". . . with the shirt about his face," see Kendall, *Narrative*, 555.

For ". . . another feast for the buzzards and prairie wolves!" see Kendall, *Narrative*, 558; the emphasis is Kendall's.

For ". . . accordingly redoubled the blows" see Kendall, *Narrative*, 561.

Both Kendall and Falconer report the incident of the killing of Golpin.

"Callous too we had become" is from Kendall, *Narrative*, 559.

For information about Kendall's hearing of Kirker see R. A. Smith, *Borderlander*, 119.

That Salazar later faced charges is from *El Siglo*, vol. 19, and can be found in Falconer, *Letters and Notes*, 97.

Magoffin's journals, written for her private use, were first published in 1926. See Magoffin, *Down the Santa Fe Trail.*

For Ruxton's story see his *Adventures in Mexico and the Rocky Mountains, 1846–1847*. There is an inconsistency on just when Ruxton met Doniphan. I have relied on Magoffin's diary rather than Ruxton's memory of the date a year later.

For Susan's being waited on by a servant girl see Magoffin, *Down the Santa Fe Trail*, 53.

"One must have great faith in their Creator" is from Magoffin, *Down the Santa Fe Trail*, 69.

On Magoffin's feelings about her servant girl see Magoffin, *Down the Santa Fe Trail*, 174.

On buying the Mexican boy see Magoffin, *Down the Santa Fe Trail*, 163.

On Ruxton at Point of Rocks see his *Adventures in Mexico and the Rocky Mountains*, 172.

That traders who ventured into the Jornada would surely be "cut to pieces" is from Magoffin, *Down the Santa Fe Trail*, 176–77.

Much of my information on Doniphan is from Hughes, *Doniphan's Expedition*; Dawson, *Doniphan's Epic March*; and Edwards, *A Campaign in New Mexico with Colonel Doniphan*.

The quote about the soapweed fires is from Hughes, *Doniphan's Expedition*, 257–58, and can be found in Edwards, *A Campaign in New Mexico with Colonel Doniphan*, 49.

The description of the Taos Rebellion is from Grinnell, "Bent's Old Fort and Its Builders."

On the strange men who visited her camp, see Magoffin, *Down the Santa Fe Trail*, 191–93.

The *Santa Fe Republican* praised Kirker as a "free and kind-hearted man" who was "highly intelligent" in issues on October 24 and November 20, 1847.

11. COFFEE ON THE PORCH OF THE BAR CROSS RANCH
Some information on what was first known as Martin's Well comes from my interview with Ben and Jane Cain in June 2001.

Information about Bernard Gruber and the quote are from a Spanish document dated September 1, 1670, and taken from Kessell, *King, Cross, and Crown*, 214–15.

Thanks to Dean Anderson for additional information regarding oryx.

Information and quotes concerning the camel caravan were provided to me through the kindness of Dean Anderson and can be found in Beale, *Wagon Road from Ft. Defiance to the Colorado River*, and Lesley, *Uncle Sam's Camels*.

For information about schools in nineteenth-century New Mexico see Meyer, "Early Mexican-American Responses to Negative Stereotyping." Additional information is from my interviews with Flo Martin (June 2000), Bill O'Connell (April 2004), and Hazel Johnson (July 2001), and from Eidenbach and Hart, *School Days*.

See Thoreau's essay "Succession of Trees" (in *Essays*, 245–58) as well as his *Journal*.

I am indebted to Carolyn Dickerman for alerting me to Adolph Wislizenus and for her inspiring and useful article "Mid-Nineteenth Century Botanical Exploration in New Mexico." The Wislizenus journal can be found in *Memoir of a Tour of Northern Mexico*. Additional information on Wislizenus is from Smith and Judah, *Chronicles of the Gringos*, 139.

The Nahuatl origin of the word *coyote* is from Chavez's "Aztec or Nahuatl Words."

12. VALVERDE

In writing this chapter I found John Taylor's masterful *Bloody Valverde* indispensable.

The quote from the man on the roof at Fort Craig is from Bell, "The Campaign in New Mexico," 57.

Most of the information about Fort Craig is from U.S. Department of Interior, *Fort Craig*, and from Giese, *Forts of New Mexico*; additional information can be found in Grinstead, *Life and Death of a Frontier Fort*.

Information regarding Sibley's drunkenness can be found in Taylor, *Bloody Valverde*, 74.

All material concerning Alfred Peticolas is from Alberts, *Rebels on the Rio Grande*. Two years after Valverde, Peticolas appeared before a Texas military medical board and was found to be "unfit for field service." He returned to Victoria, Texas. He married, but his wife and infant daughter died of yellow fever. He remarried, raised three sons, and quietly practiced law in Victoria, where he died "peacefully" in 1915.

Rafael Chacón (1833–1925) was in his seventies when he decided to preserve his memoirs for his family. His remarkable work was first published in English as *Legacy of Honor: The Life of Rafael Chacon, a Nineteenth Century New Mexican*, edited by Jacqueline Dorgan Meketa. During his later service in the Civil War in New Mexico, Chacón repeatedly distinguished himself, even though he never mastered English. He commanded volunteer companies, including one at the Battle of Valverde, fought Indians under Kit Carson, escorted the first officials to the newly established territory of Arizona, and, as one of the few Hispanics to attain the rank of major, commanded Fort Stanton at the end of the war. Following discharge, he served several terms in the territorial legislature before homesteading near Trinidad, Colorado.

All material concerning Alonzo Ickes is from *Bloody Trails along the Rio Grande: A Day-by-Day Diary of Alonzo Ferdinand Ickes*, edited by Nolie

Mumey. Shortly after Valverde, on a Union expedition into Texas, Ickes was captured and was later released. After being mustered out of the army in 1864 he returned east to Creston, Iowa, where he married and lived on a farm. Late in life he and his wife moved to Denver, where he died in 1917.

That the Texans called the Jornada "Horn Alley" is from Alberts, *Rebels on the Rio Grande*, 58.

Most of my information about Graydon can be found in Jerry D. Thompson's *Desert Tiger*.

Taylor's quote regarding the lancers can be found in his *Bloody Valverde*, 67.

The quote from Colonel Tom Green at the start of the Confederate charge is from Taylor, *Bloody Valverde*, 84.

The quote about Carson's single-handed fighting can be found in Bell, "The Campaign of New Mexico," 71. After Valverde, Carson remained in New Mexico and led several battles against the Apaches and Navajos, including the famous battle in Canyon de Chelly. He died in 1868 in Colorado.

For an excellent look at the issue of New Mexican fighters see Meketa and Meketa, "Heroes or Cowards?"

13. THE LIFE AND DEATH OF VICTORIO

The best account of Victorio's life is Thrapp, *Victorio and the Mimbres Apache*. Additional information is found in Thrapp, *The Conquest of Apacheria*.

"No white man knew him well" can be found in Thrapp, *Victorio and the Mimbres Apache*, 313.

Information about the history of the Buffalo Soldiers is from Billington's *New Mexico's Buffalo Soldiers*.

For much of my information about Victorio's battle I relied on Laumbach's *Hembrillo: An Apache Battlefield of the Victorio War*; on interviews I conducted with him during the summer of 2001; and on his April 24, 1999, "Hembrillo Battlefield Briefing," a copy of which he provided me.

The information about the origin of Victorio's name is taken from Thrapp, *Victorio and the Mimbres Apache*, 6.

Lieutenant Conline's description of the battle at the mouth of the canyon is from John Conline, *The Campaign of 1880 against Victorio*, quoted in Laumbach, *Hembrillo*, 170–73.

I obtained the information about the Zuni word for *Apache* from the Handbook of Texas Online at http://www.tsha.utexas.edu/handbook/online.

That the Spanish used Apaches as slaves is found in Welsh and Marshall, *El Camino Real de Tierra Adentro*, 8.

Emory's quote can be found in Ross, *Lt. Emory Reports*, 96–101.

The civilian quoted from the spring of 1880 is from Thrapp, *Victorio and the Mimbres Apache*, 273.

Baylor's quote concerning the official Confederate policy can be found in Barrett, *Geronimo*, 21.

The quote from Victorio after the Civil War can be found in Thrapp, *Victorio and the Mimbres Apache*, 91.

The quote from Drew is in Thrapp, *Victorio and the Mimbres Apache*, 101.

Although John P. Clum's self-serving account of Victorio was written forty-five years after the fact, some readers may find the agent's story of interest. See "Victorio."

That Victorio was "the greatest commander white or red who ever roamed these plains" is from Mills, *Forty Years in El Paso*, 134.

The historian who called Victorio's opening strategy "a classic V-shaped defensive trap" was Karl Laumbach.

"I am sure that I did not kill any Indians" is quoted in Thrapp, *Victorio and the Mimbres Apache*, 187.

The soldier's letter to his mother is quoted in Laumbach, *Hembrillo*, 180.

According to Laumbach, between 135 and 150 Chiricahua and Mescalero Apaches fought against 150 Buffalo Soldiers, 106 Apache scouts, 75 Anglos, and 5 or 6 Hispanic guides. See Laumbach, *Hembrillo*, 253.

Information about the group of mostly Apache scouts that killed thirty of Victorio's people can be found in Dunlay, *Wolves for the Blue Soldiers*, 101.

The quote that the women would eat Victorio's body is from Parker, head of scouts, and is found in Thrapp, *Victorio and the Mimbres Apache*, 278.

For the eyewitness account of Victorio's death see Ball, *In the Days of Victorio*, 102.

Payment for Victorio's scalp as well as for those of sixty-one men and sixteen women and children is from R. A. Smith, *Borderlander*, 233–34.

Quote about searching the record to find why no one listened to the Apaches is from Thrapp, *Victorio and the Mimbres Apache*, 99.

14. TWO WRITERS OF THE PURPLE SAGE

Some of my information about Crawford comes from Darlis Miller's fine biography *Captain Jack Crawford: Buckskin Poet, Scout, and Showman*.

My account of Crawford's meeting with Billy the Kid is based on Crawford's typescript of his 1880 diary and on his typescript "How I Met Billy the Kid," both in the John Wallace (Captain Jack) Crawford Papers, Rio Grande Historical Collections, New Mexico State University Library, Las Cruces. For an excellent view of Billy the Kid see Robert Utley's *Billy the Kid: A Short and Violent Life*.

That Crawford "taught Americans what they knew about the Western experience" can be found in Miller, "Captain Jack Crawford," 230.

The contemporary quote about Crawford's dress and manner of speech is in Miller, *Captain Jack Crawford*, 33.

On Crawford's speaking like a workingman see Miller, *Captain Jack Crawford*, 197.

Crawford's regret that he could not be buried at Fort Craig is quoted in Miller, *Captain Jack Crawford*, 266.

For information about Crawford and the Armendaris lawsuit see Miller, *Captain Jack Crawford*, 101 and 266.

Crawford's comment about Maria is quoted in Miller, *Captain Jack Crawford*, 119.

Information about Eugene Manlove Rhodes is drawn from Dearing, *Novels and Stories*; Hutchinson, *A Bar Cross Man*; Clark, *Sandpapers*; and materials found in the Eugene Manlove Rhodes Collection, Rio Grande Historical Collections, New Mexico State University Library, Las Cruces.

The "soulless tobacco corporations" quote can be found in Dearing, *Novels and Stories*, 126.

That no man was more of a loyal friend than Rhodes can be found in Hutchinson, *A Bar Cross Man*, 6.

May Rhodes's description of her husband can be found in her 1938 biography *The Hired Man on Horseback* and is quoted in Clark, *Sandpapers*, 33.

The quote about Rhodes facing up to his responsibilities is from Clark, *Sandpapers*, 43.

"May and I are flourishing like two bay horses" is from Clark, *Sandpapers*, 138.

For a beautiful description of the Jornada see "The Perfect Day" in Dearing, *Novels and Stories*, 427–50.

The quote from Rhodes about Alamogordo is from Clark, *Sandpapers*, 82

The nearly unintelligible, hand-written manuscript of Rhodes's history of the Jornada, "The Desert Road," can be found in Eugene Manlove Rhodes Papers, Rio Grande Historical Collections, New Mexico State University, Las Cruces.

"Here and now" quote is from "The Desire of the Moth" in Dearing, *Novels and Stories*, 347.

"We're in eternity now" is from "Beyond the Desert" in Dearing, *Novels and Stories*, 455.

Rhodes's obituary is quoted in Clark, *Sandpapers*, 84.

Rhodes's wishes for an epitaph can be found in "Say Now Shibboleth" and in "Paso por aqui" in Dearing, *Novels and Stories*, 531 and 42, respectively.

15. VIRTUAL FENCES AND REAL NEIGHBORS

The Ben and Jane Cain section is based on my interviews with the Cains during the summer of 2001 and on information from *History of Sierra County*.

Some of the information about the Space Port is from "Spaceport Plans Concern Ranchers," *Las Cruces Sun-News*, December 10, 1994, A-2.

The rail stop at the Bar Cross Ranch is where Eugene Rhodes came upon two men who were wanted for the murder of a local judge. Rhodes talked them into giving themselves up. "They hadn't shaved in several months and had long beards and he took their guns and he went with them and took them on the train to Las Cruces from right here," Ben told me.

The "worlds of cattle" quote can be found in Fredrickson et al., "Perspectives on Desertification," 199.

Information about the Jornada Experimental Range is taken from "A Laboratory without Walls."

Information about the extent and speed of the invasion of creosote and other shrubs is from Fredrickson et al., "Perspectives on Desertification," 204.

The history of Cutter can be found in *History of Sierra County*, 61.

Material regarding virtual fences and the scientific information in that section was obtained in 2001 during my interviews with Dean Anderson, Ed Fredrickson, and Al Rango at the U.S. Department of Agriculture Headquarters in Las Cruces. I also used information found in Fredrickson et al., "Perspectives on Desertification." Fredrickson is conducting the cross-breeding experiments and is also the chief scientist involved in the reintroduction of prairie dogs on the Jornada.

Dean Anderson's concept of combining sheep and goats with cattle to create flerds can be found in his article "Pro-active Livestock Management."

For more information on Wilson Waddingham see Remley, *The Bell Ranch*, 115–24; additional information regarding the past owners of the Armendaris can be found in *History of Sierra County* and in Bowden, "Private Land Claims in the Southwest."

Information about Elephant Butte Dam and the water issues near the Jornada can be found in Autobee, *Rio Grande Project*, and in *History of Sierra County*.

That the Engle dam "will do much for Mexico and a great deal for the U.S." is from Hall, *Discussion of Past and Present Plans*. For information on the death of San Marcial see "The Town Destined to Die – and That Was the End of San Marcial," *Socorro Defensor Chieftain*, September 26, 1985, 11.

For more information on the flu epidemic see Melzer, "A Dark and Terrible Moment," and Marshall and Walt, *Rio Abajo*, 283–84.

For a view of Oppenheimer Industries see *History of Sierra County*, 62.

Much of the material for the Turner section was taken from my interviews with Tom Waddell in 2000 and 2001.

Bob Eveleth, senior mining engineer for the New Mexico Bureau of Mines, told me that Pedro de Aballos's mine is the only surviving Spanish grant of a mine in New Mexico. Thought to have once held silver, all that remains in the mine is useless manganese oxide.

16. FLO MARTIN PUTS DOWN HER MONKEY WRENCH

The bulk of the material for this chapter comes from my 2000 interviews with Florence Wesner Martin. Additional materials regarding Flo are taken from Eidenbach and Hart, *School Days*, and Eidenbach and Morgan, *Homes on the Range*. The description of the destruction of her belongings and the killing of her cat is from "Florence Martin, interview by Michelle Nawrocki, Jan. 29, 1994," 21, 30–32, Rio Grande Historical Collections, New Mexico State University Library, Las Cruces.

I am deeply indebted to Jane O'Cain of the New Mexico Farm and Ranch Museum for directing me to several additional sources for this chapter. I am especially grateful for being alerted to the article she wrote with Beth Morgan, "Displaced Ranchers of New Mexico."

Information about the search for the Trinity site is from Szasz, *The Day the Sun Rose Twice*, 27–30. Additional information about that period is from the *Post Guides: White Sands Missile Range* and from materials provided me by Jim Eckles, director of Public Affairs, White Sands Missile Range.

Regarding the naming of Trinity, Bob Eveleth told me that only one mine in New Mexico was ever named Trinity and it was a lead-zinc prospect "a long ways off" of the Jornada. The story that Oppenheimer named it after reading a John Donne poem was secondhand, told years later. Oppenheimer himself never commented about the origin.

That only single women were allowed to teach is from Eidenbach and Hart, *School Days*, xv.

That they were ordered off their ranch with two weeks' notice is from "WSMR Wants Land," *Albuquerque Journal*, January 5, 1975, A-1.

For a good summary of the issues surrounding the White Sands War see Sonnichsen, *Tularosa: Last of the Frontier West*. For Edward Abbey's fictional account see *Fire on the Mountain*.

The quote from Assistant U.S. District Attorney Grant is from "WSMR Wants Land," *Albuquerque Journal*, January 5, 1975, A-8.

Some information about Flo and the Dave McDonald standoff is from "They Threw Us Out!" *Socorro Defensor Chieftain*, August 3, 1982, 1, and from "Area Ranchers Rally in McDonald Support," *Alamogordo (NM) Daily News*, October 14, 1982, 1. The initial news story, "Rancher Retakes Home on the Range," can be found on page 1 of the October 14, 1982, *Albuquerque Journal*.

Jim Eckles told me that many people assumed the government never paid Dave McDonald for his property, when actually it started paying right away in 1942. The trouble was that Dave refused to sign the checks. He wanted his ranch back. Jim said other partners in the McDonald interest had to go to court so they could get the money. "I think people misunderstood him," Jim said of McDonald and the 1982 incident. "He didn't want more money, he wanted his ranch back-but it got twisted around-his niece may have had something to do with making him look like he was sacrificing out there for the good of all the other ranchers." Jim met Dave a few times and confirmed that ranching was McDonald's entire life and that when he was forced to do other things he never quite recovered. "Now he is dead, and his niece died too. The bill sponsored by Congressman Skeen and with the support of I think both New Mexico senators, never made it out of committee," Jim told me.

That an advisory committee of ranchers would be formed is from the *Socorro Defensor Chieftain*, October 21, 1982, 1. Additional information about the standoff is from my July 2001 interview with Dale Green, the retired chief of Stallion Station.

"It is not our policy . . ."; the quote from the official at the Ballistic Missile Defense Organization is from the *Socorro Defensor Chieftain*, January 14 and 15, 1995, 1.

That interviewers were not allowed to talk about taking land was told to me by Jane O'Cain.

That the government had acted as a service to taxpayers is from *Hearing before the Subcommittee on Public Lands and Reserved Water of the Committee on Energy and Natural Resources*.

Information about the Trinity site comes from "The Road to Stallion" and from my tour of the area with Jim Eckles in 2001.

"In failing to allow ranchers to return . . ." is from O'Cain and Morgan, "Displaced Ranchers of New Mexico," 23.

17. THE GEORGIA GREEN STORY

An 1896 version of the Death Waltz folktale can be found in Botkin, *Pocket Treasury of American Folklore*, 299.

I am deeply indebted to Bill O'Connell for sharing much of the information about his half sister Georgia Green in a series of phone conversations. Additional information came to me through the generous help of Rolf Sinclair and through archivists at the New Mexico Institute of Mining and Technology, the University of New Mexico, and the New Mexico School for Visually Handicapped as well as through conversations with several elderly residents in the Socorro area. Additional information is from Sinclair, "The Blind Girl Who Saw the Flash of the First Nuclear Weapons Test," 63–67; Lamont, *Day of Trinity*; "Socorro Lighted and Shaken When Alamogordo Magazine Explodes – No One Injured," *Socorro Defensor Chieftain*, July 19, 1945, 1; and "Alamogordo Base Explosives Blast Jolts Wide Area," *Albuquerque Journal*, July 17, 1945, 1.

I wish to thank Illene Renfro, rare books archivist at the University of New Mexico, who determined that Georgia Green received her Bachelor of Arts in Education in 1948.

Information about the events at Trinity is taken from several sources, including "Trinity Site, July 16, 1945"; Szasz, *The Day the Sun Rose Twice*; Lamont, *Day of Trinity*; and "The Road to Stallion."

The Fermi story can be found in Jungk, *Brighter than a Thousand Suns*, 199. For a fascinating look at other experiments at Trinity see Merlan, *The Trinity Experiments*. Fermi, Oppenheimer, and other Trinity scientists called themselves "knights of Columbus in reverse." Instead of returning to the Old World with legends of riches and discoveries, the European-trained scientists brought to the New World dreams of wealth from the unexplored world of atomic physics. Like the conquistadores, however, once they set foot on the forlorn Jornada such dreams proved to be far more complex and troublesome. See Jungk, *Brighter Than a Thousand Suns*, 20.

For a description of the growing ball of fire and those who thought it might engulf the entire world, see Jungk, *Brighter Than a Thousand Suns*, 200.

That many Trinity-area ranchers died of cancer is from Bartimus and McCartney, *Trinity's Children*, 19, and from materials found in the oral history archives at Rio Grande Historical Collections, New Mexico State University Library, Las Cruces.

The information about the permanent danger of nuclear sites is from "Nuke Sites Spoiled for Eternity," *Burlington Free Press*, August 8, 2000, 1.

Information about the cancer-related deaths is from *Burlington Free Press*, February 28, 2002, 2, and March 2, 2002, 2.

18. THE FINAL WALK

Information regarding the belief in Venus can be found in translations of the Mayan Dreisden Codex.

The Merton quotes are from *The Wisdom of the Desert*. For "a trackless wilderness" see 7–8. For the quote about society as a "shipwreck" see 3–4.

19. JOE

In addition to my 2001 interview with Joe Turner (and Walter Slayter), I have used material about Joe's life and times from my interview with Hazel and Wayne Johnson, from *History of Sierra County*, and from the interviews of Lewis Cain and Flo Martin in the Rio Grande Historical Collections, New Mexico State University, Las Cruces.

Joe Turner passed away on Christmas Day 2002, at the age of ninety-four.

Bibliography

In my work I have favored the words and actions of people directly involved in the Jornada over the writings of later historians and biographers. Likewise, I have tended to favor the contemporary accounts of eyewitnesses over eyewitnesses' later recollections. Finally, because of the Jornada's rich and complex history, many other fascinating tales have been left untold.

PRIMARY SOURCES

Archaeological Records Management. New Mexico Historical Preservation Division, Santa Fe.

John Wallace (Captain Jack) Crawford Papers. Rio Grande Historical Collections, New Mexico State University Library, Las Cruces.

"Florence Martin, interview by Michelle Nawrocki, Jan. 29, 1994." Rio Grande Historical Collections, New Mexico State University Library, Las Cruces.

"Human Systems Research Inc White Sands Missile Range Oral History Legacy Project." Rio Grande Historical Collections, New Mexico State University Library, Las Cruces.

"Official Surveys: General Court of Private Land Claims." State Records Office, Santa Fe.

Eugene Manlove Rhodes Collection. Rio Grande Historical Collections, New Mexico State University Library, Las Cruces.

Southwest Collection. University of New Mexico, Albuquerque.

Spanish Archives of New Mexico, Santa Fe.

SECONDARY SOURCES

Abbey, Edward. *Fire on the Mountain*. New York: Dial Press, 1962.

Abe, Masao. *A Study of Dogen: His Philosophy and Religion*. Albany: State University of New York Press, 1992.

Ackerley, Neal W., et al. *Ranching in the Tularosa Basin: The White Sands Oral History Legacy Project*. Tularosa NM: Department of Defense, 1987.

Bibliography

Alberts, Don E., ed. *Rebels on the Rio Grande: The Civil War Journal of A. B. Peticolas.* Albuquerque: University of New Mexico Press, 1984.

Alfred, Kelly. "A Field Guide to the Flora of the Jornada Plain." Bulletin 739, Las Cruces: New Mexico Agricultural Experimental Station, n.d.

Anderson, Dean M. "Pro-active Livestock Management: Capitalizing on Animal Behavior." *Journal of Arid Land Studies* 39 (1998): 113–16.

Ashcroft, Bruce. "Socorro's Boom Town Decade." *New Mexico Historical Review* 87 (summer 1981): 3–9.

Austin, Mary. *The Land of Little Rain.* New York: Houghton, Mifflin, 1903.

Autobee, Robert. *Rio Grande Project: Historic Reclamation Projects Book.* N.p., n.d.

Ball, Eve. *In the Days of Victorio: The Recollections of a Warm Springs Apache.* Tucson: University of Arizona Press, 1970.

Bandelier, Adolph F. *The Discovery of New Mexico.* Tucson: University of Arizona Press, 1981.

Barrett, S. M. *Geronimo: His Own Story.* New York: Meridian, 1966.

Bartimus, Tad, and Scott McCartney. *Trinity's Children: Living along America's Nuclear Highway.* Albuquerque: University of New Mexico Press, 1991.

Beale, E. F. *Wagon Road from Ft. Defiance to the Colorado River.* 35th Cong., 1st sess., House of Representatives, Ex. Doc. 124.

Beck, Warren A. *Historical Atlas of New Mexico.* Norman: University of Oklahoma Press, 1969.

Beck, Warren A., and Ynez D. Haase. *Historical Atlas of the American West.* Norman: University of Oklahoma Press, 1989.

Beckett, Patrick H., and Regge N. Wiseman, eds. *Jornada Mogollon Archaeology: Proceedings of the First Jornada Conference.* N.p., 1979.

Bell, Joseph M. "The Campaign in New Mexico, 1862." In *War Papers Read before the Commandery of the State of Wisconsin, Military Order of the Loyal Legion of the United States.* 1:50–61. Milwaukee: Burdick, Armitage and Allen, 1891.

Bennett, Charles. "Ft. Craig, Key Civil War Site Celebrates 150 Years." *New Mexico Magazine* 82, no. 3 (2004): 56–59.

Bhikkhu, Thanissaro. "Hunting and Gathering the Dharma." *Tricycle* 11, no. 1 (2001): 78.

Billington, Monroe Lee. "Black Soldiers at Fort Seldon; New Mexico 1866–1891." *New Mexico Historical Review* 62 (January 1987): 65–80.

——. *New Mexico's Buffalo Soldiers, 1866–1900.* Niwot: University of Colorado Press, 1991.

Binkely, William Campbell. "New Mexico and the Texas Santa Fe Expedition." *Southwestern Historical Quarterly* 27, no. 2 (1923): 85–107.

Bibliography

Bloom, Lansing B. "Who Discovered New Mexico?" *New Mexico Historical Review* 15 (1940): 101–32.

Bolton, Herbert E. *Coronado: Knight of Pueblos and Plains.* Albuquerque: University of New Mexico Press, 1990.

———. *The Spanish Borderland.* Albuquerque: University of New Mexico Press, 1987.

———. *Spanish Exploration in the Southwest, 1542–1706.* New York: Scribner, 1916.

Botkin, B. A., ed. *The Pocket Treasury of American Folklore.* New York: Pocket Books, 1950.

———. *Treasury of Western Folklore.* New York: Crown, 1951.

Bowden, J. J. "Private Land Claims in the Southwest." Master's thesis, Southern Methodist University, 1969.

Brown, Vinson. *Wildlife of the Intermountain West.* Healdsburg CA: Naturegraph, 1958.

Buffington, Lee C., and Carlton H. Herbel. "Biological Feedbacks in Global Desertification." *Science* 247 (March 1990): 1043–48.

———. "Vegetational Changes on a Semidesert Grassland Range." *Ecological Monographs* 35 (spring 1965): 139–64.

Burton, E. B. "Texas Raiders in New Mexico in 1843." *Old Santa Fe*, April 2, 1915, 407–29.

Carlson, Alvar W. "New Mexico's Sheep Industry, 1850–1900: Its Role in the History of the Territory." *New Mexico Historical Review* 44, no. 1 (1969): 25–49.

Carmony, Neil B. *The Civil War in Apacheland – Sergeant George Hand's Diary.* Silver City NM: High Lonesome, 1996.

Castañeda, Pedro de. *The Journey of Coronado.* Ed. Frederick Webb Hodge and George Parker Winship. New York: Dover, 1990.

Cavalli-Sforza, Luigi Luca. *Genes, Peoples, and Languages.* New York: North Point, 2000.

Chavez, Fray Angelico. "Aztec or Nahuatl Words in New Mexico Place Names." *El Palacio*, April 1950, 109–12.

Chidsey, Donald Barr. *The War with Mexico.* New York: Crown, 1968.

Clark, Frank. *Sandpapers: The Life and Letters of Eugene Manlove Rhodes and Charles Fletcher Lumis.* Santa Fe: Sunstone, 1994.

Clum, John P. "The Apaches." *New Mexico Historical Review* 4, no. 2, (1929): 108–27.

Combs, Franklin. "Combs' Narrative, 1841." *New Mexico Historical Review* 5, no. 3 (1930): 305–14.

Bibliography

Comis, Don. "The Cyber Cow Whisperer and His Virtual Fence." *Agricultural Research* 48, no. 11 (2000): 4–7.

Conley, Marsha Reeves, and Walt Conley. "New Mexico State University College Ranch and Jornada Experimental Range: a summary of Research 1900–1983." Las Cruces NM: Special Report 56, New Mexico Agricultural Experimental Station, 1984.

Connor, Seymour V. "Attitudes and Opinions About the Mexican War, 1846–1970." *Journal of the West* 11 (April 1972): 361–66.

"A Contribution to the Bio-Diversity of the Armendaris Ranch." Privately printed, 1999.

Convey, Cyclone. *Cabeza de Vaca's Adventures*. New York: Collier, 1961.

Cortes, José. *Views from the Apache Frontier: Report on the Northern Provinces of New Spain*. Ed. Elizabeth A. H. John. Norman: University of Oklahoma Press, 1989.

Coues, Elliot, ed. *The Expeditions of Zebulon Montgomery Pike in Two Volumes*. New York: Dover, 1987.

Cress, Lawrence D. ed., *Dispatches from the Mexican War, by George Wilkins Kendall*. Norman: University of Oklahoma Press, 1999.

Crouch, Brodie. *Jornada del Muerto: A Pageant of the Desert*. Spokane: Arthur H. Clark, 1989.

Dary, David. *The Santa Fe Trail: Its History, Legends, and Lore*. New York: Knopf, 2000.

Dawson, Joseph G., III. *Doniphan's Epic March: The First Missouri Volunteers in the Mexican War*. Topeka: University of Kansas Press, 1999.

Dearing, Frank, ed. *The Best Novels and Stories of Eugene Manlove Rhodes*. Boston: Houghton Mifflin, 1908.

DeVoto, Bernard. *The Year of Decision, 1846*. Boston: Houghton Mifflin, 1943.

Dickerman, Carolyn. "Mid-Nineteenth Century Botanical Exploration in New Mexico." *New Mexico Historical Review* 60, no. 2 (1985): 159–71.

Dickinson, Patti. *Hollywood the Hard Way*. Lincoln: University of Nebraska Press, 1999.

Dinges, Bruce J. "The Victorio Campaign of 1880: Cooperation and Conflict on the United States–Mexico Border." *New Mexico Historical Review* 62, no. 1 (1987): 81–94.

Dobie, J. Frank. *The Voice of the Coyote*. Bison, 1961.

"Documentos para servir a la historia del Nuevo Mexico 1538–1778." Madrid: Porrua Turanzas, 1962.

Donnell, F. S. "When Texas Owned New Mexico to the Rio Grande." *New Mexico Historical Review* 8, no. 2 (1933): 65–75.

Douglas, Boyd. *Paraje de Fra Cristobel: Investigation of a Territorial Period Hispanic Village.* United States Dept. of Interior, Amarillo: Bureau of Reclamation, 1986.

Dozier, Edward P. *The Pueblo Indians of North America.* New York: Holt, Rinehart, Winston, 1970.

——. "Spanish Catholic Influences on Rio Grande Pueblo Religion." *American Anthropologist* 60 (June 1958): 441–48.

Dreifus, Claudia. "Noble Tycoon – Magnate Ted Turner Likes to Put His Money Where His Heart Is." *Modern Maturity*, September–October 2000, 14–20.

Dufour, Charles L. *The Mexican War: A Compact History, 1846–1848.* New York: Hawthorn, 1968.

Dunlay, Thomas W. *Wolves for the Blue Soldiers: Indian Scouts and Auxiliaries with the United States Army, 1860–1890.* Lincoln: University of Nebraska Press, 1982.

Dunne, John S. *Time and Myth: A Meditation on Storytelling as an Exploration of Life and Death.* London: University of Notre Dame Press, 1973.

Duran, M. S. "Patterns of Prehistoric Land Use in Dona Anna County, New Mexico." *Cultural Resources Management Division, Report 471.* Las Cruces: New Mexico State University, 1982.

Eardley, A. J. *Structural Geology of North America.* New York: Harpers, 1951.

Earle, W. Hubert. *Cacti of the Southwest.* Phoenix: Rancho Arroyo, n.d.

Edwards, Frank S. *A Campaign in New Mexico with Colonel Doniphan.* 1847. Reprint, Albuquerque: University of New Mexico Press, 1996.

Eidenbach, Peter L., and Linda Hart, eds. *School Days: Education during the Ranching Era on the U.S. Army White Sands Missile Range, New Mexico.* Tularosa NM: Department of Defense Legacy Management Program, Ranching Oral History Project, 1997.

Eidenbach, Peter L., and Robert Hart. *A Number of Things: Baldy Russell, Estey City and the Ozane Stage, Historic Ranching and Mining on the US Army White Sands Missile Range.* Tularosa NM: Department of Defense Legacy Management Program, Human Systems Research Project 8824, 1997.

Eidenbach, Peter L., and Beth Morgan, eds. *Homes on the Range: Oral Recollections of Early Ranch Life on the US Army White Sands Missile Range, New Mexico.* Tularosa NM: Department of Defense Legacy Management Program, Ranching Oral History Project, 1994.

Eiseley, Loren, *The Firmament of Time.* New York: Atheneum, 1972.

Eisenhower, John S. D. *So Far from Heaven: The U.S. War with Mexico, 1846–1848.* New York: Random House, 1989.

Elephant Butte Dam, 1911–1986: Construction and History. N.p., n.d.

Elmore, Francis H. *Shrubs and Trees of the Southwest Uplands*. Tucson: Southwest Parks and Monuments Association, 1976.

Emory, William Hemsley. "Notes of a Military Reconnaissance from Ft. Leavenworth in Missouri, to San Diego in California including part of the Arkansas, Rio del Norte and Gila Rivers." U.S. Congress, Senate Executive document 7, 30th Cong., 1st sess., 1848, serial set 505.

Engstrand, Iris Wilson. "Land Grant Problems in the Southwest: The Spanish and Mexican Heritage." *New Mexico Historical Review* 53, no. 4 (1978): 317–36.

Erdoes, Richard, and Alfonso Ortiz, eds. *American Indian Myths and Legends*. New York: Pantheon, 1984.

Ernenwein, Leslie. "Wild Man of the San Andres." In *Legends and Tales of the Old West – by Members of the Western Writers of America*, ed. S. Omar Barker, 275–79. Garden City NY: Doubleday, 1962.

Espinosa, J. M., and Charles Bennett Jr. "Don Diego de Vargas: Portrait of a Seventeenth-Century Conquistador." *New Mexico Historical Review* 64 (July 1989): 305–17.

Falconer, Thomas. *Letters and Notes on the Texan Santa Fe Expedition, 1841–1842*. New York: Dauber and Pine, 1930.

Fletcher, Sherry. *Cultural Heritage of Sierra County*. Truth or Consequences NM: Sierra National Bank, n.d.

Florin, Lambert. *Ghost Towns of the West*. Salt Lake: Promontory, 1970.

Franzwa, Gregory M. *Maps of the Santa Fe Trail*. St. Louis: Patrice, 1989.

Frazier, Donald S. *Blood and Treasure: The Confederate Empire in the Southwest*. Lubbock: Texas A&M Press, 1995.

Fredrickson, Ed, et al. "Perspectives on Desertification: Southwestern United States." *Journal of Arid Environments* 39 (1998): 191–207.

Gallahar, F. M. "Official Report of the Battle of Temascalitos." *New Mexico Historical Review* 3, no. 4 (1928): 385.

Geisler, Norman L. *What Augustine Says*. Grand Rapids MI: Baker, 1982.

"Geronimo Trail Scenic Byway" (brochure at Geronimo Museum, Truth or Consequences NM). N.p., n.d.

Gerson, Noel. *Kit Carson, Folk Hero and Man*. New York: Avon, 1961.

Giese, Dale F. *Forts of New Mexico*. N.p., 1995.

Gilpin, Laura. *The Rio Grande, River of Destiny*. New York: Duell, Sloan and Pearce, 1949.

Glick, Wendell, ed. *Great Short Works of Henry David Thoreau*. New York: Harper, 1993.

Greenland, David, and John Anderson. "Jornada Basin." http://lternet.edu/.

Greenleaf, Richard E. "The Inquisition in Eighteenth-Century New Mexico." *New Mexico Historical Review* 60, no. 1 (1985): 29–60.

Gregg, Andy. *Drums of Yesterday: The Forts of New Mexico*. Santa Fe: Press of the Territorian, 1968.

Gregg, Josiah. *Commerce of the Prairies in Two Volumes*. New York: Henry G. Langley, 1844.

Grinnell, George Bird. "Bent's Old Fort and Its Builders." *Kansas State Historical Society Collections* 15 (1919–22): 78–81.

Grinstead, Marion C. *Life and Death of a Frontier Fort: Fort Craig New Mexico, 1854–1885*. Socorro NM: Publications in History, Socorro County Historical Society, 1973.

"Guide to Three Rivers Petroglyph Site and Picnic Area." Bureau of Land Management, U.S. Department of Interior, Caballo Resource Ares, Las Cruces NM, n.d.

Gutierrez, Ramon A. *When Jesus Came, the Corn Mothers Went Away: Marriage, Sexuality, and Power in New Mexico, 1500–1846*. Stanford: Stanford University Press, 1991.

Hackett, Charles W., ed. *Historical Documents Relating to New Mexico, Nueva Vizcaya, and Approaches Thereto, to 1773*. 3 vols. Washington DC: Carnegie Institution of Washington, Publication no. 330, 1923–37.

Hackett, Charles W., ed., and Charmion C. Shelby, trans. *Revolt of the Pueblo Indians of New Mexico and Otermin's Attempted Reconquest, 1680–1682*. 2 vols. Albuquerque: University of New Mexico Press, Coronado Cuarto Centennial Publications, 1540–1940, 1942.

Hall, B. M. *A Discussion of Past and Present Plans for Irrigation of the Rio G Valley*. Washington DC: U.S. Reclamation Service, 1904.

Hallenbeck, Cleve. *The Journey of Fray Marcos de Niza*. Dallas: Southwestern Methodist University Press, 1987.

Hammond, George P., and Agapito Rey, eds. *Don Juan de Oñate and the Founding of New Mexico*. Historical Society of New Mexico Publications in History no. 2. Santa Fe: El Palacio Press, 1962.

——. *Don Juan de Oñate: Colonizer of New Mexico, 1595–1628*. 3 vols. Albuquerque: University of New Mexico Press, Coronado Cuarto Centennial Publications, 1953.

——. *Narratives of the Coronado Expedition, 1540–1542*. Albuquerque: University of New Mexico Press, Coronado Cuarto Centennial Publications, 1940.

——. *The Rediscovery of New Mexico, 1580–1594: The Explorations of Chamuscado, Espejo, Castano de Sosa, Morlete, and Leyva de Bonilla and Humana.*

Albuquerque: University of New Mexico Press, Coronado Cuarto Centennial Publications, 1966.

Havstad, K. M. "Legacy of Charles Travis Turney: The Jornada Experimental Range." *Archaeologist Society of New Mexico Annual* 22 (1996): 77–92.

Hearing before the Subcommittee on Public Lands and Reserved Water of the Committee on Energy and Natural Resources. U.S. Senate, 98th Cong., 1st sess., November 18, 1983, Acquisition of Land. U.S. Government Printing Office.

Hendricks, Rick, ed. *The Text and Concordance of "By Force of Arms: The Journals of don Diego de Vargas New Mexico 1691–93."* Albuquerque: University of New Mexico Press, The Vargas Project microfiche series 2, 1992.

——. *The Text and Concordance of "Correspondence of don Diego de Vargas 1675–1706."* Albuquerque: University of New Mexico Press, The Vargas Project microfiche series 1, 1988.

Hendricks, Rick, Jose Ignacio Avellaneda, and Meredith D. Dodge, eds. *The Text and Concordance of "To the Royal Crown Restored: The Journals of don Diego de Vargas New Mexico 1692–1694."* Albuquerque: University of New Mexico Press, The Vargas Project microfiche series 3, 1993.

Hernandez, Salome. "The U.S. Southwest: Female Participation in Official Spanish Settlement Expeditions: Specific Case Studies in the Sixteenth, Seventeenth, and Eighteenth Centuries." Ph.D. diss., University of New Mexico, 1987.

Hertzog, Peter. *Outlaws of New Mexico.* Santa Fe: Sunstone, 1984.

Hillerman, Tony, ed. *The Best of the West: An Anthology of Classic Writing from the American West.* New York: Harper, 1991.

Hiss, Tony. *The Experience of Place.* New York: Random House, 1990.

History of Sierra County, New Mexico. Truth or Consequences NM: Sierra County Historical Society, 1979.

Hitchcock, A. S. *Manual of the Grasses of the United States.* Washington DC: U.S. Department of Agriculture, 1950.

Hodge, Frederick W. *Handbook of American Indians North of Mexico.* Bureau of American Ethnology, Smithsonian Institution Bulletin 30. 2 vols. Washington DC: Government Printing Office, 1907–10.

——, ed. *Spanish Explorers in the Southern United States, 1528–1543.* New York: Scribners, 1907.

Hollon, W. Eugene. *The Great American Desert.* Oxford, 1966.

Horgan, Paul. *Great River: The Rio Grande in North American History.* New York: Rinehart, 1954.

Houk, Rose. *Mogollon – Prehistoric Cultures of the Southwest.* Tucson: Southwest Parks and Monuments Association, 1992.

Bibliography

Hughes, John T. *Doniphan's Expedition; Containing an Account of the Conquest of New Mexico; General Kearny's Overland Expedition to California; Doniphan's Campaign Against the Navajos; His Unparalleled March Upon Chihuahua and Durango; and the Operations of General Price at Santa Fe.* Cincinnati: J. A. and U. P. James, 1847. Reprint, Albuquerque: Rio Grande Press, 1962.

Hunner, Jon. *A Selective Bibliography of New Mexico History.* Albuquerque: University of New Mexico Center for the American West, 1992.

Hutchinson, W. H. *A Bar Cross Man.* Norman: University of Oklahoma Press, 1956.

Irwin-Williams, Cynthia. *The Oshara Tradition: Origins of Anasazi Culture.* Portales: Eastern New Mexico University Press, 1973.

——. "Picosa: The Elementary Southwestern Culture." *American Antiquity* 32 (1967): 441–57.

James, Henry. *The Curse of the San Andres.* New York: Pageant, 1953.

Jennings, Francis. *The Founders of America, from Earliest Migrations to the Present.* New York: Norton, 1993.

Jimenez Codinach, Guadalupe. *The Hispanic World, 1492–1898: A Guide to Photoreproduced Manuscripts from Spain in the Collections of the United States, Guam, and Puerto Rico.* Washington DC: Library of Congress, 1994.

John, Elizabeth A. H. *Storms Brewed in Other Men's Worlds: The Confrontation of Indians, Spanish, and French in the Southwest, 1540–1795.* Lincoln: University of Nebraska Press, 1975.

Jornada Bibliography, 1850–1999. Las Cruces NM: Jornada Experimental Range Report, January 11, 2000.

Josephy, Alvin M. *War on the Frontier: The Trans-Mississippi West.* Alexandria VA: Time Life, 1987.

Jungk, Robert. *Brighter Than a Thousand Suns.* New York: Harcourt Brace, 1958.

Kaplan, Robert D. *An Empire Wilderness.* New York: Vintage, 1999.

Keenan, Jerry. *Encyclopedia of American Indian Wars, 1492–1890.* New York: Norton, 1999.

Kendall, George Wilkins. *Dispatches from the Mexican War.* Chicago: Lakeside, 1929.

——. *Narrative of the Texan Santa Fe Expedition.* Chicago: Lakeside, 1929.

Kessell, John L. *King, Cross, and Crown: The Pecos Indians of New Mexico, 1540–1840.* Washington DC: U.S. Department of Interior, National Park Service, 1979.

Kessell, John L., and Rick Hendricks, eds. *By Force of Arms: The Journals of don Diego de Vargas, 1691–1693*. Vargas series 2. Albuquerque: University of New Mexico Press, 1992.

Kessell, John L., Rick Hendricks, and Meredith D. Dodge, eds. *Blood on the Boulders. The Journals of Don Diego de Vargas, New Mexico, 1694–97*. Albuquerque: University of New Mexico Press, 1998.

——. *To the Royal Crown Restored: The Journals of don Diego de Vargas, New Mexico, 1692–1694*. Vargas series 3. Albuquerque: University of New Mexico Press, 1995.

Kirkpatrick, David T., and Meliha S. Duran. "Prehistoric Peoples of the Northern Chihuhuan Desert." *New Mexico Geological Society Guidebook, 49th Conference*, 1998, 41–45.

"A Laboratory without Walls: Jornada Experimental Range" (brochure). Las Cruces NM: U.S. Department of Agriculture, 2000.

Lamont, Lansing. *Day of Trinity*. New York: Athenaeum, 1965.

Laumbach, Karl. *Hembrillo: An Apache Battlefield of the Victorio War*. Human Systems Research Report no. 9730. Tularosa NM: White Sands Missile Range, 2001.

Leckie, William H. *The Buffalo Soldiers, A Narrative of the Negro Cavalry in the West*. Norman: University of Oklahoma Press, 1967.

Lehmer, Donald J. *The Jornada Branch of the Mogollon*. Tucson: University of Arizona, Social Science Bulletin 17, *University of Arizona Bulletin* 19, no. 2 (1948).

Lesley, Lewis Burke. *Uncle Sam's Camels*. Glorieta NM: Rio Grande Press, 1970.

Longacre, William A., ed. *Reconstruction Pueblo Societies*. Albuquerque: University of New Mexico Press, 1970.

Loyola, Sister Mary. "The American Occupation of New Mexico, 1821–1852 (part one)." *New Mexico Historical Review* 14, no. 1 (1939): 34–75.

——. "The American Occupation of New Mexico, 1821–1852 (part two)." *New Mexico Historical Review* 14, no. 2 (1939): 143–99.

——. "The American Occupation of New Mexico, 1821–1852 (part three)." *New Mexico Historical Review* 14, no. 3 (1939): 230–86.

Luca Cavalli-Sforza, Luigi. *Genes, Peoples, and Languages*. New York: North Point, 2000.

Magoffin, Susan Shelby. *Down the Santa Fe Trail and into Mexico: The Diary of Susan Shelby Magoffin*. Ed. Stella M. Drummm. New Haven: Yale University Press, 1926.

"Mammals and Reptiles of the Pedro Armendaris Lava Field." Privately published, n.d.

Marshall, Michael P., and Henry J. Walt. *Rio Abajo: Prehistory and History of a Rio Grande Province*. Santa Fe: New Mexico Historical Preservation Program, 1984.

Matlock, Gary. *Enemy Ancestors: The Anasazi World with a Guide to Sites*. Northland, 1988.

Matlock, Gary, and Scott Warren. *The Enemy Ancestors: The Anasazi World with a Guide to Sites*. Northland, 1988.

McGregor, John C. *Southwestern Archaeology*. 2nd ed. Urbana: University of Illinois Press, 1985.

Meketa, Charles, and Jacqueline Meketa. "Heroes or Cowards? A New Look at the Role of Native New Mexicans at the Battle of Valverde." *New Mexico Historical Review* 62, no. 1 (1987): 33–46.

Meketa, Jacqueline Dorgan, ed. *Legacy of Honor: The Life of Rafael Chacon, a Nineteenth Century New Mexican*. Albuquerque: University of New Mexico Press, 1984.

Melzer, Richard. "A Dark and Terrible Moment: The Spanish Flu Epidemic of 1918 in New Mexico." *New Mexico Historical Review* 57, no. 3 (1982): 213–36.

Memoir of a Tour of Northern Mexico. 30th Cong., 1st sess., Senate, Misc. no. 26.

Mera, H. P. "Population Changes in the Rio Grande Glaze-Paint Area." Santa Fe: Technical Bulletin no. 9, Laboratory of Anthropology, 1940.

Merlan, Thomas. *The Trinity Experiments*. Human Systems Research Report 9701. Tularosa NM: White Sands Missile Range, 1997.

Merton, Thomas. *The Monastic Journey*. Kansas City: Sheed, Andrews and McMeel, 1977.

———. *The Other Side of the Mountain: The Journals of Thomas Merton*. San Francisco: Harper, 1998.

———. *The Wisdom of the Desert*. New York: New Directions, 1970.

Meyer, Doris L. "Early Mexican-American Responses to Negative Stereotyping." *New Mexico Historical Review* 53, no. 1 (1978): 75–91.

Miller, Darlis A. "Captain Jack Crawford: A Western Military Scout on the Chautauqua Circuit." *South Dakota History* 3 (fall 1991): 230–46..

———. *Captain Jack Crawford: Buckskin Poet, Scout, and Showman*. Albuquerque: University of New Mexico, 1993.

Mills, W. W. *Forty Years in El Paso: 1858–1898*. El Paso: Hertzog, 1962.

Moorhead, Max L. *New Mexico's Royal Road: Trade and Travel on the Chihuahua Trail*. Norman: University of Oklahoma Press, 1958.

Morris, Richard. *Time's Arrows: Scientific Attitudes toward Time*. New York: Simon and Schuster, 1984.

Mumey, Nolie, ed. *Bloody Trails along the Rio Grande: A Day-by-Day Diary of Alonzo Ferdinand Ickes*. Denver: The Old West, 1958.

"Native American History of Corn." Native Tech: Native American Technology and Art, http://www.nativetech.org/cornhusk/cornhusk/htlm.

Nelson, Maraget, C. *Mimbres during the Twelfth Century*. Tucson: University of Arizona Press, 1991.

Nolan, Paul T. *John Wallace Crawford*. Boston: Twayne, 1981.

Norton, Hana Samek. "Apaches and the Mining Menace; Indian-White Conflicts in Southwestern New Mexico, 1800–1886." In *New Mexico Geological Society Guidebook*, 55–60. Las Cruces NM: 49th Field Conference, 1998.

Noyes, Peter T. "A Cultural Resources Survey for a Proposed Mountain Bell Buried Cable through Bosque del Apache National Wildlife Refuge in North Central New Mexico." Washington DC: U.S. Department of Interior, 1985.

O'Cain, Jane, and Beth Morgan. "Displaced Ranchers of New Mexico: The Taking of Land for the Defense Effort at White Sands Missile Range." N.p., n.d.

Opler, Morris. *An Apache Life Way*. Lincoln: University of Nebraska Press, 1996.

——. *Myths and Legends of the Jicarilla Apache Indians*. Lincoln: University of Nebraska Press, 1994.

Oppenheimer, J. Robert. *The Open Mind*. New York: Simon and Schuster, 1955.

Ortiz, Alfonso. *The Tewa World: Space Time, Being, and Becoming in a Pueblo Society*. Chicago: University of Chicago Press, 1991.

Ortiz, Roxanne Dunbar. "Colonialism and the Role of Women: The Pueblos of New Mexico." *Southwest Economy and Society* 4 (winter 1978–79): 28–46.

Page, James K., Jr. "Rebellious Pueblos Outwitted Spain Three Centuries Ago." *Smithsonian Magazine* 112 (October 1980): 95.

Patterson, Alex. *A Field Guide to Rock Art Symbols of the Greater Southwest*. Boulder: Johnson, 1992.

Piper, June-el, ed. *El Camino Real de Tierra Adentro*. Santa Fe: U.S. Department of Interior, Bureau of Land Management, 1999.

Post Guides: White Sands Missile Range. San Diego: Marcoa, 1994 and 2001.

Quinn, Daniel. *Ishmael: An Adventure of the Mind and Spirit*. New York: Bantam, 1992.

Reb, Everett. "Armendaris Grant Is Local History." N.p., n.d.

Remley, David. *The Bell Ranch: Cattle Ranching in the Southwest 1824–1947*. Albuquerque: University of New Mexico, 1993.

Reno, Philip. "Rebellion in New Mexico, 1837." *New Mexico Historical Review* 40, no. 3 (1965): 197–213.

Revel, Jean-Francois, and Matthieu Ricard. *The Monk and the Philosopher.* New York: Schocken, 1998.

Rhodes, Eugene Manlove. *Paso por Aqui.* Alamogordo NM: Friends of Alamogordo Public Library, 1963.

——. *Recognition: The Poems of Eugene Manlove Rhodes.* Alamogordo NM: Friends of Alamogordo Public Library, 1997.

Richter, Donald H., et al. *Mineral Resources of the Jornada Del Muerto Wilderness Study Area, Socorro and Sierra Counties, New Mexico.* U.S. Geological Survey Bulletin 1734, 1989.

Rifkin, Jeremy. *Time Wars: The Primary Conflict in Human History.* New York: Holt, 1987.

Riley, Carroll L. *Rio del Norte: People of the Upper Rio Grande from Earliest Times to the Pueblo Revolt.* Salt Lake City: University of Utah Press, 1995.

Rittenhouse, Jack. *New Mexico Civil War Bibliography.* N.d., n.p.

The Roads of New Mexico. Fredericksburg TX: Shearer, 1990.

"The Road to Stallion – A Guide to RR 7." White Sands Missile Range Public Affairs Office, n.d.

Roberts, David. *In Search of the Old Ones.* New York: Touchstone, 1996.

——. *A Newer World: Kit Carson, John C. Fremont, and the Claiming of the American West.* New York: Simon and Schuster, 2000.

Ross, Calvin, ed. *Lt. Emory Reports: A Reprint of Lt. W. H. Emory's Notes of a Military Reconnaissance.* Albuquerque: University of New Mexico Press, 1951.

Russell, John. *Personal Narrative of Exploration and Incidents in Texas, New Mexico, California, Sonora and Chihuahua, Connected with the United States and Mexico Boundary Commission during the Years 1851–53.* Appleton NY, 1854.

Ruxton, George A. F. *Adventures in Mexico and the Rocky Mountains, 1846–1847.* New York: Harpers, 1855.

Sanchez, Joseph P. *The Rio Abajo Frontier, 1540–1692: A History of Early Colonial New Mexico.* Albuquerque: Albuquerque Museum, 1987.

Sauer, Carl Ortwin. *Sixteenth Century North America: The Lands and the People as Seen by the Europeans.* Berkeley: University of California Press, 1971.

Schroeder, Albert H. "A Re-Analysis of the Routes of Coronado and Oñate into the Plains in 1541 and 1601." *Plains Anthropologist* 7 (1962): 2–23.

Scurlock, Dan, "The Rio Grande Bosque: Ever Changing." *New Mexico Historical Review* 63, no. 2 (1988): 131–40.

Sherman, James E., and Barabara H. Sherman. *Ghost Towns and Mining Camps of New Mexico*. Norman: University of Oklahoma Press, 1975.

Silber, Irwin, ed. *Songs of the Great American West*. New York: Dover, 1967.

Silverberg, Robert. *The Pueblo Revolt*. Lincoln: University of Nebraska Press, 1994.

Simmons, Marc. *Coronado's Land: Essays on Daily Life in Colonial New Mexico*. Albuquerque: University of New Mexico Press, 1991.

———. *The Last Conquistador: Juan de Oñate and the Settling of the Far Southwest*. Norman: University of Oklahoma Press, 1991.

Sinclair, Rolf. "The Blind Girl Who Saw the Flash of the First Nuclear Weapons Test." *Skeptical Inquirer* 18 (fall 1993): 63–67.

Singletary, Otis A. *The Mexican War*. Chicago: University of Chicago Press, 1960.

Smith, George W., and Charles Judah, eds. *Chronicles of the Gringos: The U.S. Army in the Mexican War, 1846–1848, Accounts of Eyewitnesses and Combatants*. Albuquerque: University of New Mexico Press, 1968.

Smith, Justin H. *The War with Mexico*. New York: Macmillan, 1919.

Smith, Ralph A. *Borderlander: The Life of James Kirker, 1793–1852*. Norman: University of Oklahoma Press, 1999.

———. "The King of New Mexico and the Doniphan Expedition." *New Mexico Historical Review* 38, no. 1 (1963): 29–55.

———. "The Scalp Hunters of Chihuahua 1849." *New Mexico Historical Review* 40, no. 2 (1965): 116–40.

Smith, Thomas F., ed. *A Dose of Frontier Soldiering: The Memoirs of Corporal A. E. Bode*. Lincoln: University of Nebraska Press, 1994.

Sonnichsen, C. L. *Tularosa: Last of the Frontier West*. Albuquerque: University of New Mexico Press, 1980.

Spence, Lewis. *The Myths of the North American Indians*. New York: Dover, 1985.

Spielmann, Katherine A., ed. *Migration and Reorganization: The Pueblo IV Period in the American Southwest*. Anthropological Research Papers 51. Tucson: University of Arizona Press, 1998.

Stanley, F. *Ciudad Santa Fe: Spanish Domination, 1610–1821*. Denver: World, 1958.

Stebbins, Robert C. *Western Reptiles and Amphibians*. New York: Houghton Mifflin, 1985.

Steiner, Stan. *Fusang: The Chinese Who Built America*. New York: Harper, 1980.

Stoeser, Douglas, Michael K. Senterfit, and Jeanne E. Zelten. *Mineral Resources of the Little Black Peak and Carrizozo Lava Flow Wilderness Study Areas, Lincoln Co.* NM. U.S. Geological Survey Bulletin 1734, 1989.

Szasz, Ferenc Morton. *The Day the Sun Rose Twice.* Albuquerque: University of New Mexico Press, 1984.

Taylor, John. *Bloody Valverde: A Civil War Battle on the Rio Grande, February 21, 1862.* Albuquerque: University of New Mexico Press, 1994.

Thomas, Alfred B. *After Coronado; Spanish Exploration of New Mexico, 1696–1727.* Norman: University of Oklahoma Press, 1966.

Thompson, Jerry D. *Desert Tiger: Captain Paddy Graydon and the Civil War in the Far Southwest.* El Paso: University of Texas at El Paso Press, 1992.

Thoreau, Henry D. *The Essays of Henry D. Thoreau.* Ed. Lewis Hyde. New York: North Point, 2002.

———. *Journals of Henry D. Thoreau.* Ed. Bradford Torrey. New York: Dover, 1989.

Thrapp, Dan L. *The Conquest of Apacheria and His Victorio and the Mimbres Apaches.* Norman: University of Oklahoma Press, 1968.

———. *Victorio and the Mimbres Apache.* Norman: University of Oklahoma Press, 1967.

Timmons, W. H. *El Paso: A Borderlands History.* El Paso: Texas Western Press, 1990.

Trafzer, Clifford E. *The Kit Carson Campaign: The Last Great Navajo War.* Norman: University of Oklahoma Press, 1982.

"Trinity Site, July 16, 1945." U.S. Government Printing Office, no. 2000-844-916, n.d.

Twitchell, Ralph Emerson. *Old Santa Fe.* Santa Fe: New Mexican, 1925.

Tyler, Dan. "Anglo American Penetration of the Southwest: The View from New Mexico." *Southwestern Historical Quarterly* 75 (January 1972): 325–38.

Underhill, Evelyn. *Mysticism.* 4th ed. London: Methuen, 1912.

Undreiner, George J. "Fray Marcos de Niza and His Journey to Cibola." *The Americas* 3 (1947): 415–86.

U.S. Department of Interior. Bureau of Land Management. *Fort Craig.* BLM-NM-GI-89-0030-4340, n.d.

Utley, Robert M. *Billy the Kid: A Short and Violent Life.* Lincoln: University of Nebraska Press, 1991.

———. "The Final Days of Billy the Kid." *New Mexico Historical Review* 64, no. 3 (1989): 401–26.

———. "O. O. Howard." *New Mexico Historical Review* 62, no. 1 (1987): 55–63.

Van Bruggen, Theodore. *Wildflowers, Grasses, and Other Plants of the Northern Plains.* Interior SD: Badlands Natural History Association, 1992.

Bibliography

VanDyke, John C. *The Desert*. New York: Scribner, 1901.

Vehik, Susan C. "Oñate's Expedition to the Southern Plains: Routes, Destinations, and Implications for Late Prehistoric Cultural Adaptations." *Plains Anthropologist* 31 (1986): 13–33.

"Vertebrate Animals and Their Habitats in the Fra Cristobel Mountains of New Mexico." Privately printed, n.d.

"Victorio." *Arizona Historical Review* 2, no. 4 (1930): 74–90.

Waldman, Carl. *Atlas of the North American Indian*. New York: Facts on File, 1985.

Walker, A. S. *Deserts: Geology and Resources*. Washington DC: U.S. Geological Survey, n.d.

Walsche, M. O'C., ed. *Meister Eckhart: Sermons and Treatises*. Vol. 1. New York: Element, 1979.

Warner, Ted J., ed., and Fray Angelico Chavez, trans. *The Dominguez-Escalante Journal: Their Expedition through Colorado, Utah, Arizona, and New Mexico in 1776*. Salt Lake City: University of Utah Press, 1995.

Weber, David J. *The Spanish Frontier in North America*. New Haven: Yale University Press, 1992.

Weber, R. H., and G. A. Agogino. "Mockingbird Gap Paleoindian Site: Excavations in 1967." In *Layers of Time: Papers in Honor of Robert H. Weber*, ed. Meliha Duran, 123–27. Albuquerque: Archaeological Society of New Mexico, 1967.

Wells, Spencer. *The Journey of Man*. Princeton NJ: Princeton, 2002.

Welsh, Larry, and Mike Marshall. *El Camino Real de Tierra Adentro: Public Report and Archaeological Investigation*. Santa Fe: New Mexico Historic Preservation Division Archaeological Survey Project, 1991.

Welsh, Michael E. "The U.S. Army Corps of Engineers in the Middle Rio Grande Valley, 1935–1955." *New Mexico Historical Review* 60, no. 3 (1985): 295–316.

Weyer, J. K. "An Archaeological Survey of Nine Seismographic Test Lines for Exxon Company in Dona Ana and Luna Counties, NM." Las Cruces: New Mexico State University, Report 227, Cultural Resources Management Division, 1978.

Whalen, Michael E. *Turquoise Ridge and Late Prehistoric Residential Mobility in the Desert Mogollon Region*. Anthropology Papers 118. Salt Lake: University of Utah Press, 1994.

Wheat, Carl I. *Mapping the Transmississippi West, 1540–1861*. Vol. 1, *The Spanish "Entrada" to the Louisiana Purchase, 1540–1804*. San Francisco: Institute of Historical Cartography. 1957.

Bibliography

White, Richard, and Patricia Nelson Limerick. *The Frontier in American Culture*. Berkeley: University of California Press, 1993.

"White Sands Fauna." http://www.wsmr.army/mil/paopage/Pages/fauna.htm.

Widdison, Jerold G., ed. *The Anasazi: Why Did They Leave? Where Did They Go?* Albuquerque: Southwest Natural and Cultural Heritage Association, 1991.

Wills, Nirt Henry. "Early Agriculture in the Mogollon Highlands of New Mexico." Ph.D. diss., University of New Mexico, 1985.

Wilson, James C. *Itzatenango and Friends*. Santa Fe: Moo Cow, 1974.

Wilson, John P. "How Settlers Farmed: Hispanic Villages and Irrigation Systems in Early Sierra County, 1850–1900." *New Mexico Historical Review* 63, no. 4 (1988): 333–56.

Winship, George P. *The Journey of Coronado, 1540–1542*. Foreword by Donald C. Cutter. 1896. Reprint, Golden CO: Fulcrum, 1990.

——, ed. *The Coronado Expedition, 1540–1542*. Bureau of Ethnology, Smithsonian Institution, Annual Report, 14. Washington DC: Government Printing Office, 1896.

Wislizenus, Frederick Alfred. "Memoir of a Tour to Northern Mexico Connected with Col. Doniphan's Expedition in 1846 and 47." U.S. Senate Misc. Doc. 26, 30th Cong., 1st sess., 1848, serial set 511.

Young, Jane, M. "Images of Power and Power of Images: The Significance of Rock Art for Contemporary Zunis." *Journal of American Folklore* 98 (1985): 187–93.

Zolbrod, Paul. *Dine bahane': The Navajo Creation Story*. Albuquerque: University of New Mexico Press, 1984.